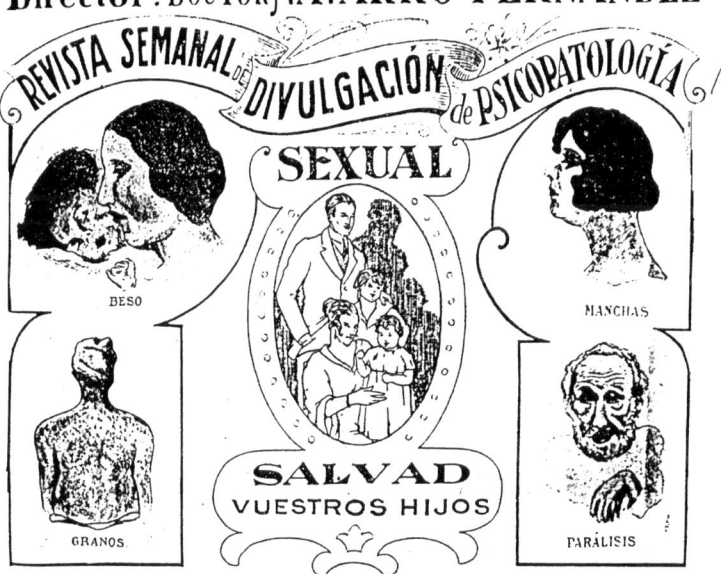

IBERIAN AND LATIN AMERICAN STUDIES

Sex and Society in Early Twentieth-Century Spain

Series Editors
Professor David George (University of Wales, Swansea)
Professor Paul Garner (University of Leeds)

Editorial Board
David Frier (University of Leeds)
Lisa Shaw (University of Liverpool)
Gareth Walters (University of Exeter)
Rob Stone (University of Wales, Swansea)
David Gies (University of Virginia)
Catherine Davies (University of Nottingham)

IBERIAN AND LATIN AMERICAN STUDIES

Sex and Society in Early Twentieth-Century Spain

Hildegart Rodríguez and the World League for Sexual Reform

ALISON SINCLAIR

UNIVERSITY OF WALES PRESS
CARDIFF
2007

© Alison Sinclair, 2007
Reprinted 2011

All rights reserved. No part of this book may be reproduced, stored in a retrieval system, or transmitted, in any form or by any means, electronic, mechanical, photocopying, recording or otherwise, without clearance from the University of Wales Press, 10 Columbus Walk, Brigantine Place, Cardiff CF10 4UP.

www.uwp.co.uk

British Library Cataloguing-in-Publication Data
A catalogue record for this book is available from the British Library.

ISBN   978-0-7083-2017-4
e-ISBN   978-0-7083-2470-7

The right of Alison Sinclair to be identified as author of this work has been asserted by her in accordance with the Copyright, Designs and Patents Act 1988.

Frontispiece: 'Front cover of *Sexualidad* (1925–8)'. Reproduced with kind permission of the Hemeroteca Municipal, Madrid.

Typeset by Columns Design Ltd, Reading
Printed in Great Britain by Antony Rowe Ltd, Chippenham, Wiltshire

Dedicated to the memory of Edith Lees

Contents

Series Editors' Foreword	ix
Acknowledgements	xi
Introduction	1
Chapter One: The Face of Reform in Europe and the Spanish Case	5
Chapter Two: Conception of Reform	23
Chapter Three: Growing up under the Dictatorship	41
Chapter Four: Coming to Maturity and the Limits of Tolerance	63
Chapter Five: Hildegart's 'child', the Spanish Liga	85
Chapter Six: The Liga Speaks	103
Chapter Seven: Writing to the 'fairy god'	123
Chapter Eight: Filicide: Perfection and Eugenic Death	147
Appendix I: Hildegart's Letters	163
Appendix II: Brief Bio-Bibliographical Guide to Figures Mentioned in the Text	217
Bibliography	233
Index	245

Series Editors' Foreword

Over recent decades, the traditional 'languages and literatures' model in Spanish departments in universities in the United Kingdom has been superceded by a contextual, interdisciplinary and 'area studies' approach to the study of the culture, history, society and politics of the Hispanic and Lusophone worlds – categories which extend far beyond the confines of the Iberian Peninsula, not only to Latin America but also to Spanish-speaking and Lusophone Africa.

In response to these dynamic trends in research priorities and curriculum development, this series is designed to present both disciplinary and interdisciplinary research within the general field of Iberian and Latin American Studies, particularly studies which explore all aspects of **Cultural Production** (*inter alia* literature, film, music, dance, sport) in Spanish, Portuguese, Basque, Catalan, Galician and the indigenous languages of Latin America. The series also aims to publish research on the **History and Politics** of Hispanic and Lusophone worlds, both at the level of region and that of the nation-state, as well as on **Cultural Studies** which explore the shifting terrains of gender, sexual, racial and postcolonial identities in those same regions.

Acknowledgements

This book would never have come into being had Tom Glick not introduced me to the work of Hildegart, and had I not had long conversations with Richard Cleminson on the world of sexual reform in which she figured so briefly. These conversations have continued throughout the drafting of this book. I am particularly grateful to the staff of the British Library, the University Library, Cambridge, and the Hemeroteca Municipal, Madrid. The support of friends and colleagues has been invaluable, and I would particularly like to thank Julia Biggane, Beatriz Caañamo, Angeles Carreres, Ivan Crozier, Richard Cleminson, Nigel Dennis, Philip Ford, Tom Glick, Lesley Hall, Belén Jiménez, Jo Labanyi, Kurt Lipstein, Anja Louis, Roy Porter, Mike Richards, Francisco Vázquez García, Lorna Sinclair, Anne Summers and Sarah Wright. I would like to thank Simon Masterton for his assistance with the transcription of the letters and Maruja Rincón for friendship, hospitality and conversation in Madrid. I am as ever indebted to my family for their tolerance and support.

I am especially indebted to Professor François Lafitte for his help and generosity in directing me to the location of the letters now in the British Library. The letters of Hildegart to Havelock Ellis are reproduced by permission of The British Library (ADD.70542). I am also grateful to the British Library for permission to reproduce the copy of their photograph of Hildegart from the Ellis collection for the jacket cover and to the Hemeroteca Municipal, Madrid, for permission to reproduce the front page of *Sexualidad* for the frontispiece.

I would like to acknowledge warmly the support of the British Academy (2001–3) for my 'Centres of Exchange' project, and of which the exchanges between Hildegart and Havelock Ellis and the work on the dissemination of eugenics form a part.

Earlier versions of parts of this book have been given as conference papers at the Institute for Romance Studies, the

MMLA, the Wellcome Institute, London, Hispanic Lesbian and Gay Studies (Bradford), Medical Anthropology Group of the Royal Anthropological Institute, and in seminars at the universities of Aberdeen, Cambridge, Lancaster, and Sheffield. I am grateful for permission to draw on articles published in the following three journals:

'Hildegart: the Paradox of the Eugenic Dream', *Journal of the Institute of Romance Studies* 7: 127–44 (1999); 'The World League for Sexual Reform in Spain: Founding, Infighting and the Role of Hildegart Rodríguez', *Journal of the History of Sexuality* (University of Texas Press) 12(1): 98–109 (2003); 'Setting up the Interlocutor: Two Case Studies in the Construction of Self in 1930s Spain', *Anthropology and Medicine* 10(2): 223–238 (2003).

Introduction

In this book I set out to tell a double story. I track the development of movements concerned with sexual reform and eugenics in early twentieth-century Spain, and in order to do so with particular focus, I take a specific case history, namely that of Hildegart Rodríguez (1914–33) who came to be one of the central players in the Spanish chapter of the World League for Sexual Reform (WLSR). The book traces how Hildegart's conception, life and early death can be mapped in uncanny manner onto the rise, organization and decline of the Sexual Reform movement in Spain.

Hildegart was conceived deliberately in 1914 as a 'eugenic' child (at a time when writing on eugenics was well under way in both England and Spain), and received her early education from her mother who in turn had received her own from her father's library, rich in works of utopian socialism. Subsequently and formally, Hildegart's education through the 1920s coincided with a period in Spain when writing on eugenics and sex reform became particularly intense. Her studies encompassed both law and medicine (favoured disciplines for those involved in the sex reform movement) and her teens provided a social education within the meetings and publications of the Campaña Sanitaria (Hygiene Campaign) of Navarro Fernández in the 1920s. Hildegart's own rise to a position of prominence in the world of eugenics and sex reform undoubtedly relates to her concentrated and impressive publishing activity from 1930 onwards, at a time when writings of others involved in sex reform also reached heightened activity. The coming of the Second Republic in 1931 further facilitated this publishing activity, and made possible the organization of the Spanish chapter of the WLSR in Spain (the Liga Mundial Para la Reforma Sexual) in March 1932 with Gregorio Marañón as its president, and the youthful Hildegart (age seventeen) as its secretary.[1] The Liga gathered together the groupings of hygienists, eugenicists, lawyers and educational reformers who were already part of a wider international scene, and who had been promoting ideas of eugenics and sexual reform in Spain for some time, and particularly through the 1920s.

Both Hildegart and the movements with which she was associated in Spain came to an untimely and premature end during the Second Republic. In June 1933, little more than a year after the Liga was founded, Hildegart was murdered by her mother, Aurora Rodríguez. It is hard to assert that this shocking event caused the death of the Liga but the movement in Spain seems not to have survived in coherent manner beyond 1933, although individual members continued to be active in various ways.

In telling this double story I have drawn on a striking record of the private life of Hildegart, one that illuminates issues of the movements with which she was associated, and that also allows us to gain some perception of her exceptional personal life. In October 1931 she wrote to Havelock Ellis, asking for advice on setting up the Spanish chapter of the WLSR. The correspondence developed far beyond the initial simple request for advice, and it lasted until a month before Hildegart's death. The letters include Hildegart's record of the foundation meeting of the Liga, and give details of discussion of the ten planks of belief of the WLSR, revealing the inbuilt power struggles between professional factions in the organization. At the same time as the letters provide this key documentation they provide something much more personal. Written (with one exception) in English, they are full of Hildegart's character: her style moves between business-like discussion, an endearing and ingenuous flirtatious manner, distress, and even paranoia. Above all the letters reveal a side of this youthful sexual reformer never documented elsewhere, and their extraordinary discursive nature encapsulates the paradoxes and conflicts in Spain at the time relating to thoughts on sexuality and reform. They form a text with a dramatic subtext, one that allows us to glimpse in poignant and dramatic detail the personal tensions and anxieties of this young woman as she related to others in public life and as she related to the dominating and unsettled woman who would eventually murder her. At the same time the letters also testify to Hildegart's strong and touching attachment to Ellis as mentor in the setting up of the Liga and, more personally, as a father-figure. The correspondence (reproduced in full in Appendix I, discussed in detail in Chapter Seven, and used as supporting material throughout the preceding chapters)[2] thus provides a unique window onto a complex movement and a striking individual and provide pointers to the links between ideas and sexuality in England and the way such ideas were explored in Spain.

NOTES

[1] The World League for Sexual Reform will be referred to as the WLSR and the Spanish chapter of it as The Liga.
[2] Hildegart's written report of the foundation meeting of the Liga, sent on to Ellis, is not included in the appendix, but its contents are discussed fully in Chapter Five.

Chapter One

The Face of Reform in Europe and the Spanish Case

> You see what my work is. I am reading a great quantity of books over sexual things. Lindsey, Forel, Bloch, Van de Velde, Ellen Key, Marie Stopes, Kollontay, Renato Kohl, Sanger, and a lot of several others. But the special motive of my writing to you is to beg your help for me in the work which I have enterprised. I would desire to know the laws, the propositions, the ideas and the books which are given to publicity in all countries but specially in England where you can so well know the developpement of people in this interesting object. (Hildegart to Havelock Ellis, 23 October 1931)[1]

In his summary of broad republican aims in Spain in the early twentieth century, Álvarez Junco indicates how certain features of 'España negra' [Black Spain] were to be set aside, and new, rational aims and ideals were to be adopted. The rowdy Spain depicted in the bullfight, alcoholism, lotteries and executions was to be discarded in favour of sanitary and hygienic progress, cremation, criminology and modern prisons, women's legal emancipation, a rethinking of marriage with provision for divorce, urban planning, and progress on a variety of other fronts, including phonetic spelling (Álvarez Junco, 1989: 356). This was a special agenda for Spain, arising from its history, its geography and the particularities of its social and political structures. Yet in the early decades of the twentieth century its social and political aims and activities also had striking resonances with what could be found in the rest of Europe. Spain's involvement with broad and international political movements such as socialism, communism and anarchism clearly had impact. In the intellectual world writers and thinkers such as Unamuno and Ortega pioneered, whether by personal activity and example or by organizational drive, the links between Spain and Europe, the foundations for which had been laid by the tradition of the Institución Libre de Enseñanza (ILE) set up by Francisco Giner de los Ríos*.[2] A canonical picture of Spain's engagement with Europe has existed by which the prime players were institutions such as the Junta para Ampliación de Estudios (JAE) [Committee for the Broadening of Study], the Residencia de Estudiantes, and publications such as the *Revista de Occidente*. In relation to this a much broader field of exchange with a wider range of participants has still to be fully recognized.[3] Numerous routes through to intellectual activity in Europe were forged through publishing houses, newspapers, and reviews. Not all exchanges were within the most traditionally educated classes, and socialist and anarchist groups were significant in extending the possibilities for the autodidact. The real prominence of popular culture as a factor for our understanding of modern Spain has now been articulated (Graham and Labanyi, 1995), and the role of elites is being nuanced (Sinclair, 2004c).

The modernizing aims highlighted by Álvarez Junco above show a role of rationality being claimed as necessary: what has to be set aside is untidy tradition. Obvious areas for the importation of practices and tendencies from Europe in the process of modernization were education, the economy and political structures, while concepts of sociology, historiography and philosophy underpinned the formal framework of such study. Psychoanalysis was similarly imported, albeit less well documented (Glick, 1981, 1982). The enthusiasm of Giner de los Ríos for the advantages of study in Europe, with first Germany, and then England being his preferred pattern (Castillejo, 1997: 192), relates to formal, academic education, but both his ideals, and those of Ortega later, came from a concept of education in society that would give access to a whole culture, and would allow for informed decisions and choices on the part of those who received benefit from it.

It should not come as a total surprise that Spain participated in wider European concerns relating to social reform as it affected matters of sex.[4] Indeed, as Cleminson shows, the ILE was a case in point (Cleminson and Vázquez García, 2007. Yet this participation is not well known. It can be glimpsed partially through the struggles to bring in divorce reform under the Second Republic but it is possible that the difficulties of achieving divorce provisions in a Catholic country have eclipsed our view of other fundamental movements towards reform in related areas including sex, hygiene and sex education.

The importation of ideas is more subject to local adaptation than is the case with material objects, and the manner of adaptation tells us more about local conditions and custom than it does about the ideas themselves. With this in mind, my intention in this chapter is to give a brief overview of how specific issues in Spanish public life in the period made it receptive to particular interests and enthusiasms elsewhere. I then place this in a broader context, first that of the general climate in the early twentieth century relating to reform in eugenics and sexual matters in Europe, with specific but not exclusive reference to England, and second in relation to the founding and development of the World League for Sexual Reform.

The life and activity of the reformer Hildegart Rodríguez (1914–33) offer a suggestive time-line for tracking the development of the sex reform movement in Spain as it developed alongside major political changes in the country, and this is followed through subsequent chapters. There are three main phases: from the turn of the century to 1923; Primo de Rivera's dictatorship 1923–30; the Second Republic 1931–36. The first two phases have a particular style of input into the development of thought about eugenics and sex reform, while the third phase made a substantial change in what supporters of sex reform could do and publish, and made it possible for the Spanish chapter of the World League for Sexual Reform to get its official foundation.[5] Hildegart's life, from its 'eugenic' conception, through its intense and idealistic education, and its practical application of social ideas and ideals, puts flesh onto these developments and highlights conflicts and paradoxes.

Ripe for Eugenics

There is little doubt that impetus to the growth of eugenics in Spain came with regenerationist ideas (Álvarez Peláez, 1988: 183; Cleminson, 2000: 68–76; Nash, 1992: 742–3). These in turn relate to the various manifestations of public disquiet about Spain's national standing at the turn of the century, linked habitually to the loss of Cuba in 1898, but generally accepted to be rooted at an earlier date. The ideas of degeneration contained in Nordau* (certainly known in Spain) and of Lombroso* (equally well known, if not fully acknowledged) made a good match for feelings of national despondency at Spain's condition.[6] Nash puts a date of 1918 on the association between the crisis being made articulate in a work about national decline, *En defensa de la raza* [In defence of the race] by Martínez Vargas (Nash, 1992: 742), but it is also there in key 1898 essays such as Unamuno's *En torno al casticismo* (1902) [On Authenticity], and is embodied in numerous works by Baroja, from his 1900 essay on the 'Patología del golfo' [Pathology of the Rogue] to his novel *El árbol de la ciencia* (1911) [The tree of Life].

In her foundational essay Álvarez Peláez tracks how eugenics in Spain was well under way in the early years of the twentieth century, and shows clear links between Spain and England in the field from 1912 onwards (Álvarez Peláez, 1988: 184). Eugenics would not really flower in Spain until the 1920s, and arguably became part of a general phenomenon of political displacement in the regime of Primo de Rivera by which left-wing public political activity was put into abeyance, and new outlets were characteristically found. The Residencia de Estudiantes, for example, trod a path of circumspect intellectual exploration, while the *Revista de Occidente*, founded in 1923, the year the dictatorship began, had the desire – according to Ortega's mission statement in the first number – to speak to a readership with a curiosity that was neither purely aesthetic, cultural nor political, although the journal included articles on the structure of society, gender and national characteristics. Meanwhile the Residencia's lectures, wide-ranging in cultural terms, offered a way to connect to European thought in a way that could not be politically irrelevant (Sinclair, 2004c: 755–61, Sinclair forthcoming). So too with the activity of eugenics, which developed within the field of social medicine, and which would go a step too far in its first attempt to hold the Jornadas Eugénicas [Eugenics Conference] in 1928. As Glick (1982: 566) observes, one of the most startling aspects of the reception of Freud is that most of the discussion of his ideas took place under Primo de Rivera. The coming of the Second Republic made much possible, but the delicate political balance between different political and social groups, and the fact that both conservative and traditional aims were to be found among the reformers themselves, meant that the sex reform movement in the 1930s was set on a course of conflict and difficulty.

Eugenic Ideals

Throughout this book the terms 'eugenics' and 'sex reform' will be used. They are not intended to be mutually exchangeable, and the high degree of overlap between the two requires some explanation and ongoing attentiveness (Cleminson, 1994: 729). Some of the overlap between terms derives simply from personalities in that many were affiliated to a number of organizations, with different parts of the agendas of such organizations appealing to them. Hildegart will be a prime example of this overlap, her case illustrating some of the resultant complications. There were social peculiarities pertaining to these activists and reformers. Lyndsay Farrell comments of the Eugenic Education Society founded in England in 1907 that it was 'one of a network of organisations representing a common front of social activists who might be doctors, teachers or social workers, or simply ladies interested in social problems. Many were active in more than one society; social activism did not confine itself to a single remedy, though a given society might be specialised in its interests' (1970, cited by Mazumdar, 1992: 9). This pattern is as characteristic of Spain in the early twentieth century as it was of England. The different circles of the universities, the Residencia de Estudiantes, the inner circle of the JAE, the ILE and the Ateneo de Madrid made for numerous informal exchanges, influences and points of stimulation. Meanwhile in popular series such as *La novela proletaria* [The Proletarian Novel] Hildegart rubbed shoulders with Ángel Pestaña* (although the series *El libro del pueblo* [The Book of the People] had a predominance of elite names such as Marañón*, Juarros*, Baeza* and Santullano*). The *Cuadernos de la Cultura* (Culture Notebooks) published in Valencia by the energetic Marín Civera* made a wide range of writings by the lettered available to a less cultured *pueblo*.

The degree to which individuals carry their individuality over to the organizations in which they participate, rarely if ever losing their personal passions and anxieties in the process of participation, means that nuancing and shifts of emphasis within broad organizations are bound to occur, and the case of eugenics and sex reform is no exception. The existence of overlapping networks is, however, not fully sufficient to explain the interaction between the terms. The word 'eugenics' comes from the Greek *eugenes* (well-born) leading to Galton's 1883 definition, 'the study of agencies under social control *that may improve or impair* the racial qualities of future generations, either physically or mentally'. This contrasts with the 1904 definition offered by Karl Pearson of eugenics as the 'science which deals with all influences *that improve the inborn qualities of a race*, also with those that *develop them to the utmost advantage*' (emphases mine). Freeden points out how Pearson's implied umbrella of reform appealed to many, and would account for the differences between a 'pure' form of eugenics (as defined by Galton) and a form that had built into it the prospect of a programme of social reform (Freeden, 1979: 645–6).

The precision of the term 'eugenics' for a specific movement or specific set of beliefs is also usefully challenged by Adams on four points: that eugenics was a 'single, coherent, principally Anglo-American movement with a specifiable set of common goals and beliefs', that it was necessarily bound up with Mendelian genetics, that it was a pseudo-science, and that it was essentially right wing or reactionary (Adams, 1990: 217). The Spanish case shows the justification of Adams's challenges and bears out his denial that there is a unitary form of eugenics. As detailed by Stepan (1991: 2), eugenics is a set of beliefs and practices with highly variable local forms, within which Spain forms part of the 'Latin' tradition, along with Italy, France, Belgium and Latin America, in which there is an emphasis on education, on the improvement of social conditions, and on puericulture. But there are also strong similarities between the style of eugenics in Spain and England, particularly as articulated by Havelock Ellis. Despite the general assignation of Spain to the 'Latin' tradition it also has elements of hard-line eugenics (not least in Hildegart, and to a greater degree in her mother Aurora). Finally, in agreement with Adams's fourth point, the political and social persuasions of reformers in Spain ranged over a wide and complex spectrum.[7]

Eugenics in England is of course not solely represented by Ellis, but in the light of his correspondence with Hildegart it is illuminating to see how he drew back from certain positions in the movement, and to observe the degree of congruity between his approach and the tendencies to be observed in the movement in Spain. The Eugenics Education Society was founded in 1907, and – of some anecdotal interest when we consider the position of Hildegart Rodríguez in the Liga – was founded by a young woman, Sybil Gotto, aged twenty-one and recently widowed (Mazumdar, 1992: 7). The Society was predominantly of the great and the good: Farrell (1970) found that nearly 80 per cent of its members were listed in the *Dictionary of National Biography* and that they were predominantly associated with university education, two thirds of them coming from the biological or social sciences (Mazumdar, 1992: 8). Kevles characterizes the membership in the US and England as 'white, Anglo-Saxon, predominantly Protestant, and educated' (Kevles, 1985: 64), noting also that half the members and a quarter of the officers were women. A more outspoken view was that of a Brighton physician who observed that meetings of the Society would contain 'all the neo-Malthusian, antivaccinationists, antivivisectionists, Christian Scientists, Theosophists, Mullerites (who have strange ways of having a bath and of breathing deep breaths), vegetarians, and the rest!' (Kevles, 1985: 58). In similar vein to this (unnamed) physician, Chesterton launched a savage attack on the movement and its adherents in *Eugenics and Other Evils* (1922).

Whatever the taunts of outsiders, the Society had muscle when it came to firm recommendations. In 1914 the Mental Deficiency Act came into force, by which education authorities were required to place mentally deficient children in special schools (Mazumdar, 1992: 24), and in 1917 the Society would take a strong line on the treatment of venereal disease, urging that the Poor Law Amendment Act of 1867 be used to compel those who fell under the act and suffered from venereal disease to be detained in order for treatment to be carried out (Mazumdar, 1992: 34). In 1930 the Eugenics Society would set up a committee for legalizing compulsory sterilization (Freeden, 1979: 666).

Not all members of the Eugenics Society were hard-liners, however, and Ellis in particular drew back from compulsion. One is tempted to say that he drew back decisively, but such terminology hardly fits his general approach in his writings, always careful, circumspect and usually finding means of avoiding outright conflict. What we can see of his attitude in general is suggestive of his likely responses to Hildegart's letters (which unfortunately have not survived). An example of his tact is shown in his dealings with the frequently provocative and tetchy Unamuno over a difference in opinion on Ferrer (Sinclair, 2001: 25–6). In relation to some issues he could however be outspoken, as when he wrote in protest in 1930 to Dr C. P. Blacker, secretary of the committee for legalizing sterilization, declaring that to 'propose a law to authorise a voluntary act which is already being practised is a retrograde and stupid notion. Sterilization is becoming recognised as simple, harmless, in many ways beneficial. It will certainly continue to grow in favour. To invite ignorant and prejudiced legislators to meddle with an open medical question of this kind is a proceeding we ought not to encourage and are entitled to resent' (Grosskurth, 1980: 412). His view on the issuing of a health certificate before marriage was again that it should be voluntary, stating that both this and sterilization only had worth if they were 'intelligent and deliberate, springing out of a widened and enlightened sense of personal responsibility to society and to the race' (Ellis, 1912: 31). He took a broad view of the obligations eugenics suggested to society, and stated that 'to assume that social reform is unnecessary because it is not inherited is altogether absurd' (Ellis, 1912: 13). Anticipating an observation made by Marañón in his *Tres ensayos sobre la vida sexual* (1926) [Three Essays on Sexual Life], Ellis pointed out that a high birth-rate was inextricably linked to a high death-rate so that reducing births of unwanted children would in itself reduce infant mortality.[8] Ellis took an educational approach to eugenics, seeing it as 'the scientific study of all the agencies by which the human race may be improved' (Ellis, 1912: 29), and, as emphasized by Galton before him and Hildegart and others later, he laid stress on the need for human beings to do what they did consciously, voluntarily, and responsibly (Ellis, 1912: 30). He clearly saw a pathway by which feeble-mindedness and criminality were both inherited (no doubt drawing on Lombroso, whose 1888 work *The Man of Genius* he had translated in 1891) but clearly opposed 'any compulsory elimination of the unfit or any centrally regulated breeding of the fit' since to do so would 'impair the legitimate authority of eugenic ideals' (Ellis, 1912: 44).

Ellis's brand of eugenics, as articulated in *The Task of Social Hygiene*, is very much woman-centred. In one respect this is part of the internal logic of eugenics: if there was to be concern for improving the lot of the race by improving the conditions in which children were born (and Ellis is progressive and forward-thinking in his concern for maternal care both before and after the birth of a child), then a concentration on woman was natural. But, for all his even-handedness about women, and his openness that would envisage the companionate marriage as an ideal (and one that he put into practice with his lesbian wife Edith Lees), Ellis fundamentally saw women as mothers. He reminds readers of *The Task* of the theories of Bachofen about *mutterrecht* (Ellis, 1912: 92) and embarks on a lengthy exposition of the works of Ellen Key*, the Swedish reformer for whom marriage and motherhood were equally ideals. It is not fortuitous, I believe, that it is to Key that Hildegart will write at the same time as she writes to Ellis. Indeed one could trace much of what Hildegart has to say in her publications to the lines of thought explored by Ellis in *The Task*. The fact that she had access to it is revealed in her mention to Ellis in the letter of 1 May 1932 of the Italian version of this work (a translation published in 1922).

Ellis is a central example of the networking of different groups in the areas of eugenics and sexual reform. He is in at the foundation of the Eugenics Society, but in 1929 (when he was seventy) his wider range of interests also makes him one of the three honorary presidents of the WLSR. Robinson (1976) casts him as being at the forefront of 'sexual modernism', and emphasizes his openness: to pleasure, to varieties of sexuality, to the possibilities of human experience. It is doubtless this openness to the range of experience and sexuality, and which comes across in the *Studies in the Psychology of Sex* (works that Hildegart had read), that made him approachable. Yet as a 'modernist' he will also, in Robinson's terms, be open to issues of homosexuality, and it is clear that this is an initial point of difference between himself and Hildegart. Her early letters to him demonstrate that this is an area in which – for all her progressiveness – she is not at ease. By contrast, *Sexual Inversion*, the first of the *Studies in the Psychology of Sex*, is termed by Robinson as a 'classic example of Ellis's lifelong effort to broaden the spectrum of acceptable sexual behaviour' (Robinson, 1976: 4).

Structures and Varieties of Eugenics

Eugenics had no single set of beliefs, no agreed agenda of action, and the case of Ellis and his differences with other colleagues in England brings this sharply into focus. Eugenics societies of different areas of emphasis sprang up in the interwar years in England, Italy, France, Japan, Soviet Union, Sweden, Peru and Australia (Stepan, 1991: 2) and in 1921 the International Federation of Eugenics Societies was formed (Stepan, 1991: 5). Stepan, whose main area of interest is Brazil and Latin America, proposes a broad line of differentiation between the style of eugenics in different countries, distinguishing between 'hard eugenics' and 'soft eugenics', the latter being known as 'Latin eugenics', and according to which in Latin America eugenics would be 'preventive, hygienic, social' (Stepan, 1991: 85). In France, where a local eugenics society was formed after France had participated in the First International Eugenics Congress, London 1912, the style of eugenics was firmly towards the positive aims of puericulture and of prevention, rather than the adoption of Anglo-American tendencies towards sterilization and legislation (against which, as we have seen, Ellis made his protests) (Stepan, 1991: 80). In France the influence of Lamarck (with his theories of the possible inheritance of acquired characteristics) generally held more sway than the Mendelian approach prominent in some of the more extreme Anglo-American eugenicists. As a result, education and the provision of good social conditions were of more weight than active legislation that would restrict the birth or indeed the fertility of the feeble-minded, the criminal or the disease-stricken.

The idea of eugenics as 'Latin' or otherwise perhaps offers us some way through the difficulties of distinguishing between 'hard' and 'soft' eugenics, and the difficulties are outlined in some detail by Cleminson (2007). While 'hard' and 'soft' (and indeed 'positive' and 'negative') are terms used to qualify eugenics in ways that can be problematic, we need to retain the idea that such terms indicate a possible inflection or grouping, rather than a definitive indication of the scope of ideology and practice.

Where does Ellis fit in all this? Clearly, by the exceptions that he took towards the moves of others towards controlling legislation, he was in fact more in affinity with the 'Latin' eugenics of France and other Mediterranean and Latin American countries than he was with some of the more strident English eugenicists. H. G. Wells*, for example, in his 1906 essay 'Socialism and the Family' took the view that 'the children people bring into the world can be no more their private concern entirely, than the disease germs they disseminate or the noises a man makes in a thin-floored flat' (cited in Kevles, 1985: 92). Ellis would never have made such presumption about the boundaries between public and private, something which is made particularly evident in his attitude to sexual reform rather than eugenics. This also explains his association (albeit never very close) with the WLSR.

Importing Sexual Reform from Europe

For Glick, Freud was the thinker who most set the rationale for sex reform in Spain and there is no doubt that, by the time Hildegart wrote to Ellis, Freud was – whether in the original, or in some other European language – well known in Spain. In 1922 Biblioteca Nueva had begun to publish a translation of Freud's *Complete Works* by Luis López Ballesteros (the first translation into a foreign language). The 1893 *Studies on Hysteria* (Freud and Breuer) had had their first translation into Spanish (Jagoe *et al*, 1998: 347), and it is clear that both before the *Complete Works* edition and in the first years of its publication there were numerous volumes of single works by Freud in English or French available in Spain.[9] Yet Glick's further comment that 'Ellis was not much read in Spain' (Glick, 2003: 71) requires further examination. Reception of these thinkers is complicated. As mentioned above, Hildegart had already read Ellis's *Studies in the Psychology of Sex* when she wrote to him. Most of these works had been published by Hijos de Reus in 1913, with some parts of this having appeared earlier.[10] The only section of the *Studies* not to appear in Spanish was *Eonism and Other Supplementary Studies*. Simply from the dates of publication one could argue that Ellis was well known in Spain before Freud, although to take the 1922 publication of the complete works of Freud as the measure of how Freud was imported to Spain is to miss the degree to which many non-Hispanic writers were known initially in Spain either through their works in the original language, or through a language that was relatively accessible, such as French.[11] A further example of Ellis's mark on Spain comes from the private library of Ricardo

Baeza which contains no fewer than twelve works by Ellis, published between 1894 and 1936, while his collection – with the exception of volumes acquired after the Civil War – contains significantly fewer items by Freud.[12] Ellis also had useful connexions. It was through the friendship (and intervention) of Unamuno that *The Soul of Spain* was rapidly translated into Spanish, having been serialized in *La España Moderna* between April 1908 and December 1909 (Davies, 2000: 84–5).

The WLSR

The WLSR had a portfolio of concerns that to some degree overlapped with the broad agenda of eugenics. But just as eugenics was variable from country to country, so too would the agenda of the WLSR vary. The authoritative article by Ralf Dose on the history of the WLSR (2003) dates its official inception as 1928 when the Copenhagen Congress was held. Later the 1921 Congress of Berlin would be counted as part of the movement. Founded by Magnus Hirschfeld*, the movement had the following congresses: Berlin, September 1921; Copenhagen, July 1928; London, September 1929; Vienna, September 1930; Brno, September 1932. A meeting was planned for Paris for September 1933, and a further one for the US.[13] Dose notes that membership of WLSR reached 190,000 members, of which 182 were individual members. He lists 190 British members for 1932–3 (Dose, 2003: 3). This compares with the initial membership of fifty-one for the Spanish chapter in Spain in 1932, and which Hildegart in March 1932 hoped would soon rise to 100.

The WLSR is best understood through the framework of its 'planks' of belief. So termed by Norman Haire*, an Australian who rose to prominence in the English branch of the movement (Crozier, 2003: 20), the planks are listed in the proceedings of the Copenhagen 1928 Congress (WLSR, 1929: 10):

1. Political, economic and sexual equality of men and women.
2. The liberation of marriage (and especially divorce) from the present Church and State tyranny.
3. Control of conception, so that procreation may be undertaken only deliberately, and with a due sense of responsibility.

4. Race betterment by the application of the knowledge of Eugenics.
5. Protection of the unmarried mother and the illegitimate child.
6. A rational attitude towards sexually abnormal persons, and especially towards homosexuals, both male and female.
7. Prevention of prostitution and venereal disease.
8. Disturbances of the sexual impulse to be regarded as more or less pathological phenomena, and not, as in the past, as crimes, vices or sins.
9. Only those sexual acts to be considered criminal which infringe the sexual rights of another person. Sexual acts between responsible adults, undertaken by mutual consent, to be regarded as the private concern of those adults.
10. Systematic sexual education.[14]

From the planks the overlap between eugenics and the sexual reform movement can be divined. Plank 4 is the prime common factor. But planks 5, 7 and 10 are also common factors, within a 'Latin' form of eugenics as is plank 3, in that they form part of a pattern of provision of protection of women, education and provisions to improve the activity of motherhood and the social conditions of women and children. Of the remaining planks, 1 and 2 state a political and social agenda, while planks 6, 8 and 9 announce a reform of social attitude and legislative provision most clearly associated with sex and society. The planks therefore encapsulate a prime aim of eugenics, but frame it clearly in an approach of pedagogy and care, while at the same time announcing aims of liberal belief in the area of sexuality. This spectrum of aims, encompassing eugenics and sexual reform, makes the existence of Ellis as a significant mover wholly credible. In the case of the Liga in Spain, different planks clearly would have appeals to different members. Hildegart herself, while subscribing fully to the Liga as an organization and showing in her publications and lectures strong commitment to many of the planks, would also have reservation about some of the elements of plank 8, as revealed in her letters to Ellis. She would back the idea of homosexuality as pathology, but recommend that homosexuals be shut away.

The 'planks' never reached the state of being an integrated whole. Just as the discussion of them at the founding of the Liga (and doubtless in the founding moments of other branches) provoked a sense of difference between individuals and factions, so the different agendas contained in the various planks continued to satisfy some groups and not others. The attempts to provide a sense of unity through organization failed through the lack of adequate (and agreed) leadership. Hirschfeld, Ellis and Forel* were put onto the executive board at the Copenhagen Congress, and would later appear as honorary presidents (1930) (Dose, 2003: 6). Hirschfeld and Ellis had been aware of one another since 1904. Hirschfeld's works *Die Transvestiten* [Transvestites] and *Homosexualität* [Homosexuality] (1914) were undoubtedly of interest to Ellis, who would give his own version of the former in his theory of Eonism. Yet Ellis, who combined what seems to be endless patience with some individuals with irritation at others, came to avoid Hirschfeld, and was in fact (diplomatically) absent from the 1929 Congress of the WLSR in London (Grosskurth, 1980: 379–80). One might surmise that Hirschfeld's work on homosexuality would have been of interest to Ellis, but it did not seem sufficient to allow them to transcend personal lack of ease with one another.

The question of language at the congresses, and the manner of its resolution, is an example of how something rough and ready was put together that would continue to emphasize difference, rather than a clear language policy being agreed. Leunbach*, as general secretary of the Copenhagen Congress announced that the three main languages of English, French and German would be used (while Esperanto continued to be an option favoured by some). The solution of having the congress card printed in English, the programme in German and the list of participants in Esperanto seems quirky to say the least. French was omitted because there was only one French delegate to that Congress.[15]

Notwithstanding these areas where difference was manifest, the records of the various congresses show attempts to think of overarching ways in which the WLSR saw its mission. Hirschfeld's presidential address to the London Congress of 1929 spoke of the four areas of sexology (the newly defined branch of learning with which the WLSR concerned itself): sexual biology; sexual pathology; sexual ethnology; sexual sociology (WLSR, 1930: xii). The programme for that congress bears out this broad coverage, and Hirschfeld's words map out the terrain of investigation. It is in Haire's address of welcome at the same event that dissent is made evident, and he emphasized how the establishment of the 'planks' was crucial in holding together an organization with potentially quite disparate aims. Haire's words are above all forward looking. He refutes the view of some outsiders that the WLSR seeks the 'abolition of sexual morality'. He announces instead a type of sexual modernity, by which the aim of the WLSR is 'the substitution of a new sexual ethic, in consonance with the scientific knowledge of the social and economic circumstances of this century, for the old outworn sexual ethic which has descended to us from the civilization of Biblical times, mutilated and patched up by generation after generation, but never submitted to a really adequate or thoroughgoing revision' (WLSR, 1929: xvii–xviii).

For some, and this includes Hirschfeld as prime originator and mover, there was a more precise aim, in that they saw that the impulse for the WLSR would be largely to bring about the emancipation of homosexuals within society. This would use two routes: scientific knowledge about homosexuality, and integrating the homosexual movement with other related movements of sex reform. Appealing though this strategy seems it did not meet with success (Dose, 2003: 8–9). It had been a major topic at the 1921 Berlin Congress, but by the 1928 Copenhagen Congress was barely there (Crozier, 2003: 33). For those who gave priority to sex education, spread of information about abortion, birth control and venereal disease on the other hand, the papers offered at the congresses indicate success, albeit one that would continue in uneven manner in the countries involved (Dose, 2003: 11–12).

Leunbach and Haire decided to dissolve the WLSR (in its international form) in 1935, after the death of Hirschfeld, their underlying, or perhaps their prime idea being that national chapters of the organization should decide their own futures (Brandhorst, 2003: 51). National differences were already in evidence. The emphasis in English eugenics was closely linked to Mendelian ideas of heredity (Stepan, 1991: 65), although, as the case of Ellis demonstrates, not all were hard-liners about preventive legislation. In France, by contrast, the emphasis was on neo-Lamarckian theory, resulting in social provisions to improve the lot of mothers and children, and the combination of activities that would become known as 'puericulture'.[16] This was no mere attempt to ameliorate conditions for birth and infancy, but – in the light of the intervention of the state – appeared almost industrial in its functioning, and was bent on 'the need to keep women *in* reproduction, healthily rearing their children according to modern medical principles for the good of the country' (Stepan, 1991: 68). Spain would essentially follow in the Latin tradition as exemplified by France, in the intention if not in the realization. It would maintain two differences from other European countries. No congress of the WLSR was held in Spain, although the 1933 Eugenics Conference and the two numbers of *Sexus* (discussed in Chapter Six) met the broad aims of the WLSR. Homosexuality would again be pushed to the margins. Divorce would also cause complication. A divorce law was brought in by the Republic on 25 February 1932, but some of its provisions exercised a number of reformers. They were concerned lest 'equal' treatment for men and women in divorce proceedings might – paradoxically – open the way for women to be inferior, because judged hysterical, or superior, because their emotions, or feelings that a state of marriage was intolerable, would be allowed to weigh in the issue of whether the divorce were granted or not (Glick, 2003: 89–91). Reform was never simple, and least of all in Spain.

NOTES

1. Hildegart's letters to Havelock Ellis, discussed in detail in Chapter Seven, are housed in the Manuscripts section of the British Library. In addition to the letters there are numerous press cuttings, some of them annotated by Ellis, and a number of other letters pertaining to Hildegart and her mother. The press cuttings include items from France, Germany and Sweden. The collection also contains Ellis's notes on the trial of Aurora. Quotations from Hildegart's letters written in English retain the original spelling and punctuation, apart from proper names. In her letter written in Spanish the accents have been modernized.
2. References marked with an asterisk have an entry in Appendix II.
3. See for example Trend, 1921, 1934; Cacho Viú, 1962; Carr, 1966; Bécarud, 1978; Sánchez Ron, 1988.
4. See for example the case of Tardieu as background to this, cited by Cleminson and Vázquez García (2007: Chapter Three, note 1).
5. See Chapter Four for background to the Liga, and Chapters Five and Six for details of the setting up of the Liga and its publishing activities.
6. See Maristany, 1973 for background, and Nóvoa Santos, 1929 for an example of the application of theories of Lombroso.
7. See Richards, 2004 for an examination of the complexities of attitude

The Face of Reform in Europe and the Spanish Case 21

underlying the development of psychiatry in Spain, not least in its reception of German psychiatry.

8   Marañón's point would be more detailed, referring to the fact that the death rate of infants born to a specific mother rose as the number of births increased (Richards, 2004: 842).

9   See, for example, *Psychopathology of Everyday Life* (London, Fisher Unwin, 1914), *The Interpretation of Dreams* (London, Allen and Unwin, 1920), *Introduction à la psychanalyse* (Paris, Payot, 1922), *Trois essais sur la théorie de la sexualité* (Paris, La Nouvelle Revue Française, 1923), *Totem et tabou. Interprétation par la psychanalyse de la vie sociale des peuples primitifs* (Paris, Payot, 1924), *Psychologie collective et analyse du moi* (Paris, Payot, 1924).

10 The following works of Ellis appeared singly (translations here are of the Spanish title given): *El impulso sexual de la mujer*, trans. Ginés de San Telmo (Madrid: Antonio Marzo, 1905) [The Sexual Impulse in Women]; *Amor y dolor: estudio sobre el sadismo y el masoquismo*, trans. Ginés de San Telmo (Madrid: Viuda de Rodríguez Serra, 1906) Col. Biblioteca de ciencias penales 5 [Love and Pain: Study of Sadism and Masochism]; *El impulso sexual en la especie humana y en los animales* (Madrid: Antonio Marzo, 1909) [The Sexual Impulse in Humans and Animals]; *El mundo de los sueños* (Barcelona: Araluce, 1929) [The World of Dreams]. Works that are part of the *Studies* and appear in the series Biblioteca médica de autores españoles y extranjeros of Hijos de Reus in 1913 are: Vol. 1, *Hombre y mujer* [Man and Woman], trans. J. López Oliván; Vol. 2, *La evolución del pudor* [The Evolution of Modesty]; *Fenómenos de periodicidad sexual* [Phenomena of Sexual Periodicity]; *El autoerotismo* [Auto-Erotism], trans J. J. L.; Vol. 3, *Inversión sexual* [Sexual Inversión]; Vol. 4, *El impulso sexual; Amor y dolor* [The Sexual Impulse; Love and Pain]; Vol. 5, *La selección sexual en el hombre* [Sexual Selection in Man], trans. Ceferino Palencia y Tubau; Vol. 6, *El simbolismo erótico; El mecanismo de la* detumescencia*; El estado psíquico durante la preñez* [Erotic Symbolism; The Mechanism of Detumescence; The Psychic State in Pregnancy, trans J. J. L.; Vol. 7, *El sexo en relación a la sociedad* [Sex in Relation to Society], trans. Ceferino Palencia y Tubau.

11 For fuller discussion of intellectual importations to Spain at this time, particularly those relating to gender and society, see Sinclair (2007).

12 *Man and Woman: a Study of Human Seconday Sexual Characteristics* (London: Walter Scott, 1894); *Estudios de psicología sexual: el sexo en relación con la sociedad* (Madrid: Hijos de Reus, 1913); *Estudios de psicología sexual: Hombre y mujer* (Madrid: Hijos de Reus, 1913); *The philosophy of conflict and other essays in war-time*, second series (London: Constable, 1919); *L'impulsion sexuelle* (Paris: Mercure de France, 1921); *L'inversion sexuelle* (Paris: Mercure de France, 1921); *La pudeur, la périodicité sexuelle, l'auto-érotisme* (Paris: Mercure de France, 1921); *Le Symbolisme érotique: le mécanisme de la détumescence* (Paris: Mercure de France, 1925); *El sexo en la civilización* (Madrid: Aguilar, 1930); *Le Mécanisme des déviations sexuelles: le narcissisme* (Paris: Mercure de France, 1932); *L'ondinisme: La Cleptolagnie* (Paris: Mercure de France,

1933); *Afirmaciones (Affirmations): Comentarios éticos sobre los valores humanos de grandes hombres* (Barcelona: Joaquín Gil, 1936). The works of Freud in this exceptionally well-stocked library, by contrast, are *Introduction à la psychanalyse* (Paris: Payot, 1922), and *Moisés y la religión monoteísta* (Buenos Aires: Losada, 1939; probably obtained after Baeza moved to Argentina).

13 In a letter of March 1932 Hildegart proposed Madrid as a possible venue for the 1933 meeting. The suggestion was modified to May 1934, because of funding problems, and the event did not take place.

14 This is the version of the planks discussed at the Liga foundation meeting. A longer version of the planks had initially been drafted by Hirschfeld. See Dose (2003: 7) for details, and Chapter Five.

15 A curiosity of the French position is that the eugenics movement was relatively strong, and yet France was not prominent in the WLSR. See Schneider (1990).

16 The word had been come into being around 1865, but given more precise use in 1890 by Pinard.

Chapter Two

Conception of Reform

Voy a cumplir ante todo su deseo de que le diga todo lo que me sea posible sobre mí. Nací el día 9 de Diciembre de 1914, y soy una hija eugénica, esto es, no inconsciente. Mi madre se quedó huérfana de padre cuando tenía 30 años, y un año después deliberadamente vine yo al mundo. De mi educación física le puedo dar a Vd. una idea, diciéndole que hasta los siete meses estuve acostada en mi coche cuna y que a los once meses, sin que antes hubiera puesto los pies en el suelo, me puso mi madre a andar y eché a correr sin la menor dificultad y tropiezo.

[First of all I shall do as you request and tell you everything possible about myself. I was born on 9 December 1914, and I am a eugenic child, that is, not unintentional. My mother lost her father when she was 30, and a year later I chose to come into the world. I can give you some idea of my physical development by telling you that until the age of seven months I lay in my pram, and that at eleven months, when I had never put my feet on the floor before, my mother started me walking, and I began to run without any difficulty or stumbling.] (Hildegart to Ellis, 2 December 1931)

Eugenics in Spain did not arise out of a vacuum. The project by which Hildegart was conceived and the nascent activities of eugenicists and sex reformers can be tracked to a context that is local, but it also had international echoes and influences. These areas of reform pre-date Hildegart's birth, making the exceptional style of her conception and birth possible. The activities of reformers, largely but not exclusively with a medical or educational focus, gather momentum in the first two decades of the twentieth century, building on the sort of social utopianism that filled the library shelves of Hildegart's grandfather and formed the home education of her mother: texts by Saint-Simon, Fourier,

Owen, Cabet (Rendueles, 1989: 66).[1] This chapter highlights the concerns of reformers active in those early decades, their focus falling largely on notorious areas such as prostitution, disease and degeneration , and – consistent with utopianism – on education as a prime resource for curing such ills.

An Independent Eugenic Child?

In her second letter to Havelock Ellis, written at his request in Spanish, and responding to his prompt for further information about herself, Hildegart announced that she was a 'eugenic child', adding that she was 'no inconsciente' [not unintentional]. It is striking that she clarifies this to Ellis – he of all people would have needed no introduction to the idea of conscious parenthood. Awareness of intentions and actions came uppermost in his thoughts about sexual behaviour, as evidenced in *The Task of Social Hygiene* where he had taken the view that 'breeding must proceed from impulses that arise, voluntarily, in human brains and will' (Ellis, 1912: 30). More than this, he separated himself from those who wished to achieve 'good' breeding through legislation on marriage certification or on sterilization of the unfit: such acts were only of worth if 'intelligent and deliberate' (Ellis, 1912: 31).

Hildegart's opening combines two approaches. She presents her credentials to Ellis: to one interested in eugenics being approached by another interested in eugenics, what better pedigree than to have been born a 'eugenic child'? But then, it is as if she sees the drawbacks of being one who has been produced with such control and intention, and asserts her own agency: 'deliberadamente vine yo al mundo' [I chose to come into the world]. Her position as her mother's object, and her need to declare her own independence in the light of this position is flagged up from the very start.

Hildegart was the 'eugenic' child of Aurora Rodríguez Carballeira, the mother who would murder her in 1933. But she was not the only 'eugenic' child of the period. In 1913 a baby named 'Eugenette Bolce' had been born to a London woman. This caused considerable public stir, summarized with sharp disparagement by G. K. Chesterton at the end of his blistering attack on eugenics in *Eugenics and Other Evils* (1922). He related how 'a foreign gentleman' named Bolce 'was advertised on a huge scale as having every intention of being the father of the Superman. It turned out to be a Superwoman, and was called Eugenette' (Chesterton, 1922: 180). The scorn poured by Chesterton on the attempts of the parents to provide ideal conditions for the development of the child (he sends up their attempts to cultivate a sense of humour in her) echoes the satirical treatment of similar aims in Unamuno's novel *Amor y pedagogía* (1902).

The fact that we can go back to the start of the twentieth century for a Spanish satire on eugenics demonstrates how far the topic was part of public awareness. Closer to home than the coincidence between the birth in 1913 of Eugenette and that of Hildegart in December 1914 there were other events related to Aurora's eugenic project. Nicolás Amador of Barcelona, who had belonged to the English Eugenic Society between 1912 and 1915, was to publish in 1914 an article saying that what needed attention, in the light of national decadence, was the idea of selective reproduction (Amador 1914, cited in Álvarez Peláez 1988: 185). Gómez Baquero (Andrenio) reported in *Nuevo Mundo* [*New World*] on 6 October 1910 that Federico Gómez Arias had set up a prize in 1910. His intention was that the prize money should provide a dowry of 1000 pesetas for a robust, beautiful, well-behaved, moderately educated young woman of Salamanca, between the ages of fifteen and twenty-two, about to get married to a man of similar physical and moral conditions (and of appropriate age). This prize was cited in Hildegart's history of the Liga (1932b: 107), so that whether or not her mother had been aware of it earlier, it had by 1932 entered collective knowledge in the Liga.

Aurora's Choice

Although Hildegart presented herself to Ellis as a 'eugenic' child, there is no evidence that she did so habitually in public. Aurora's choice of creating a eugenic child would, however, capture the imagination of the public after Hildegart's death, arousing speculation about the identity of the father, a topic on which she was adamantly unforthcoming.

The background of Aurora's family provides a vignette that reminds us of the level of unconventionality possible in provincial Spain. The family came from El Ferrol in Galicia. Aurora's father,

Francisco Rodríguez Arriola, married for the first time in 1866, and again in 1872, his first wife having died after only three years of marriage. This second marriage was to Aurora Carballeira, some eighteen years younger than himself (Cal, 1991a: 21).[2] Five children were born between 1873 and 1884, the oldest being Josefina, Aurora coming next (Cal, 1991a: 24).

The family background was liberal. Aurora stated on a number of occasions that her father was a mason (Cal, 1991a: 22), that when his friends came there was talk of masonic lodges in the Philippines (Rendueles, 1989: 22) and that one of her grandfathers was subject to political persecution for having taken part in 'masonic-liberal activities' against the slave trade (Rendueles, 1989: 54). At her trial she elaborated on her desire that the ideals of masonry should be followed by her daughter (Toga, 1934a). Aurora appears not to have had any formal schooling, and her account of her life given to the doctors at the asylum in Ciempozuelos where she was eventually consigned after the murder of Hildegart is that of an autodidact let loose in her father's library, reading books on travel, hygiene, marriage, the law, and classic works of literature (Rendueles, 1989: 23).[3]

A family curiosity is that Hildegart was the second illegitimate child in her family. In 1896 Aurora's sister Josefina had had a son who was left in the charge of Aurora while his mother went to Madrid. The child would become the infant pianist prodigy Pepito Arriola. It appears that Josefina collected her son from her sister when it became evident that Pepito had precocious musical talent, and this when he was just a toddler.[4] Aurora's project of having her own child that she could make into a prodigy (as it seemed she had done in the case of Pepito, who went on to perform in Buenos Aires) did not follow immediately on losing her nephew. Rather the plan was one that she conceived when her father died, and she acquired the financial means to bring up a child of her own. Pepito Arriola's first successful tour to Buenos Aires in July 1912, with further visits in November of that year and January of 1913 could possibly have acted as further stimulus to her plans.[5] Hildegart was born on 9 December 1914.

How did Aurora find the ideal father for her child? The press at the time of the trial alleged that the father was a sailor, or priest, or both, or possibly an English naval chaplain (*Daily Herald*, 28 May 1934, *Sunday Chronicle*, 27 May 1934). Guzmán's novelized version of Aurora's life suggests that she meets an ideal man, but that he is unwilling to embark on the project of creating a genius. According to his version, the two then go their separate ways, and that later a man of thirty-five is introduced to her as a sailor, which Guzmán then corrects saying that he was also a priest (Guzmán, 1933: 55).[6] Rendueles, basing himself on the clinical notes from Ciempozuelos, suggests that Hildegart's father was part of Aurora's social circle. Her words, rephrased by the doctors who saw her in the asylum, carry a strong message of scorn for the chosen father: 'Como defectos le encontraba: vago, mal amigo, incapaz de tender una mano. Egoísta. Dominante, pero con astucia hipócrita' [His defects were that he was vague, a poor friend, unable to lend a hand. Selfish. Domineering, but with hypocritical cunning], adding that his culture was extensive but shallow (Rendueles, 1989: 29). Cal offers the most detailed and convincing case, identifying the father as Alberto Pallas, a cultured man, journalist and writer, and given to unorthodox methods of trying to improve the poor, a version that broadly fits with Aurora's judgment that his culture was extensive but shallow (Cal, 1991b: 126). His reforming zeal and mixture of disciplines will be characteristic of non-scientific reformers in the period. Aurora's own version, given by Sacristán* and Prados* in their psychiatric report for the defence at her trial, is that, with some distaste, she chose a man out of five of her social circle, a range of choice notably lacking in breadth (Rendueles, 1989: 203). This version is rather more credible than that of Hackl, which refers to Aurora having placed an advert for a father in a local paper stipulating that 'she was determined not to marry him or to enter into any other relationship with him that resembled marriage'. (Hackl, 1990: 29). At her trial, when asked about the father's identity Aurora responded:

> Eso no lo sabe nadie más que yo, ni podrá saberlo nadie más que yo. Mientras los hombres no paran no podrán saber de qué hijos son padres. Hildegart no tuvo padre: aquel hombre fue mi colaborador fisiológico, porque no pude fecundar artificialmente.
>
> [This is something only I know, and no-one else can know. As long as men do not give birth they cannot know which children they have fathered. Hildegart had no father: that man was my physiological collaborator,, because I could not become pregnant by artificial means.] (Toga 1934a)

The pregnancy apparently occurred after three sexual encounters.

Aurora not only wanted her child to be a model of intellectual perfection, as the clinical report for the defence summarized, but had plans for her to bring about the reform of the human race (Rendueles, 1989: 203). Aurora's ideas might have been radical, even extreme, but they were far from being foreign to her time. Her plans to put the ideas into practice, whether in the form of a eugenic child, or in the establishment of some type of experimental community do, however, set her apart. Her concept of society was of a highly regulated hierarchy of a heterosexual nature. Thus, in relation to the idea of a 'casa de labor' [workhouse], she thought that the servants therein should be married as soon as possible, and that her institution would have model men and women who in their turn produced model families. Eventually this would form a special and distinguished race, distinct from all other Spaniards (Rendueles, 1989: 28).

Engaging with Reform

In the broader context of eugenics from which Aurora's ideas derived, biology, medicine, the law and sociology all had a part to play (Álvarez Peláez, 1988: 183–4). Relevant to Aurora's choice to have a eugenic child are the following: eugenic thought in Spain in the period, especially with regard to conscious parenting; attitudes towards the regulation or otherwise of sexual activity falling outside norms of marriage; sex education and its place in society.

Spain sits firmly in the 'Latin' tradition of eugenics with provision of puericulture, hygiene and social improvement, and it is a tradition that begins before the foundation of eugenics societies. 'Hygiene' as a significant concept in Spanish medicine dates back to the 1830s when it became vital to combat outbreaks of cholera, yellow fever and syphilis in poor quarters of cities (Jagoe, 1998: 319–20). The first chairs of hygiene were established in 1843, and the work of early hygienists almost always included sections on women and sexuality (Jagoe, 1998: 320). The major writer in this area was Pedro Felipe Monlau whose *Higiene del matrimonio* [Hygiene of Marriage] first appeared in 1853. Monlau's contribution illustrates some of the ambiguities that would characterize twentieth-century eugenics in Spain, in that he situated female sexual pleasure within the activity of maternity (see

Jagoe, 1998: 319). Part of his activity was a recuperation of the feminine from the concept of woman as passionate (and primitive) being, in order to place her centre-stage in the activity of procreation. A similar shift will be observable in the later eugenic writings on woman. The 'Latin' culture of eugenics emphasizes the physical process of procreation (whereas Ellis will retain the emotion of love at the heart of his writings on sex). Emphasis on the physical is even more noteworthy in Ángel Pulido's work, *Bosquejos médico-sociales para la mujer* [Medico-Social Studies for Women] (1876). The devotion of Pulido to his cause of hygienic motherhood was strongly affiliated to the concept of woman as the *ángel del hogar* [angel of the house]. Jagoe comments on how Pulido, who enjoined women to be modest (an attribute Ellis explores at the start of the *Studies in the Psychology of Sex*) and domesticated, combined this with an excessive interest in those women who deviated from such an ideal (Jagoe, 1998: 330). This splitting between an ideal and a fascination with those who deviated from it is found elsewhere, and could be argued to be characteristic of campaigns in sexual matters. It characterizes, for example, the work of Gladstone whose passion for redeeming fallen women was matched by his intense interest in them. It further characterizes the interest in pastoral theology in nineteenth-century Spain in those who deviated from the ideals of behaviour being promoted. Similarly, the eugenic ideal of a perfect form of motherhood has a companion interest in the fate of all those who fall short of the ideal, not least in the form of prostitutes and women impeded from realizing maternity in exalted form. The even-mindedness that will be typical of the planks of the World League for Sexual Reform is not necessarily the note that strikes within purely eugenic writings.

It is thus not by chance that Aurora's ideal of bearing a child is an ideal of a daughter, who would redeem the world, go on to be a model woman, and provide continuation, since she would proceed to have model children (Rendueles, 1989: 29). But the birth of this child was to take place in an asexual context, her conception not the result of passion or pleasure. As Aurora declared 'A mí no me ha hecho gozar ningún hombre de la cintura para abajo' [No man has given me pleasure from the waist downwards] (Rendueles, 1989: 29).

A health certificate as a prerequisite for marriage would not be proposed in Spain until 19 November 1915, but the idea of hygiene and marriage follows in an unbroken line from the nineteenth-century hygienists referred to earlier. In 1904 Dr Fernández Caro gave a lecture to open the academic year at the *Sociedad Española de Higiene* on 'El matrimonio ante la higiene' [Marriage and Hygiene], and Diego Madrazo's work, *El cultivo de la especie humana. Herencia y educación. Ideal de vida* [Cultivating the Human Race. Heredity and Education. The Ideal of Life] (1904) did all but use the actual word 'eugenics' (Álvarez Peláez, 1988: 184). Madrazo was clearly salvationist in his views of the power of medical and sexual education: scientific selection was what was needed to save the human race (Madrazo, 1904: 9, cited by Álvarez Peláez, 1988: 184). A full discussion of the dimensions and nuances of Madrazo's work is given by Cleminson (2006), providing a crucial detailed case-study of this early promoter of eugenic ideas.

I have spoken above of the tendency to split into extremes in matters of hygiene, leading to a prurient interest in the extreme deviation from that ideal. An interesting example of this in Spain relates to the eugenic prize offered in Salamanca. This was the city within closest reach of the desolate region of Las Hurdes, renowned since the sixteenth century for its population believed to be the epitome of poverty, congenital illness and dire social conditions (see Sinclair 2004a). From 1922 onwards it would become the focus of hygienic reform through Marañón and Pittaluga* (both later members of the Liga). In the lecture given by Recaséns* to open the 1928 Eugenic Conference the region reappears as the epitome of degeneration embodied in an abandoned population:

> Toda raza abandonada a sus propias fuerzas e instintos degenera sin remedio. Se llega en esta pendiente degenerativa hasta Las Hurdes, siendo el primero de nuestros deberes nacionales el evitar los procesos degenerativos que puedan llevar nuestra raza a unas Hurdes inmensas. (Noguera and Huerta 1934: 329)[7]
>
> [Any race that is left to its own strength and instincts will inevitably degenerate. This slope of degeneration leads us to Las Hurdes, and one of our prime national duties is to avoid the degenerative processes that might lead our race into being an immense region of Hurdes].

Isolated, poor, stricken with endemic goitre and malaria, with additional problems of malnutrition, dwarfism and a high mortality rate, the population of the region contained all the problems hygienists and eugenicists would seek to solve. Ironically it was as though Las Hurdes held a functional position in the nation, that of being always already forgotten and yet always held in cultural memory as that place where the really backward potential of the nation could be observed (Sinclair, 2004b: 212).

The vocabulary and attitude of Ramón Escalada, cited by Polo, expresses a full eugenic horror at the negative potential of the region:

> No busquéis allí estadística criminal . . . [sic] porque el adulterio, la violación y el incesto están tan connaturalizados entre los jurdanos, que ni los consideran como delitos, ni los permite comprender la gravedad de otros actos punibles. (Polo, 1904: 125)
>
> [Do not seek criminal statistics there . . . because adultery, rape and incest are so ingrained among the *hurdanos* that neither do they consider them to be crimes, nor do they allow them to understand the seriousness of other punishable acts.]

The options seen by Escalada for the region were regeneration or extermination. Polo, however, admonishing Escalada for his demonization of Las Hurdes, then makes his own internal split, and singles out two internal others of the region, conceding that the villages of Nuño Moral and Casares might conceivably fit Escalada's view. Here one might find men :

> agitando sus flacas piernas, mostrando al desnudo tostadas y sucias carnes, saltando de peña en peña con espantosa agilidad, llevando a hombros pesado cesto de *vicio* (abono) para el huerto . . . (Polo, 1904: 126–7)
>
> [shaking their skinny legs, showing filthy sunburned flesh to view, leaping from rock to rock with horrifying agility, carrying on their shoulders a heavy basket of *vice* (manure) for the garden] . . .

Such extreme views of those considered to be degenerate are echoed by Aurora's recollection of her own family. A prime complaint she made about her sister Josefina, the mother of Pepito Arriola, was that she was bad, in all respects. In her interviews with the clinicians of Ciempozuelos she heaped censure on her sister, with little refinement: '*Josefa* murió a los 63 años. Muy mala hermana. Rencillosa, liosa, "Mala madre y mala esposa'". [*Josefa* died aged 63. Very bad sister. Caused quarrels and confusions, 'a bad mother and bad wife']. She is classed as homosexual on the basis of there having been an incident in which she was surprised by her mother with the nursemaid (Rendueles, 1989: 18). The terminology and exaggeration used by Aurora to speak of her sister suggest that she considers her little better than the prostitutes who, in the view of those who documented *la mala vida*, were no better than street criminals: 'Josefa era desordenada, sucia, de una suciedad morbosa, en los retretes de su casa se veían las huellas de sus dedos con excrementos. No se cambiaba de ropa interior hasta que ésta estaba rota' [Josefa was untidy, dirty, fatally filthy, in the toilets of her house you could see fingermarks where she had smeared excrement. She did not change her underwear until it was worn out] (Rendueles, 1989: 19).[8]

Prostitution

One of the realities of Spain behind Aurora's reforming ideas was prostitution, and when we look at the status and control of the activity we see the difficulties involved with the nation's coming to terms with sexual and social 'untidiness'. Prostitution focalized attention in eugenics in Spain, particularly in relation to the question of whether or how to make special provision to control it. In so far as hygienists wanted to ring-fence prostitution, and to make sure that venereal disease was controlled, then legislation for prostitution was viewed as progressive. But some held that prostitution had a positive role in the sexual economy. Thus Dr J. Call, a provincial Inspector of Hygiene in his *Reglamentación higiénica de la prostitución* [Hygienic Regulation of Prostitution], referred to it as a safety valve that would deal with the natural aggressiveness of men (Guereña, 2003: 21). Prostitution was thought to be a protection for woman's virginity and family honour, and believed to be significant in the struggle against male homosexuality, and male masturbation (Guereña, 2003: 22).

Post-Tissot, masturbation was generally envisaged as an activity to be avoided, not just because it was believed to affect the individual, but because it was considered to have more far-reaching consequences. Guereña cites an 1831 Spanish translation of a French work on the topic, *Estravíos secretos o El onanismo en las personas del bello sexo* [Secret Straying or Onanism in the Fair Sex] by J. L. Doussin-Dubreuil (Guereña, 2003: 22). This author is one of the many cited by Padre Claret in his advice on masturbation in *La llave de oro* [The Golden Key] (1862: 139; see Sinclair, 1998: 165–9).[9] Monlau's *Higiene del matrimonio* [Hygiene of Marriage] left no doubt about the dire effects of masturbation on the individual and his descendants:

> Si el masturbador llega por azar a la virilidad, no cuente con buena salud, ni vida longeva: resígnese a la más vergonzosa impotencia y renuncie a la fecundidad, o sepa que, cuando más, transmitirá su menguada complexión a una prole raquítica y desgraciada. (Monlau, 1853: 624, cited by Vázquez García and Moreno Mengíbar, 1997: 125)

> [If by chance the masturbator reaches manhood, he should not rely on having good health, nor a long life: he should be resigned to the most shameful impotence and give up thoughts of fertility, or should realize that at the most he will pass on his weakened constitution to wretched and stunted offspring.]

This provides a neat and simplistic example of how characteristics acquired through behaviour were thought to then enter the line of heredity. In Monlau's view excess of copulation also brought similarly disastrous consequences for the children (Monlau, 1853, cited in Jagoe, 1998: 394)

It would seem then that, for some, prostitution had its positive side in enabling the avoidance of other ills. But institutionalizing it was not straightforward. A difficulty in obtaining abolition of the regulation of prostitution was that it was a matter for provincial or municipal control. By the middle of the nineteenth century, provincial authorities held lists of prostitutes, just as they did of criminals, and of the curiously undefined categories of 'sospechosos' and 'vagos' [suspect characters and slackers] (Guereña, 2003: 91). The term 'higiene especial' [special hygiene] was used to refer to the registration and checking of prostitutes under local administrative provisions until 1918. Tensions between police and sanitary authorities led to some confusion about systems through the early twentieth century. Thus there was a proposal by the Real Consejo de Sanidad in 1905 to have a 'Reglamento especial del Servicio de higiene de la prostitución' [Special Regulation of the Service of Hygiene of Prostitution] one of the intentions of which was to separate sanitary matters from police matters. Retaliation from the police side was virtually simultaneous, as by a Reglamento de la Policía Gubernativa in 1905 they set up a special brigade whose function it was to ensure that regulations of the 'higiene de la prostitución' [hygiene of prostitution] met with full compliance (Guereña, 2003: 235–6). In 1909, however, regulation was back with provincial commissions, and listing of prostitutes was voluntary and 'gratuito' [free] (Guereña, 2003: 237). Running contrary to the spirit of regulation, which gave recognition to the activity of prostitution was the criminalization in 1904 of 'proxenetismo' [pimping]. This modified the 1870 Penal Code, and would be taken up again in Primo de Rivera's 1928 code. In 1918 there was an important move to establish medical officers whose responsibility was public hygiene, and to establish VD clinics, which would take in prostitutes suffering from venereal disease, and more generally would head the measures against such infections. Such clinics began to be set up from 1920 onwards (Guereña, 2003: 241–3).

Taking the view that 'boys will be boys' (or indeed that 'girls would be girls') embedded in earlier attitudes to the regulation of prostitution (which gave official recognition to its existence) for many reformers was, however, a cynical step too far. The major argument that would be levelled against 'regulation' by sexual reformers was that to control the activity in this way was to acknowledge that it existed and, implicitly, to tolerate it. Despite his views on masturbation, Monlau declared early on that regulation was immoral and thus anti-hygienic (Monlau, 1847: 292). Yet it was not until 1922 that the Sociedad Española del Abolicionismo [Spanish Abolitionist Society] was set up by César Juarros,* who ten years later would be one of the founding members of the Liga. The Society was to campaign against the regulation of prostitution, and the inclusion of what was termed the 'delito sanitario' [health crime] in the Penal Code (Guereña, 2003: 385). Abolition of regulation was finally achieved in 1935, albeit in a form much more cautious than originally envisaged, and in the event was not effective in suppressing brothels. It did away with the need for prostitutes to undergo regular medical examination and the requirement that they should have sanitary certificates. At the same time it required those who contracted venereal disease to have it treated and – should they be reluctant to do so – there was a provision for doctors to impose hospitalization on them (Guereña, 2003: 394–6).

Sex Education

Characteristic of attitudes to sex education among the sex reformers of this period is the espousal of openness about imparting sexual knowledge to children. In relation to eugenics in general, and in accord with the 'Latin' variety of eugenics to be found in Spain, sex education is a key factor in providing the positive face of eugenics. Education of the young (and indeed of the sexually mature) relies on a belief in the power of people to learn. It stands in contrast therefore with the coercive approaches and agenda of negative eugenics; compulsory sterilization of the mentally feeble, the insane or the criminal, attempts to 'reform' or 'cure' homosexuals, avoidance of inadvisable unions by compulsory pre-nuptial medical certificates, closure of premises associated with 'pathological' behaviour, such as brothels (see Vázquez García and Moreno Mengíbar, 1997: 170).[10] Aurora's account of her own education fits in with progressive attitudes, although it seems to have come about more by a failure to conceal than by any direct intention to educate. 'Yo ya conocía el cuerpo y la sexualidad, pues los amigos de mi padre hablaban ante mí sin tapujos, sin ocultaciones, no como se hace con otros niños y además yo me había enterado de la sexualidad por los libros.' [I already knew about the body and sexuality as my father's friends used to speak in front of me openly, hiding nothing, not as happened with other children, and besides, I had found out about sexuality from books] (Rendueles, 1989: 64). This ideal of openness in sex education (and the consciousness that it was an ideal) was passed on to Hildegart, who tells Ellis with some pride of her own early sex education, based, it would seem, on an understanding of more than simple heterosexual relations. At the age of three, she tells him, she came across the concept of 'hermaphrodite' when studying natural history, the example being that of a rose. When she then told their maid, Rosa, that she was hermaphrodite, and explained that it meant being male and female at the same time, it gave rise to uproar. Her comment to Ellis, that 'Nadie pensaba por aquel entonces en España en ninguno de estos apasionantes problemas de iniciación sexual'

[In those days no-one thought about these fascinating problems of sexual initiation] (2 December 1931), and her account of the incident curiously suggests that she had had a sexual education that other children had not, but that it was one where the information had not been fully understood and integrated. The possibility that there could be problems in being precocious (a suggestion Rendueles makes about Aurora's own education) clearly had not been entertained (see Rendueles, 1989: 65).

For those involved in eugenics and sex reform, sex education took the form of something more extensive than the simple enlightenment of children. A new discourse of sex education appears to come in at the start of the twentieth century, partially displacing a nineteenth-century Foucauldian discourse of surveillance and correction. The idea of warning the population about some of the less pleasant aspects of sexual life continued to be important. But there was a slight emphasis in the battle, away from focus on 'dangerous individuals' and towards the use of statistics related to behaviour and conditions thought to be adverse to individual and community health (Vázquez García and Moreno Mengíbar, 1997: 130–2). Clearly high on the agenda was the issue of spreading information about disease and practices that could harm individuals or their offspring. The emphasis was now not on excessive practices (the examples of masturbation and copulation warned of by Monlau) but of contagion. Hildegart herself would become involved with this, through the Campaña Sanitaria [Hygiene Campaign] of the 1920s, and through her own publications, a number of which were in pamphlet form. In the line of this preventive education, Sainz de Aja*, for example, another founder member of the Liga, produced in 1920 his popularizing pamphlet, *Sífilis, blenorragia y matrimonio* [Syphilis, Blennorrhagia and Marriage]. Its popularizing intent would become yet more evident in later editions, and continued publication into the early Franco years under the title of *Lo que todo el mundo debe saber sobre la sífilis* [What Everyone Needs to Know about Syphilis].

Arguably more effective than single pamphlets were periodical publications that had an agenda of sex education. Thus *Salud y Fuerza* [Health and Strength], a Barcelona anarchist review that appeared between 1904 and 1914, placed emphasis on sex education, but did so in the form of raising broad awareness of issues concerning sexual life and health that had a bearing on the health of the population (Cleminson, 2000: 31). It thus did more than provide sex education: it offered an education in eugenics, and published articles from outside Spain, including two by Rémy Perrier on race improvement and eugenics (Cleminson, 2000: 151).

Sex education is – in terms of the way it will be considered within the context of the WLSR – more than a simple imparting of knowledge about procreation, and in the period that concerns us, was viewed as education into good eugenic practice. Having said this, there is a degree to which 'simple' is the operative guiding word, and the crucial part of the title of the WLSR is the subtitle that alerts us to the idea of thinking about sex 'on a scientific basis'. As Vázquez García and Moreno Mengíbar point out, the coming of sex education, in its widest understanding, and not restricted to the infants of the population, moves sexual knowledge over a pivotal point. Instead of sex being the domain of the informed and the professional (as implied by the presence of a regulating society), sex education moves knowledge to the community. This wider access to knowledge about sex comes about in Spain from the 1920s (Vázquez García and Moreno Mengíbar, 1997: 131). Enlightenment of course did not have to come from Spanish sources. As they point out, and as is evidenced by Hildegart's own background in matters of eugenics and sex reform, many of Havelock Ellis's works had been translated, as had the educational work of Forel (1911). In Spain itself in this period, works of sex education had appeared: Ciro Bayo, *Higiene Sexual del soltero* [Sexual Hygiene of the Bachelor] (1902, reprinted 1919), Antonio Piga Pascual, *Higiene de la pubertad* [Hygiene of Puberty] (1910), Genaro González Carreño, *La educación sexual* [Sexual Education] (1910) and César Juarros, *Educación física y moral del niño en la familia como preparación de su futuro desenvolvimiento integral* [Physical and Moral Education of the Child in the Family as Preparation for His Future Comprehensive Development] (1918). The creation of the Instituto de Medicina Social [Institute of Social Medicine] was a crucial move in the direction of social enlightenment, and in its foundation there is an initial grouping of those who will later be associated with the Liga. Among the twenty signatories of its foundation document we find Luis Huerta*, whose book *Eugénica* [Eugenica] was published in 1918. The Institute was set up after an exchange of letters between Juarros and Antonio Aguado Marinoni. Founding members included Huerta, Sebastián Recaséns, Gustavo Pittaluga and Gregorio Marañón (Álvarez Peláez, 1988: 190–1), all later founding members of the Liga. The four sections of the Institute, research in medico-social matters (including everything from strike action to healthy reproduction), popular and professional education, 'social propaganda' and 'political action' shows a strong presence of a pedagogical intent. The fact that the Institute did not have success at this point is possibly due to the coming of the Dictatorship, but – as seen by the contrast with the relative success of the Liga – it may have also suffered from a combination of an over-ambitious programme and lack of international support, as Álvarez Peláez suggests (1988: 192–3).

Eighteen years would pass between the conception of Hildegart and the conception of the Liga. But two things are clear. Hildegart was born into a world already sensitized to the message of eugenics, a message that was being promoted with energy in 'hygienic' circles in Spain. Awareness of disease, of the possible negative burdens of heredity (and a concomitant sense that there could be 'positive' aspects of humanity passed down through the genes) was firmly entrenched in reformist areas of Spanish society. By the time Hildegart was born a significant number of the Liga's future members were already in the public eye. Some were already publishing in the early years of the twentieth century, their publications firmly within the field of medicine. These included Sánchez Covisa's* work on syphilis, *Los pseudo-chancros sifilíticos y el tratamiento abortivo de la sífilis* [Pseudo-Syphilitic Chancres and the Abortive Treatment of Syphilis] (1919) and numerous works by Sainz de Aja on the use of salvarsan in the treatment of syphilis. Concentration on the darker side of eugenics was reinforced by awareness of the fates awaiting children: Huerta published *Por qué mueren los niños* [Why Children Die] (1914), and Lafora*[11] focused on *Los niños mentalmente anormales* [Mentally Abnormal Children] (1917). At the same time, the idealism that led Aurora to her project of redemption was also present. In 1917, Huerta lectured in Gijón on *La conquista del bienestar* [Achieving Well-Being], and Ortiz de Pinedo* brought out *El afán de vivir* [Desire for Life] (1917). Greater public attention was secured through the daily press. A sample scan of *El Sol* for 1920 reveals numerous articles on or by Marañón, Pittaluga, Juarros and Haro* while Lafora wrote every two or three weeks on topics relating to medicine, psychiatry, and medical education. As Hildegart would grow and mature, so would the organization of the Liga.

NOTES

1. The exposition by Poldervaart (1995) of the attitudes of utopian socialists to sexuality explains some of the idealism underlying Aurora's ideas, making more evident the extremity of what would be revealed about her views on sexuality.
2. Cal gives the date of the first marriage as 1886, when Francisco Rodríguez was 33, but given that he was born in 1833 this date should be 1866.
3. The clinical notes from Aurora's time in the asylum, providing much of our information about Aurora's life, are reproduced by Rendueles (1989), as is the psychiatric report on her by Sacristán and Prados.
4. Pepito apparently played before the Congress of Psychology in Paris in 1900 (see *Revue Scientifique*, 6 October 1900, 432).
5. See accounts of Pepito Arriola's performances in Buenos Aires in *Nosotros* (Buenos Aires), 6 (42) (July 1912), 242–4; 6 (43) (November 1912), 96–9; 7 (45) (January 1913), 145–6; 7 (55) (November 1913), 222–3; 15 (143) (April 1921), 561; 16 (155) (April 1922), 573–4. He was sponsored in his visits by the Blüthner piano company.
6. Guzmán's version of Aurora's life is given some credence by his having been chosen by her to write it. To this end he visited her in prison, after the murder, with Ezekiel Endériz. His fictionalized account served as the basis for that of Hackl.
7. Cited from the text of the lecture as repeated for the 1933 Eugenics Conference. José Goyanes, who had accompanied Marañón on his 1922 visit to Las Hurdes, would also give a lecture in the 1933 series on Las Hurdes as a centre of racial degeneration (Noguera and Huerta, 1934: 412–23).
8. Some of Aurora's hostile comments on her family derived from her perception that she was fundamentally abandoned by her mother (Grau, 1934a).
9. For the lengthy history of earlier concern within the Church about masturbation see Vázquez García and Moreno Mengíbar, 1997: 70–94, and for attitudes post-Tissot, 94–116.
10. For a full survey of attitudes towards homosexuality in Spain, and in particular to the medical attitudes towards homosexuality, see Cleminson and Vázquez García (2007: Chapter Two).
11. Note that Lafora is the name by which Gonzalo Rodríguez Lafora was habitually known.

Chapter Three

Growing up under the Dictatorship

Los padres . . . abandonan el deber moral de educadores de sus hijos, y asusta pensar en los hogares que las generaciones así formadas constituirán en no lejano plazo.

Recordemos a este intento la sublime máxima del Zende-Avesta;

'Instruid cumplidamente a vuestros hijos, si anheláis ser perfectos, porque el mundo, después, de sus acciones, os hará responsables y no a ellos.' (Hildegart, 'Instruid cumplidamente a vuestros hijos' [Instruct your children properly], *Sexualidad*, 22 August 1926)

[Parents . . . abandon the moral duty of educating their children, and it is terrifying to think of the homes thus resulting that will exist in the near future.

Let us remember on this topic the sublime maxim of Zende-Avesta;

'If you wish to be perfect, instruct your children properly, because the world will later hold you and not them responsible for their actions.'

la obra de la educación no tiene término fijo, período determinado, pues el espíritu puede siempre ensancharse y el corazón mejorar constantemente. (Hildegart on education, *Sexualidad*, 23 October 1927)

[the task of education has no fixed ending, no limited period, since the spirit can always be broadened and the heart always improved.]

El hombre tiene un radio de acción para su desenvolvimiento; mas dentro del reducido círculo de sus medios puede llevar a cabo una de las más grandes obras en beneficio de la Humanidad, cumpliendo sus deberes, que le reportarán la estabilidad de su posición social, material y moral. Por lo tanto, sus deberes más ínfimos, cumplidos, sus virtudes más mínimas, bien ejecutadas, son los cimientos del edificio espiritual del carácter. (Hildegart, on character and duty, *Sexualidad*, 15 January 1928)

[Man has a sphere of action in which to develop; but within the limited scope of his means he can bring about one of the greatest works for the benefit of Humanity by fulfilling his duties, and which will yield him stability in his social, material and moral position. Thus, his most minor duties, if attended to, and his least virtues, if well put into practice, are the foundations of the spiritual dwelling of the character.]

La Pedagogía sexual del niño y del adolescente ha de ser *puritana*; para que – a su hora – la Ética sexual del adulto pueda, sin riesgo, ser *liberal*. (Saldaña, *La sexología*, 1930)

[The sexual education of the child and the adolescent should be *puritan*, so that in due time, the sexual Ethics of the adult may, without risk, be *liberal*.]

When Primo de Rivera's dictatorship began in 1923, Hildegart was nine years old. She would briefly go to a convent school to prepare her for entering the Instituto for her secondary education, and at this point – a sign of her precocious development – was just four years away from beginning her university studies. Surprisingly she took her first communion when at the convent school, an event marked by her mother with a ring inscribed May 1923 (Cal, 1991a: 61). Aurora's explanation for this – that she did not wish Hildegart to forego the pleasure of dressing up in white for the event (Grau, 1934a) – seems barely credible. The idea that Hildegart wanted to know what other companions were talking about when they spoke of going to Mass seems more plausible, as does the decision that some years mother and daughter would go to Mass, so that she would understand what it was about (Cal, 1991a: 62).[1]

Hildegart's entry into public education did not mean that Aurora took a diminished interest in it. A mother whose daughter was at the same school as Hildegart spoke of how, on collecting her from school, Aurora habitually told her daughter off for minor faults and shortcomings (Cal, 1991a: 61). Aurora's own account of her educational role is that of an exacting taskmaster: 'Yo le exigía catorce horas de trabajo intelectual que yo seleccionaba para ella: derecho, anatomía, humanidades, sexología (yo siempre le hablé del tema a Hildegart) y también actividades físicas, caminar, cuidar a los animales' [I made her do fourteen hours intellectual work a day on topics selected by me: law, anatomy, humanities, sexology (I always spoke to Hildegart on this subject) and physical activity: walking, looking after animals]. In this exacting, even punishing regime, rest was clearly meant just to be a change: 'Le inculqué que descansar es cambiar de actividad y no dejar la cabeza a pájaros' [I drummed it into her that to rest is to change activity and not a matter of leaving the brain to idle musings] (Rendueles, 1989: 100). The curriculum appears to come straight out of a sex reform manual, crossed with one of progressive education as at Beacon Hill, the progressive boarding school set up by Bertrand and Dora Russell in 1927 and whose activities would be reported in the first number of *Sexus* ([Hildegart?], 1932).[2] Aurora's approach, however, seems far removed from the self-determination encouraged at the school, and well distant from that of another theorist whose progressive ideas were much in vogue, Rudolf Steiner.[3]

Hildegart's entry into public activity comes within a eugenic framework, and we find a further layer of her education in the company she keeps and the speakers alongside whom she finds herself. Later, in 1929, she will join the Unión General de Trabajadores (UGT) (at the age of fourteen) and will take part in the Congreso de las Juventudes Socialistas [Conference of Socialist Youth] the following year (Rendueles, 1989: 106). But in March 1926, at the age of eleven, we find her making her debut in the Campaña Sanitaria [Hygiene Campaign] of Antonio Navarro Fernández. A specialist in dermatology and venereology, Navarro Fernández's bent of social and hygienic reform is evident from 1909, the date of two publications: *La prostitución en la villa de Madrid* [Prostitution in the City of Madrid] and *Conciencia y voluntad sociales* [Social Will and Conscience]. Slightly later his dermatological and forensic interests surfaced in *Dactiloscopia en España: Estudio médico forense de la identidad* [Fingerprinting in Spain: Forensic Study of Identity] (1912), while *El porvenir de la raza blanca* [The Future of the White Race] (1912) signalled his interest, in common with others of the period, in issues of race and nation. His hygienist commitment is further evidenced by his being a contributor to the review *Archivos De Higiene y Sanidad Pública* [Archives of Hygiene and Public Health] from its inception in January 1925. Navarro Fernández appears in the activities of the *Archivos* with a number of others who, like himself, will be founding members of the Liga. This group includes the manager of the publication, Mario Sánchez Taboada*, who also wrote as medical correspondent for *El Liberal*, other contributors being Pittaluga, Juarros, Marañón and Bravo Sanfelíu*.[4]

Contrasting with the somewhat parochial nature of aspects of the Hygiene Campaign, the *Archivos* had a strong international character. Pittaluga, listed as one of the regular contributors, was also on the Comité de Higiene de las Naciones [Hygiene Committee of the Nations]. The sections on bibliography and reviews in the *Archivos* are overwhelmingly international in content: in 1925 some 105 items are reported of which only twenty-one are Spanish in origin (20 per cent). Nor are they restricted to items from Europe, but include material from the US, Canada and Japan, and in August 1925 carry two British items reporting on material from Siam, South Africa and New Zealand (taken from *The Lancet* and the *British Medical Journal*). In that same number there is a brief item that flags up what will be a recurrent interest for eugenicists and sexual reformers, namely the possibility of adopting an international language: it was judged of interest to the readers of the *Archivos* therefore to mention in the section of current news items that the Esperanto Centre in Madrid had made Carlos Cortezo president.[5]

The activities of the Hygiene Campaign were published in *Sexualidad*, a journal of signal importance that ran from 1925 to 1928. As noted by Cleminson (2000: 79) a full study of this review is still to come.[6] It occupies an interesting middle ground in that it aims at providing straightforward information on sex with an attitude to the family that is clearly moral, albeit not overtly Catholic. It declared itself as engaged with the 'task of regeneration', one that entailed racial improvement (Cleminson, 2000: 79). In 1925 when *Sexualidad* begins publication, the participation of those who would become key players in the Liga is evident: Jiménez Asúa, Juarros, Macau*, Marañón, Pittaluga, Saldaña*, Recaséns, Haro and – with particular prominence – Jaime Torrubiano Ripoll*. There are a number of single appearances that are quite striking. Ellen Key, the Swedish reformer to whom Hildegart writes at the same time as Ellis, published an article on free love on 25 July 1926, a year in which numerous pieces by Hildegart herself (then aged thirteen) appear. Shortly after this, on 12 September 1926, Margarita Nelken* wrote on how to educate future Spanish mothers, a piece wide-ranging in examples, particularly from Germany. Less expected still are contributions from better known figures. Azorín, for example, writes supportively in 'La propaganda sanitaria' [Sanitary Propaganda] about measures of public health (1 August 1926). Even Ortega makes an appearance on 5 December 1926, albeit with 'Para una antropología filosófica: Darwin y el principio de los contrastes' [Towards Philosophical Anthropology: Darwin and the Principle of Contrasts], an article less directly linked to the main concerns of *Sexualidad* than to the sort of publications appearing at the time in his own *Revista de Occidente*.

In addition to those who published in *Sexualidad* we can get a sense of the surrounding spectrum of support from the list of those published on 28 June 1925 who took part in the 'mitines de propaganda sanitaria' [Meetings of Sanitary Propaganda]. A further founding member of the Liga is there, Rocamora*. The cast of supporters includes Joaquín Noguera, brother of Enrique Noguera*, one of the two editors of the proceedings of the Eugenics Conference of 1933, and himself a writer on eugenics, publishing *Moral, eugenesia y derecho* [Morality, Eugenics and Law] in 1930. The world of mainstream newspaper publishing represented by Ortega is further reinforced by the presence of Ricardo Gasset, the director of *El Imparcial*. Criminology is embodied in Bernaldo de Quirós, author of *La mala vida en Madrid* [Low-life in Madrid] (1901), and Rafael Salillas, Director of the School of Criminology. Medicine, in addition to the presence of various Liga founders who had medical affiliation (Marañón, Haro, Rocamora, Juarros and Macau) was strengthened by an official presence in the form of Ignacio Baüer, President of the Colegio de Médicos [College of Doctors].

We can regard *Sexualidad* as a sort of discussion going on around Hildegart, a context into which we can fit her own interventions, an intellectual first home (that is, one that might be outside her mother's influence, although this is not certain). *Sexualidad* is the place where she would first have heard of the WLSR, given its reports on 31 October and 7 November 1926 of the 1921 Berlin Congress (claimed after the event to be part of the series of the WLSR events) (Dose, 2003: 1).

Two figures of interest in *Sexualidad* are Torrubiano Ripoll and Saldaña, because of their particular brand of morality and commitment to the study of sexuality. Torrubiano Ripoll, an academic theologian, had his own specialism, a subject defined as 'Teología sexual' [Sexual Theology], and a section of this name carried items by him through 1925 and the first part of 1926. He opposed education run by the Church, and proposed as the 'reading list' for 'Teología sexual' items including Havelock Ellis, *Estudios de Psicología Sexual* [Studies of Sexual Psychology] and Iwan Bloch, *La vida sexual contemporánea* [Contemporary Sexual Life] (Torrubiano Ripoll, 1925: 2–3). Although he can be viewed as the major writer to offer reconciliation between religious belief and the aims of sex reformers (Vázquez García and Moreno Mengíbar 1997: 150, n. 302) the degree to which he was not a religious conformist is evidenced by his being prepared to contemplate sterilization for the delinquent or mentally deficient (Vázquez García and Moreno Mengíbar, 1997: 171). His major contribution to the field surrounding Hildegart would be his *Teología y eugenesia* [Theology and Eugenics] (1929).

Quintiliano Saldaña, who would eventually supervise Hildegart's thesis when she studied law, publishes four pieces in 1925 and 1926, not on law but sexuality: 'La vida sexual' [Sexual Life] (14 June 1925), 'Una civilización sexual' [Sexual Civilization] (3 January 1926), and two companion pieces on 'Una civilización asexual' [Asexual Civilization] (10 and 17 January 1926). Later, in his *Siete ensayos sobre sociología sexual* [Seven Essays on Sexual Psychology] (1929) and *La sexología (Ensayos)* [Sexology (Essays)] (1930), he would expound a position of interest in sexual matters, but caution in action. He did not support birth control, believing that 'riman sexualidad y fecundidad' [sexuality and fertility rhyme] (Saldaña 1929: 12). His attitude towards birth control, unlike that of Hildegart who would be his pupil, was of disapproval: it was a matter for concern that the birth-rate was going down. Noting that neo-Malthusian methods were being publicized through the Barcelona publication *Salud y Fuerza* he sourly commented that the publication did not justify its motto in terms of either literature or hygiene (1929: 43). His stance on Spain and sexuality was not unlike that of Unamuno: a vision that was austere, moral, lacking in sensuality. His comments on love in Iberia are typical (1929: 27). According to this, ancient Iberian man was necessarily chaste, occupied with hunting, athletic and virgin, far from the weakening influence of women, and Saldaña laments the passing of this fundamentally pure national being (1929: 29). Nonetheless he adopts a position of radical denial in relation to the idea of homosexuality in Spain: 'felizmente, no existen formas estables de inversión sexual' [fortunately there are no stable forms of sexual inversion]. Above all, Saldaña's commitment was to sex and love within marriage. Consequently for him 'free love' was a love that freely engaged in the commitment of marriage (1929: 71).

Saldaña is not an anarchist, and yet his ideal of the chosen commitment of the couple has a strong resonance with the anarchist ideal of the companion. His position on divorce (an essay originally of 1924) is surprising if we look at his traditionalism, yet less so if we think of him in quasi-anarchist terms. He is reluctant to contemplate it, and yet does so, in a lengthy discussion of possible conditions for it (1929: 92–106).

Saldaña's position in the *Siete ensayos* is quaint, yet *La sexología* must be regarded as a major work of dissemination of current thinking and trends in sexology. He exemplifies for us how being a progressive in the area of sex reform does not mean necessarily subscribing to a canon of ideas, but rather indicates adherence to a movement some of whose goals prompt approval. *La sexología* combines a Catholic moral attitude in which traditional and biblical reference is part of the apparatus of persuasion, but it also abounds in international reference. Saldaña cites Ellis repeatedly, Freud less so, and somewhat more unexpectedly, a 1923 essay by Melanie Klein in *Imago* (1930: 91–2). Yet his strong moral line on prohibition of sex outside marriage is based on Exodus 20: 14 and Saint Paul (1930: 30), and he shows himself at home with a vast and unusual array of saints when discussing the sexual origins of the psychosis of mystics (1930: 164–6). Meanwhile his view on sex education, as indicated in the epigraph, has a strong base in the need to keep childhood pure in order to make a later liberalism a 'safe' option (1930: 123).

Also of note in *Sexualidad* is Haro, the man who would spark tremendous feelings of paranoia and anxiety in Hildegart in July 1932 because of the threat he appeared to pose to her position in the Liga. We have no record of Hildegart's thoughts on the identity of her father, but Haro's article of 27 June 1926 'Por la infancia abandonada. La investigación de la paternidad' [For abandoned childhood. The investigation of paternity] could have had particular resonance for her at this point when she was in her early teens.

Hildegart's Debut

The array of those who would become prominent in the discussions of sex reform and eugenics and who are associated with *Sexualidad* can be interpreted, as above, in terms of their national and international significance, and their intellectual outreach. But the actual meetings of the Hygiene Campaign, and Hildegart's presence in them, are of a more reduced world. A snapshot of the people involved in the campaign is provided by a writer named 'Espectador' [Spectator] who wrote 'Pro cultura sanitaria' [For Sanitary Culture] in *Sexualidad* on 22 January 1928 (apropos of a meeting on 27 November 1927). The gathering he describes is composed of well-intentioned middle-class people, not unlike those associated with the Eugenics Society, if rather more tame: 'Un público limpio, sereno, sufrido, casi manso' [a clean, serene, long-suffering, almost docile audience]. Notable by his absence from the gathering is the 'obrero' [worker], since neither he nor the aristocracy (also absent) judge the meeting of any social importance. The problem here is that – for this observer at least – the 'obrero' is caught up with issues of politics, unconvinced by issues of education and public hygiene (Espectador, 1928: 3).[7] An astute further comment by this writer is that there is an excess of young people among the campaign speakers: they want to make a name. This included Hildegart, and the jockeying for position between the speakers certainly bears this out. Whether the real protagonist here is Hildegart or – as in the case of beautiful baby competitions, her mother – is a matter for conjecture.[8]

Between 4 April 1926 and 1 December 1928 Hildegart appeared forty-seven times in *Sexualidad*, and there are twenty articles by her, all in connection with the Hygiene Campaign. Some of the articles, primarily those at the start of this period, are written versions of speeches that she made in the Sunday meetings. The brief summaries of her articles show that she spoke on major 'moral' topics (character, duty), with an admixture of philosophy and ethics, and a proportion of topics that link to eugenics. In her pieces on women it is evident that she espoused a eugenic valuation for the importance of women in that she spoke of their maternal destiny and duty, but – in a manner consonant with the fundamentally conservative persuasions of those about her, including Marañón – she restricted her comments on women to those maternal zones. None of the articles are outstanding in terms of their interest or import. They resemble youthful essays on topics that are abstruse and theoretical, and certainly too detached (in terms of experience) from her own life. What they suggest, by their nature and their subject-matter, is the idea that Hildegart was producing work if not to order, then at a prompting.

The restricted social stratum of the campaign where Hildegart makes her debut accounts in part for the careful manner of her presentation and conceivably for the limitation of her views. This is a context into which she steps. She is presented as one of two new speakers, wrongly called 'Señorita Hidelgart'. (Misspellings characterize her appearances in the reports of the campaign, a sign perhaps of not quite managing to be taken seriously.) At the first mention, 28 March 1926 (when she is thirteen), her intervention is reported briefly, but it is sweeping in its aim, as she calls on Spanish women to join the campaign whose main aim is the defence of women and children.[9] A week later, however, on 4 April 1926, her range of comment – on the need to protect plants and animals – seems to be more within the remit of the child. Notwithstanding the juvenile nature of her speech, she is obviously being primed for prominence, in that she speaks immediately after the campaign's organizer, Navarro Fernández. Misnamed once again on 25 April 1926, speaking next but one after Navarro Fernández, Hildegart is reported as making a rather prim appeal to young women not to be taken in by modern fashion and to aim at being perfect wives and mothers. By 2 May 1926 she speaks on the fire service. Here, in the painstaking and indeed painful simplicity of her speech, recorded one assumes to some degree verbatim, she praises the fire brigade: 'un organismo valeroso y abnegado' [a valiant and selfless organization].

It is on 22 August 1926 that something of greater length appears, this time what appears to be the complete text of a speech with the title 'Instruid cumplidamente a vuestros hijos' [Instruct your children properly]. The general direction of her speech is simple: society needs to give its children appropriate moral instruction in order to combat the wave of selfishness threatening the future of Spain. Hildegart is responding to a speech by Juarros, but although this gives a context for her words, the overriding impression is a mixture of high rhetoric, intellectual emptiness, and internal lack of coherence. The conclusion is either that she has not produced it herself, or that she is producing something parrot-fashion, a feature that argues for the close interest and influence of her mother.[10] Here, for the first time, Hildegart makes reference to a type of deity, referred to simply as 'Aquél que todo le obedece' [The One that all obey]. Her title comes from the Zende-Avesta, the sacred book of Zoroastrianism, and this, with other references to Eastern religions that occur later in her offerings, suggest that she has been given some orientation in these areas, although the depth of it is not at all apparent.[11]

By 13 February 1927, however, Hildegart seems to have emerged from the position of the child prodigy into one of some prominence. Speaking in the Cinema Real (a venue that is typical of the campaign), she comes first after Navarro Fernández, and speaks on the inequalities of the law as it affects women. Her discourse is now more abstract, and indeed it is reported as 'discourse'. She takes woman above that of a being in need of protection (enjoining her to aspire to 'elevación cultural' [cultural elevation]), and her syntax is more complex.

From this point, Hildegart makes a rapid rise. Characteristically the first speaker to come after Navarro Fernández, she provides the exotic and elevated cultural note in proceedings. It is not always obvious that what she has to say is closely related to the campaign, and the range of her references is striking. In an authored piece her view of philosophy (27 March 1927) is that it is a way of combating 'el príncipe de la oscuridad espiritual' [the prince of spiritual darkness], and in the report of her Sunday speech of the same day she combines the law and Confucius, suggesting that one should study the former through the latter. This is followed up a week later on 3 April when she looks at the problem of woman in relation to her legal status, with assistance from the Vedas. And if she is happy to have recourse to Eastern religious systems (not always specified), she also draws on some sort of humanist tradition. Initially (9 January 1927) the aims seem remarkably like traditional Catholic ones, yet Hildegart is anxious to dissociate herself from philanthropic or charitable activities run by religious groups. When she turns again to the image of woman on 5 June 1927, her language becomes flowery, and not far removed from the sentimental discourse of the *novela rosa*. She speaks on the desirability of breastfeeding. Her tone is elevated, her syntax complex (even contorted), her expression saccharine, and her sentiments those of the sentimental novel, as she refers to the rosebud to be placed in the mouth of the infant to receive life and 'divine nectar'. This could easily come from a late nineteenth-century conduct manual.

Where is all this wide range of reference coming from, not to mention the odd mix of traditions on which Hildegart seems to draw? Not obviously from the other major figures connected with *Sexualidad* that are mentioned earlier. But the utopian nature of the volumes in her grandfather's library will have had some input (via Aurora), and in addition to this Hildegart is a new student, officially in 'filosofía y letras' [philosophy and letters], and also studying law.[12] It would be surprising if the curriculum of her course did not contain various general manuals of knowledge. The recommended book selection of the Bibliotecas Populares when they were instituted by the Residencia de Estudiantes in 1918 demonstrates how general guides were much in vogue, and likely also to provide material for at least first and second year university students. Hildegart makes a reference on 10 April 1927 to her friend and mentor Méndez Bejarano* (Álvarez Peláez and Huertas, 1987: 80), for whom forty-five works are listed in the Biblioteca Nacional catalogue, many of them general literary works but also including a *Historia de la filosofía en España hasta el siglo XX* [History of Philosophy in Spain up to the Twentieth Century]. A further source of Hildegart's references appears to be freemasonry. Her reference to the 'Sér Supremo que a todos nos ha creado' [Supreme Being who has created us all] (16 October 1927), and the 'Sumo Artífice' [Great Architect] (30 October 1927) both suggest this, and would not be surprising given Aurora's masonic background (see Chapter Two).

A salient feature of the short articles of Hildegart in *Sexualidad* is the brief encapsulating sentence. We might see this as an early form of the sound bite, something Hildegart learned from an early point to manipulate as a useful ploy on public occasions. But it is also possible that this indicates her use of general manuals of information, freely plundered to produce her utterances at the

Sunday meetings and their publication. Thus on 4 December 1927, her piece opens with an epigraph from Samuel Smiles and follows with definitions of duty and the law:

> El Deber es la necesidad racional de cumplir libremente el bien, exigido por el orden social.
>
> Por el contrario, el derecho se considera como actividad o poder moral de hacer o exigir el bien, según razón y libertad.
>
> [Duty is the rational need to do good freely, as required by social order.
>
> By contrast, the law is the moral activity or power of doing or requiring good, according to reason and liberty.]

Her statements appear to have emerged direct from the dictionary. Their lapidary style of definition is typical of these early pieces, and may indicate the methods adopted to write the pieces, as well as – perhaps – a choice of reading that is itself structured, simplified, and in manual form.

Hildegart's recorded public appearances in the Hygiene Campaign came to an end on 25 December 1927 when, aged just thirteen, she was shunted back to the wings and a gendered position that took woman as its focus. The meeting for her final appearance had a strongly emotional bent, with Navarro Fernández concentrating on infanticide (with special sympathy for the mother). Hildegart herself is reported as giving 'la nota sentimental' [the sentimental note] in her plea that women should learn to be more tender, so that they would become better mothers. After the report of the Hygiene Campaign, a gushing poem by Gómez Sebastián about how he has been saddened and deceived puts the finishing touch on what has been increasingly saccharine. There is, in retrospect, more than a little irony in Hildegart's plea.

Hildegart never returns to her previous prominence in this publication, making her last appearance on 1 December 1928, her relegation being expressed in the misspelling of her name. In the meantime other young women have appeared in her slot, similarly encased in a limited gendered role. She appears briefly on 15 January 1928, with a note in the Social Hygiene section, and a routine mention of speaking up for the protection of women and children. *Sexualidad* is then suspended for a year, until

1 December 1928, when Hildegart makes her last appearance, she is misspelt as 'Hildegar' and speaking rather generally on culture and society. The UGT would provide a new arena for her activities, and a place to move on in personal terms. But other outlets for reform were available outside the domain of the Hygiene Campaign.

Vicissitudes of Reform Under Primo

Spanish law is gathered under the Penal Code and the Civil Code, with various spheres of activity falling under the jurisdiction of provincial authorities (as in the case of prostitution, discussed in the previous chapter). Primo's attitude to public life was unpredictable, and, as Carr puts it, his 'paternalistic care for the nation bordered on eccentricity' (Carr, 1966: 565). A feature of this care is arguably his decision to reform the Penal Code, a procedure rarely undertaken. The Code in force was fundamentally that of 1848, revised in 1850 and then 1870. Hildegart was reported as commenting on the planned new code on 27 February 1927, when she spoke in favour of equality before the law of the two sexes, and defending the reform of the Civil Code.[13] Her reference here is not entirely clear. There was equality of the sexes under the constitution, as pointed out by Carmen de Burgos (Louis, 2005: 42, citing de Burgos, 1927: 84–5). In the revised Penal Code of 1928 inequality was still evident.[14] A woman who caused herself to abort or went to have an abortion was liable to a sentence of between two and four years, whereas a man causing an abortion would be punished by imprisonment of between six months and four years. Distinctions were made between women considered 'honestas' [decent] (articles 605 and 606) and prostitutes (article 600), the rape of whom attracted a lower penalty than that of other women above the age of eighteen. The articles on prostitution (608–610), however, did not take up the firm abolitionist stance that would be adopted by Hildegart, Juarros, Carmen de Burgos and Concha Peña in the Semana Abolicionista [Abolition week] (Ruiz Salvador, 1976: 264), and merely set out the punishment for those involved in acting as third parties in prostitution, and for the corruption of minors. Notwithstanding the provision for making a criminal act of the deliberate contagion of venereal disease (article 538), thus following the idea of the 'health crime' as campaigned for by César Juarros in his Abolitionist Society established in 1922 (Guereña, 2003: 385–6), the revised code did little to liberalize legislation. Article 618 forbade the publication of theory or practical advice on birth control, and the provisions for public scandal outlawed homosexual acts in private and in public (article 616).[15] The Code might have been reformed, but hardly in the direction desired by sex reformers.

The 1928 Eugenics Conference

Primo's regime also flew directly in the face of the activity of sex reformers and eugenicists alike in its limitation of how the public might be informed about sexual matters. The suppression of the first Eugenics Conference in 1928, when issues of eugenics and birth control were aired publicly, could have come as no surprise, even with the unpredictability of the regime. Yet it was done with typical inefficiency and patently in response to conservative pressure. The conference was closed by decree, but this closure was after it had been in operation for seven weeks, so that a majority of the planned nine lectures had in fact taken place. The closure came about through pressure from two Catholic daily papers, *El Debate* and *El Siglo Futuro*, rather than because of unprompted intervention by the government (Noguera, 1934: 404; Pérez Sanz and Bru Ripoll, 1987: 17). Of the seven lectures, five then appeared as an appendix to the publication of the *Libro de las primeras jornadas eugénicas españolas* [Book of the First Eugenics Conference] (1934).

In setting up the conference in the first place the organizers tried to avoid conflict by including a variety of viewpoints in its speakers. Enrique Noguera commented that there was a deliberate choice to include diversity in the speakers, including Laburu, a Jesuit, Sureda (a chaplain publicly in opposition to Lafora) and Ossorio y Gallardo, a *maurista* ex-minister. At the same time there were men of the left such as Jiménez de Asúa*, Sanchís Banús* and Hoyos Sainz* (Noguera and Huerta, 1934: 402).[16] The papers not republished in the 1933 papers belonged to the two religious speakers. One of them, Laburu, had resigned from the conference after the attacks on it by clerical papers, but Noguera was careful to exempt both him and Sureda from complicity with the attack (Noguera, 1934: 405).

Glick identifies the group who put on the 1928 conference as the Spanish chapter of the WLSR, formalized as the Liga in 1932 (Glick, 2003: 70). Before this, as we have seen, various of them were involved in the Hygiene Campaign. But significant members of those involved in the conference would be involved in the 1932 grouping: Enrique Noguera, Jiménez de Asúa, Sanchis Banús, Recaséns, Marañón. The programme of lectures for the 1928 conference has a distinct emphasis on matters of procreation, maternity and the dangers posed to children by ignorance or avoidance of eugenic measures.[17]

The decree that closed the conference down stated that the closure was because of a mismatch of audience and material, in which the speakers had brought inappropriate matter to a mixed public. This included 'conceptos verdaderamente demoledores de la familia y de los fundamentos sociales, y destructivos de la santidad del matrimonio y de la dignidad de la mujer' [concepts truly ruinous for the family and social foundations, and destructive of the sanctity of marriage and the dignity of woman]. Themes such as eugenics and euthanasia (a topic not obviously present in the lectures) might go before experts, but could not go into an arena where they might turn into anti-birth propaganda. The activity was classed as 'pornographic' and liable to corrupt the young (Pérez Sanz and Bru Ripoll, 1987: 15). Ironically the lecture of Sureda, billed to be given on 22 March 1928, the day the decree was issued, was the one most likely to contain elements that could be considered pornographic: '¡No moechaberis! Discreteo ético-psíquico-religioso sobre la urgencia de la sensualidad' [Thou Shalt not Commit Adultery! Ethico-Psychic-Religious Disquisition on the Pressing Nature of Sensuality].[18]

Publishing and Not Being Damned

Under Primo a tightrope was regularly walked in the area of making revolutionary ideas public. As Hildegart points out in her history of the Liga in the first number of *Sexus* the suspension of the 1928 eugenics conference made publicity through speech seem a risky venture, while the book was as yet not subject to pre-censorship. She records an impressive core list of eugenic and reform volumes published in the Dictatorship. Some of the works seem to have sunk without trace, but many are titles published by those who would found the Liga: Marañón, *Amor, Conveniencia y Eugenesia* [Love, Compatibility and Eugenics] (1929) and *Los estados intersexuales en la especie humana* [Intersexual States in the Human Race] (1929);[19] Jiménez de Asúa, *Libertad de amar y derecho a morir* [The Freedom to Love and the Right to Die] (1928) (a work that promptly reached three editions); Hernández Catá*, *El ángel de Sodoma* [The Angel of Sodom] (1928); Nóvoa Santos*, *La mujer, nuestro sexto sentido y otros esbozos* [Woman, Our Sixth Sense and Other Sketches] (1929), *Cuerpo y espíritu* [Body and Spirit] (1930) and *El instinto de la muerte* [The Death Instinct] (1928); Juarros, *La sexualidad encadenada* [Sexuality in Shackles] (1931); Saldaña, *Siete ensayos sobre sociología sexual* (1928) and *Sexología* (1930); Torrubiano Ripoll, *Teología y Eugenesia* (1929); Ruiz Funes*, *Endocrinología y Criminalidad* [Endocrinology and Criminality] (1929) (winner of the Premio Lombroso, 1928); Vital Aza*, *Feminismo y sexo* [Feminism and Sex] (1928); Otaola*, *Sexo y matrimonio* [Sex and Marriage];[20] Roso de Luna, *Aberraciones psíquicas del sexo* [Psychic Aberrations of Sex];[21] Barcía Goyanes*, *La vida, el sexo y la herencia* [Life, Sex and Heredity];[22] López Ureña*, *El misterio de la vida* [The Mystery of Life] (1929); Oriol Anguera*, *Monogamia y poligamia* [Monogamy and Polygamy] (1930);[23] Campoy, *El amor y la patología* [Love and Pathology] (1931); Maraury, *Impotencia, esterilidad e inconsumación ante el Derecho* [The Law and Impotence, Sterility and Non-Consumption] (1931); Joaquín Noguera, *Moral, Eugenesia y Derecho* [Morality, Eugenics and Law] (1930); Bugallo Sánchez*, *La higiene sexual en las escuelas* [Sexual Hygiene in Schools] (1930). Hildegart notes other 'younger' authors, Díez Fernández, Donato and Haro, who joined in the campaign with their books, contributing with good intentions rather than other qualities.[24] Lastly, Hildegart mentions her own contributions, *El problema sexual tratado por una mujer española* [The Sexual Problem Discussed by a Spanish Woman] (1931b), *La rebeldía sexual de la juventud* [The Sexual Rebellion of Youth] (1931d) and *Malthusismo y neomalthusismo* [Malthusianism and Neo-Malthusianism] (1932c).

Hildegart's list is not exhaustive, nor does it cover the question of how various writers split their activities between what was published strictly within the professional specialism of the author, and work that dealt with matters of sexuality, eugenics or sexual reform, albeit within a framework traditional enough to seem not threatening to the regime. To some degree the split is simply chronological and it is clear that particular caution was observed during the Dictatorship. Her list, extensive though it is, omits mention of Recaséns, Rocamora, Sacristán, Sánchez Covisa, Sánchez de Rivera*, Sanchis Banús, Sainz de Aja, Pittaluga and Cansinos-Assens*. Some future members of the Liga were clearly omitted because they restricted their writing to their professional area, the case of Recaséns, Rocamora, Sacristán and Sainz de Aja. Other members, for example Pittaluga, were less obviously committed to sexual reform. Pittaluga, a committed public hygienist, would publish articles in the *Revista de Occidente* (as did Marañón) that took a conservative view of gendered behaviour (see Sinclair forthcoming). Sanchis Banús, held to be one of the best psychiatrists of his generation, had published an *Estudio medico-social del Niño Golfo* [Medico-Social Study of the Urchin] (1916), but did not move further into eugenics. Sánchcz de Rivera, however, moved from writing about *Degeneración por sífilis adquirida* [Degeneration Acquired Through Syphilis] (1911) to works that were more eugenic and sociological in import such as *Lo sexual: (peligros y consecuencias de los vicios y enfermedades sexuales)* [The Sexual: Dangers and Consequences of Sexual Vices and Diseases] (1924), and *La ruta del matrimonio* [The Path to Marriage] (1929).

Other publications from this group were more on the margins, although they fit into the broad concerns of the reformers. Juarros, for example, active as an abolitionist, produced a number of more or less popular writings: *El breviario sentimental de la madre* [Sentimental Handbook of the Mother] (1921), *El amor en España: características masculinas* [Love in Spain: Masculine Features] (1927), *Los senderos de la locura (Divulgaciones psiquiátricas)* [Paths of Madness (Psychiatric Musings)] (1927), *Los horizontes de la psicoanálisis* [Horizons of Psychoanalysis] (1928), and the more florid and popular *Los engaños de la morfina* [The Deceits of Morphine] (1929), in which a healthy sexual life is billed as being incompatible with the consumption of morphine. Cansinos-Assens's writings on eroticism are an example of what it was possible to publish within the ambit of literature (presumably deemed 'safe'), but have little direct link with eugenics and sex reform, beyond their willingness to write on sexuality.

Publication was not simply the affair of individuals, and could be supported and encouraged through institutions. That is, in Certeau's terms, we periodically find a successful move from the outsider writing of the tactician to the more protected conditions of the strategist. But such transitions were not without their setbacks, and in the period under discussion one of the features of the (admittedly numerous) charitable movements and new institutions is that they tended not to be long-lived. Their demise seems not to be related to public intervention, but perhaps more to a lack of either critical mass in terms of those supporting them, or simple lack of finance. Marinoni's Institute of Social Medicine, set up in 1918,[25] was a seedbed for the Liga, in which Huerta, Recaséns, Pittaluga and Marañón were involved, well before the 1928 conference, but there seems to have been no trace of it after 1923 (Álvarez Peláez, 1988: 190–3). The failure of this enterprise coincides with the coming of Primo's regime, but as Álvarez Peláez notes, there might have been inbuilt problems, and it disappeared because it was overreaching itself, and lacked the finance for what it wanted to achieve (Álvarez Peláez, 1988: 193). A Liga de Educación Social [League of Social Education] was set up in 1928 (Vázquez García and Moreno Mengíbar, 1997: 134).

There is an apparent mismatch between Álvarez Peláez's reading of the 1920s, in which emphasis is given to the degree to which enterprises came to nothing, and that of Vázquez García and Moreno Mengíbar who emphasize the vitality of the period. This mismatch derives from different attitudes to institutional formality, in that Vázquez García and Moreno Mengíbar, in their more positive reading, give weight to the importance of small informal gatherings. Their relatively positive reading of the period includes the degree to which lectures (even in restricted professional milieux) and journalism in the daily press contributed in significant manner to the airing of questions of reform and eugenics.

The *Gaceta Médica Española* [Spanish Medical Gazette], however, was without dispute a success story. Founded by Enrique Noguera in 1927 out of concern for infant mortality, and linked to the Sociedad de Amigos del Niño [Society of Friends of the Child], the *Gaceta* had as its prime aim the dissemination of work linked to problems of infancy and of eugenic ideas. It would be the *Gaceta* in 1928 that put forward the idea of the Eugenics Conference. While the conference would be suppressed, other material published within its pages did not meet with such difficulties. Similarly, in 1925 there had been a number of meetings at the Real Academia de Medicina concerned with eugenics (Álvarez Peláez, 1988: 194), and these seem not to have experienced problems. Interestingly, Marañón's *Tres ensayos sobre la vida sexual* [Three Essays on Sexual Life] (1926), not obviously restricted to a professional readership, also managed to avoid difficulties with the authorities, conceivably because he was a publicly approved figure. Marañón would go on to publish *Amor, conveniencia y eugenesia* (1929) and divers psychobiographies, including 'La psicopatología de Don Juan' [the Psychopathology of Don Juan] (1924), and *El Conde-Duque de Olivares: la pasión de mandar* [The Conde-Duque of Olivares: the Passion to Command] (1927).

A further success story was the establishment of the *Archivos de neurobiología, psicología, fisiología, histología, neurología y psiquiatría* [Archives of Neurobiology, Psychology, Physiology, Histology, Neurology and Psychiatry], later titled *Archivos de neurobiología* [Archives of Neurobiology]. One of the founders of this was Lafora, and the journal became an immensely important forum for exchange of ideas within science and medicine. Lafora himself had a clear public profile through his regular articles in *El Sol* (writing with some energy on the reform of medical studies in Spain in the early 1920s). His publications through the period were predominantly within the professional rather than the popularizing band, but including work on mentally abnormal children, on the treatment of syphilis and on masculine impotence. At the same time he displayed the tendency (in common with others of his profession) for straying into literature and culture, with his *Estudio psicológico del cubismo y expresionismo* [Psychological Study of Cubism and Expressionism] (1921), and *Don Juan, los milagros y otros ensayos* [Don Juan, Miracles and Other Essays] (1927).

Clearly, if eugenic talk had to be careful (or it would be suppressed, as in the 1928 conference), it was nonetheless possible. The spate of publication that would appear from 1930 onwards, as the Republic approached, is testimony to this, and key figures of the Liga would also move into positions of public power as they were elected to the 1931 Cortes.

NOTES

1 Aurora stressed that if Hildegart did take communion, she did not go to confession (Grau, 1934a).
2 The article is not signed, but seems likely to have been drafted by Hildegart.
3 There is a lack of evidence about how many of Steiner's works were available in Spain at this time. A letter from Nicolás Tasín to Ruiz-Castillo, editor of Biblioteca Nueva, of 24 November 1921 (archive in Biblioteca Nacional), provides ample information about him, with a view to negotiating translation rights for some of Steiner's works. Biblioteca Nueva would include Steiner, *La Teosofía*, in its collection 'Biblioteca del Más Allá' [Library of the Beyond], available in 1929, and possibly earlier. There is an edition of *La Teosofía* in the Biblioteca Nacional, no publisher, no date, but printed in Segovia (where Biblioteca had much of their printing done) and with a prologue by Rafael Urbano, which suggests a date in the 1920s.
4 An example of early networking in this group who would form part of the core of the Liga is that Sánchez Taboada is reported in the *Archivos* (August 1925) as having brought an article by Pittaluga from *El Liberal*. He also brings forward Pittaluga's report of the visit of the Society of Nations Committee to Spain. The *Archivos* appeared as such for a single calendar year, at the end of which it was announced that the Dirección de Sanidad would be publishing a *Boletín* from the following January. It became a *Boletín Técnico* until 1932, after which the publication became the *Revista de Sanidad*.
5 Esperanto as an interest for eugenicists recurs with some regularity. Cleminson (1994: 733) notes that the journal *Eugenia*, published in Barcelona from 1921 speaks of the need for a group that would impose morality, altruism, and makes reference to naturism, Esperanto, physical exercise, athletics as desiderata for a eugenic society. An event at the Ateneo de Madrid on 23 June 1929 was the report by Adalberto Smith on the upcoming Congreso Internacional de Esperanto in Budapest. On 15 January 1932 the Cuban esperantist and mason Julio Mangada spoke at the Ateneo on 'El esperanto como solución al problema de las lenguas' [Esperanto as the Solution to the Language Problem], on 'Esperanto y turismo' [Esperanto and Tourism], 11 May 1933, and on a course in Esperanto on 10 January 1934 (Ruiz Salvador, 1976: 253–8).
6 There is, however, some detailed discussion of *Sexualidad* in Cleminson and Vázquez García (2007: 127–31) with reference to its view of the position of 'inverts' and 'homosexuals'.
7 This observation may be true of these meetings, but the writer fails to take into account the vigorousness of workers' movements, including those of an educational and cultural nature. See Cleminson (1994).
8 When Hildegart joins the UGT, and embarks on her campaign of

political commitment to the Socialists, she bridges the social gap observed in the Hygiene Campaign, and enters a quite different milieu.
9 All the references to the Hygiene Campaign are to the accounts published in *Sexualidad*.
10 Beatriz Caamaño aptly makes references to Paulo Freire's concept of two sorts of learning: one by which there is assimilation and digestion and the other in which there is a wholesale taking in followed by regurgitation with little or no change (Caamaño, 2004: 31). This is an example of the second sort. See the discussion in Chapter Seven of Hildegart's relationship with her mother.
11 Other aspects of Zoroastrianism that relate to some of Hildegart's pieces in this period are the belief in the equality of the sexes, in the cleanliness of the environment, in hard work and charity, and the condemnation of cruelty to human beings and animals.
12 Hildegart's grandfather was a provincial professional, and became Procurador de los Juzgados de Marina en el Ferrol, and later Procurador del Juzgado de Primera Instancia (Cal, 1991: 20).
13 The mention of the civil code may be a slip here, since what came in was the 'Estatuto Penal de 1928' (Barriobero y Herrán, 1930: 181).
14 See Barriobero y Herrán (1930: 181–203) for the provisions relating to sexual offences.
15 See Cleminson and Vázquez García (2007) on the differences between Spain and other countries in legislation on homosexuality, and the fact that legal condemnation of homosexuality would only occur in Spain with the 1928 Code.
16 This account by Noguera of what happened was published in the *Gaceta Médica Española* 50 (November 1930), then reprinted with the proceedings of the 1933 Eugenics Conference.
17 See Pérez Sanz and Bru Ripoll (1987: 14) for the programme of the conference.
18 This is in the tradition of pastoral theology in Spain. The title makes reference by association to Pierre Debreyne, *Moechialogie, ou Traité des péchés contre les sixième et neuvième commandements du Décalogue* (Paris 1846) one of the authorities cited by Padre Claret in his *Llave de oro* (1862). 'Moechaberis' comes from the verb 'moechor', 'to have unnatural sexual relations', and occurs in Catullus. Sureda's use of it, however, is from the Vulgate version of the commandment prohibiting adultery.
19 For a full discussion of intersexuality see Cleminson and Vázquez García (2007: Chapter Three).
20 No publication details remain of this volume.
21 No publication details remain, but Roso de Luna had published a novel in 1924, *El trío en sí bemol (el sexo y su eterno problema)* [Trio in B flat (Sex and the Eternal Problem)].
22 No publication details remain of this volume.
23 The work in question is *Física de la psique: Monogamía, Poligamía* [Physics of the Mind: Monogamy, Polygamy], one of the many books published by Morata.

24 This slighting remark may have contributed further to the friction with Haro recorded in the correspondence with Ellis in July 1932, and it is noticeable that Hildegart does not cite his work *Eugenesia y matrimonio: El certificado médico prenupcial* [Eugenics and Marriage: the Prenuptial Wedding Certificate].
25 This was set up by an open letter to *El Siglo Médico*, October 1918, p. 886.

Chapter Four

Coming to Maturity and the Limits of Tolerance

My position is thus here a revolutionary one. They find that I am very valiant, they admire themselves to find that a girl has much more courage to enterprise a mouvement in that sense than they, and I find so accomplished that the points of view of old and new generation are fully opposed.

... I remember the tragical cases which you expose in your book which would be exemplar for Humanekind if she had a little more sense. (Hildegart to Ellis, 23 October 1931)

You will have surely heard of our Penal Director. She is a woman. She is called Victoria Kent. Well, she lives with another woman, Julia Irureta Goyena during several years and as I can know in lesbic relations. Well. Albornoz that is a widow with a daughter maintains relations with the two. ¿Don't you think it strange? I have been reading your book over 'Sexual Inversion' and I can't find a full explanation for it. But as I am studying the case and trying to apile materials so as to judge, when I have these cases finished I will tell you in several letters some of the small things that I judge decisive to know the character of these men and women.

But I have not finished yet. Mr. Galarza that has been until last 'crisis' Director of Policemen is known in public as 'Madame. Rosita'. Llopis, the director of our Primary teaching, that is to say of our schools, is also a known homosexual of the passive kind. (Hildegart to Ellis, 5 January 1932)

Did you know that many of the leading figures in the new Republican regime in Spain are homosexual? So at least I hear from a remarkable young Spanish girl lawyer in Madrid. (Ellis to Haire, 14 January 1932)

Spanish Public Life Post-Dictatorship

1930 was a watershed year for Spanish politics, in that January brought the resignation of Primo de Rivera. It was also a watershed year for Hildegart herself, and for the reform movements around her. The hesitations evident through the years of Primo's regime on the part of all but the most established figures, and the decree of 1928 that told eugenicists and sex reformers alike to keep their views to themselves (or at least to their professional colleagues) were no context to encourage a new and young reformer to go public. But from 1930 onwards, we find a surge in publication and public activity from reformers, including Hildegart, who now bursts into print in her mature phase. This chapter tracks the development of public examination of issues of sex reform and eugenics with the ending of the Dictatorship, and gives focus to the ways in which Hildegart moved on in public life. This includes her activity in politics, and charts her somewhat more problematic engagement with homosexuality.

Despite the fact that censorship under the Dictatorship applied to the press rather than to books (see Carr, 1966: 597) the coming of the Republic had manifest effect on book publication. Reformers now had the option of participating in public power: among those elected to the 1931 Cortes were Marañón, Nóvoa Santos, Juarros, Sanchís Banús and Jiménez Asúa (Glick, 1981: 8). No fewer than forty-eight of those elected were in the medical profession, more than 10 per cent of the total (Álvarez Peláez, 1988: 201), so that matters of medicine, sanitation and reform were well placed for obtaining public support.

The high degree of participation of doctors and lawyers in structures of power (both intellectual and political), and the ensuing potential competitiveness between them, leading to tensions in public life and ambiguities in publications, is a crucial factor in Spanish public life at this point. The law might be thought of as containing the excesses of the body, but in the context of sexual reform as it existed in 1920s and 1930s Spain, there was an impetus to move towards the liberation of the body. At the same time the driving model of eugenics was one of controlling and containing the excesses of disease and heredity of the body in order to 'free' the race for its betterment. Co-operation between law and medicine, each of which would be prominent in the Cortes Constituyentes of the Second Republic, was beset by a sense of conflict which was in part about whether excess was to be controlled, and if so by whom, or whether it was to be liberated. These tensions underlie, but do not necessarily dominate Hildegart's divers articulations of her position on homosexuality. They are, however, particularly prominent in the conflicts within the Liga. In both cases a significant factor is Hildegart's initial training. Having qualified as a lawyer, she began to study medicine. Those interested in eugenics habitually placed themselves in a difficult territory between the professions. Hildegart's dual career track significantly places her in the middle of this territory, something she alluded to in 1931, in *La rebeldía sexual de la juventud*, where co-operation rather than conflict was implied (Hildegart, 1931d: 258)

Professional rivalry was not the only source of problems in the development of eugenics and sex reform in the Republic. Sex education was an area of notorious difficulty. The attack on the 1928 Eugenics Conference from the Catholic right-wing press (see Chapter Three) is testimony to the resistance towards dissemination of sexual knowledge to the broad public. During the winter of 1929 to 1930, the daily newspaper *El Sol* ran a survey among its readers about sexual problems of the young. Those who answered were unanimous in declaring that problems relating to sexuality derived from lack of knowledge or an atmosphere of prejudice. 'Mi educación sexual ha sido ineducación' [My sexual education has been lack of education] (Glick, 1981: 21) was a response that summed up the reaction of many. A virtually immediate response to the departure of Primo de Rivera had been that of publications designed to meet this educational need. Hildegart joined with this drive to disseminate knowledge on sexual matters, and on birth control, and produced detailed plans of activities that would meet the need for education (see, for example, Hildegart 1930a, 1930b, 1931a, 1931b, 1931c, 1931d, 1931e). Yet despite the desire on the part of reformers to put legislation in place to ensure sex education, progress on this front was difficult. The Liga Española de Higiene Mental [Spanish

League of Mental Hygiene] handed a document to the government on sex education in early 1933, but the change of government later that year and the shift towards conservatism within the Republic meant that this was not acted upon. No provision was made for the training of teachers in sex education, and discussion was limited to the type of features such education should have, rather than leading to any practical outcome (Vázquez García and Moreno Mengíbar, 1997: 153).[1]

Meanwhile other issues did reach legislative status, a number of them with specific attention to the protection of women (as part of the 'Latin' agenda for eugenic reform). Jiménez de Asúa had defined the 'crime of venereal infection' in 1925, and this would come to the statute book in 1935. Even before this, the standing of such an offence was such that in 1932 it was declared to be grounds for divorce (Guereña, 2003: 391).

In a landmark essay that contrasted with much essentialist writing in the *Revista de Occidente* on the place of gender in society, Lafora wrote a factual and informative article in February 1933 on 'La reforma de la moral sexual' [The Reform of Sexual Morality].[2] This came out after the foundation of the Liga, but before the 1933 Eugenics Conference. Viewed with the hindsight offered by his attitude at the time of Aurora's trial, it is typical that his article makes no mention of the Liga, or of the activity of other founding members. His position is to establish himself as an internationalist, astutely weighting his presentation towards statistics and other information on sexual activity in Europe rather than offering concentrated and specific commentary upon Spain.

The abolition of prostitution became the focus of concentrated activity. A committee was set up in the summer of 1931 to draft a law concerning venereal disease that had clearly abolitionist intent. On the committee were numerous foundation members of the Liga: Sánchez Covisa, Méndez Bejarano, Sáinz de Aja, Bravo, Jiménez de Asúa. The intention was to do away with the regulation of prostitution, and to bring in compulsory treatment of venereal disease. A first step towards this was made by a 1932 decree which set up funding for anti-VD services, thus dispensing with the provision by which taxation of prostitution funded them (Guereña, 2003: 392–3).

The contribution of publishers is arguably no less significant than that of those who wrote on eugenics and sex reform. Morata*, founding member of the Liga, is of signal importance here. Of the twenty-six books of his series 'Temas de nuestro tiempo' [Themes of Our Time], twelve referred to sex, marriage or eugenics, and in a 1933 list of 'Otros libros de interés' [Other Books of Interest] consisting of seventy volumes, forty-four were on sex and marriage, and six had eugenics in their title (Álvarez Peláez, 1988: 194). Morata's activity was of particular weight for those who founded the Liga, and his publications from this group would include the following: Bugallo, *La higiene sexual en las escuelas* (1930) and *La delincuencia infantil* [Infantile Delinquency] (1932), Haro, *Eugenesia y matrimonio: El certificado médico prenupcial* [Eugenics and Marriage: the Prenuptial Medical Certificate] (1932 edition with a foreword by Marañón, the first edition having appeared in 1928)[3] and *Fases biológicas de la mujer: (Cartas a Paloma)* [Biological Phases of Woman: (Letters to Paloma) (1934), Hernández Alfonso*, *¿Miedo al porvenir?: Democracia y comunismo* [Fear of the Future?: Democracy and Communism] (1931) and *Eugenesia y derecho a vivir* [Eugenics and the Right to Live] (1933), Nóvoa Santos, *El advenimiento del hombre y otras conferencias* [The Advent of Man and Other Lectures] (1933), Ruiz Funes, *Delito y libertad* [Crime and Freedom] (1930), Torrubiano y Ripoll, *Política religiosa de la democracia española* [Religious Politics of Spanish Democracy] (1931). Joaquín Noguera López, brother of Enrique Noguera, published *Moral, eugenesia y derecho* (1930) (with a prologue by Marañón) with Morata, and the important *Libro de las primeras jornadas eugénicas españolas* [Book of the First Spanish Eugenics Conference] (1934), edited by Enrique Noguera and Luis Huerta, similarly came out with him. Even some of the provincial founding members of the Liga published work through Morata, including Oriol Anguera, *Física de la psique: Monogamía, Poligamía* [Physics of the Psyche: Monogamy, Polygamy] (1930), and Campoy Ibáñez, *El amor y la patología* [Love and Pathology] (1931), which again had a prologue by Marañón.

Hildegart, (Eugenic) Child of her Time

In the context of the above, we can see how Hildegart came to her maturity as writer and reformer at the same moment as (or stimulated by) the opportunities offered by the end of the Dictatorship and the coming of the Republic. What is most striking is the range of her activity, the breadth of her output, and the degree to which she not only had her own voice, but one that could be identified within a complex and mobile situation. Although other reformers of professional weight and experience were active in promoting reform at the level of legislation and establishing an institutional framework, she had her own track, one that becomes particularly enlivened when we read the correspondence with Ellis.

Hildegart's publishing career explodes in 1930, the year when (in December) she turns sixteen. The evidence for her publications is patchy at best, with varying titles and publishers. An extensive list is produced by Rosa Cal (1991a), but a number of the items are hard to match exactly with other sources.[4] There are two relatively short publications in 1930: *El problema eugénico: punto de vista de una mujer moderna* [The Eugenic Problem: Point of View of a Modern Woman] (57 pp.) and *La limitación de la prole: un deber del proletariado consciente* [Limiting Offspring: a Duty of the Conscientious Proletariat] (72 pp.). The first of these is a work Hildegart mentions to Ellis in her first letter to him (23 October 1931), referring to it as a pamphlet of 'divulgation'.[5] It is possible that the second is what she refers to as *Birth Control* in her letter, adding that these two works, as well as *Sexual Education* (*Educación Sexual* [63 pp.] which came out in 1931), are 'works that have been very diffused among workmen as was my desire'. *La limitación de la prole* is, however, not a how-to manual, and Hildegart refers to it as the second part of her work *El problema eugénico* [The Eugenic Problem]. The pamphlet sets out the case for eugenics, asserting that while eugenics is natural (the race will always tend towards its own betterment) economics also has its part in the case for birth control (Hildegart, 1930a: 17). She sent a dedicated copy of it to Ellis in December 1931, 'For Havelock Ellis, with the sincere admiration of his Spanish pupil and friend'. All three works are printed by Gráfica Socialista in Madrid, a sign that Hildegart's membership of the UGT has brought her into an ambience propitious for her publishing career. In the same year she managed to bring out *Tres amores históricos: estudio comparativo de los amores de Romeo y Julieta, Abelardo y Eloísa y los Amantes de Teruel* [Three Historic Loves: Comparative Study of the Loves of Romeo and Juliet, Abelard and Heloïse and the Lovers of Teruel], of over 300 pages, and published by *La Voz de Teruel*. Her habit of keeping a big work on the move at the same time as she publishes within the realm of sex reform continues. When she writes to Ellis about her publications she mentions having translated a sixteenth-century philosophical work in Latin by the Seville neo-platonist Fox Morcillo, *De Naturae Philosophia seu de Platonis et Aristotelis relatione* [On the Philosophy of Nature, or on the Relationship between Plato and Aristotle] (more than 400 pages in 8vo).

The coming of the Republic in spring of 1931 is also the moment when some of Hildegart's best known writings are published. On birth control there is the substantial *Profilaxis anticoncepcional: Paternidad voluntaria* [Contraceptive Prophylaxis: Voluntary Fatherhood] (1931c, 110 pp.).[6] Hildegart's two most famous works date from this year: *El problema sexual tratado por una mujer española* (1931b, 258 pp.) and *La rebeldía sexual de la juventud* (1931d, 336 pp.) both of them brought out by Morata. Hildegart also brings out two pamphlets with Marín Civera's Cuadernos de la Cultura in Valencia: *Sexo y amor* [Sex and Love] (1931f, 58 pp.) and *La revolución sexual* [The Sexual Revolution] (1931e, 46 pp.). In a number of her pamphlets Hildegart specifically addresses herself to workers, at other times to fellow socialists. The tone and content of these works of propaganda do not necessarily make a good match with the intended recipients. Thus *El problema eugénico* [The Eugenic Problem] (1930b) is more appropriate for popular dissemination than is *Educación sexual* [Sexual Education] (1931a).

This spate of activity is followed in 1932 by the substantial *Malthusismo y Neomalthusismo* [Malthusianism and Neo-Malthusianism] (680 pp.), again not a how-to manual, although there is a section on practical issues of birth control. The whole book is dedicated to a detailed exposition of issues surrounding population control, including substantial legal information. The printed dedication for the first edition of September 1932 situates Hildegart firmly in what will become familiar to us as the international context of the WLSR, in that it is directed to Leunbach and Haire for their part in working for the 'neo-Malthusian cause' across the world, and for leading the WLSR.

Another major work of this period is Hildegart's major political piece, *¿Se equivocó Marx . . . ?* [Was Marx Wrong?] published by Ediciones Boro of Madrid, and some 400 pages.[7] Cal records a further work, *¿Cómo se curan y cómo se evitan las enfermedades venéreas?* [How to Cure and Avoid Venereal Disease], but with no publication details (Cal, 1991a: 195).

These publications are all within the mainstream of Hildegart's adopted areas of expertise, and detailed perusal of them reveals extensive reference. A question arising from this is whether they were the product of her sole authorship, or in some way produced in collaboration with her mother. Given that Aurora's education was mainly acquired in the private library of her father, collaboration would be most likely for those works that cite largely early European references. We might surmise that these references formed the initial intellectual frame of reference that she passed on to Hildegart in the course of her education. But some of Hildegart's works contain a notable level of contemporary reference, from which we might conclude either that they are Hildegart's own, or that her mother continued her own education and intellectual exploration well after the initial years of her own foraging in her father's library. Whereas *Sexo y amor* (1931f) is barely referenced at all, much of *¿Se equivocó Marx . . . ?* (1932e) could have been referenced from the family library. By contrast *Venus ante el derecho* [Venus and the Law] (1933d) is mainly based on Hildegart's frame of reference as a lawyer, and on the work of Havelock Ellis. Dedicated to Aurora ('a mi madre, compañera insustituible en los éxitos y en los fracasos, colaboradora con su comprensión y su aliento en la obra toda de mi vida' [for my mother, irreplaceable companion in success and failure, understanding and encouraging collaborator in my whole life's work]) and published shortly before Hildegart's death, the wording of the dedication gives no hint of problems to come.

In 1933 Hildegart would concentrate her attention on prostitution and the abolitionist debate. *Venus ante el derecho* was one of a collection that year: *Historia de la prostitución* [History of Prostitution] (with advice on how to avoid venereal disease); *Estudio de la prostitución; ¿Qué es el abolicismo* [sic] *de la prostitución?; El aspecto jurídico del delito de contagio venéreo; El problema social que implica la prostitución* [Study of Prostitution; What does Abolition of Prostitution Mean?; Legal Aspect of the Crime of Venereal Contagion; The Social Problem Presented by Prostitution].[8] Clearly Hildegart is contributing to the abolitionist activity noted above. But few if any other founding members of the Liga were to write so directly (and, if the details of publication are correct, with such profusion) on the topic. Hildegart leaves a paper trail of some of her history in her dedications, including, in the case of *Venus ante el derecho*, a printed dedication to her mother.

Hildegart gave no sign of being about to stop in her tracks. Her plans for future work included: *El cáncer de la guerra, Rebelión universal, Orientaciones pedagógico-sexuales* [The Cancer of War, Universal Rebellion, Educational and Sexual Guidance], and a pair of works to be brought out in collaboration with the Brazilian eugenicist, Renato Kehl*, *Cómo escoger un buen marido* [How to Choose a Good Husband] and *Cómo escoger una buena esposa* [How to Choose a Good Wife].[9]

Hildegart and the Route of Politics

The trajectory that Hildegart follows in relation to politics is fundamentally one that shows her exploration of the possible arenas of activity. Her move out of the Hygiene Campaign (or, more probably, the way in which she was moved out of the campaign) followed by her involvement in socialist activity via the UGT from the age of fourteen can be interpreted in various ways. It can be read as her awakening to the need to engage with current organized politics (rather than with the idealistic and imprecise agenda of the campaign); it can be read as a bid for more mature and independent action (given that her position in the campaign is always one that seems the protected role of the protégé); it can be read as a feature of her involvement in university life, where she comes into contact with those she addresses as the 'mozos' [lads] of the Federación Universitaria Española (dedication of *La rebeldía sexual de la juventud*).

Within the political context the major part of Hildegart's output was in journalism and meetings at which she spoke. Months after joining the UGT in January 1929 she began writing for *El Socialista*. Having completed her degree in law in May 1932 she began writing for *La Libertad* and *La Tierra*. Her pattern of work, not restricted to her political output, is that lectures frequently appeared as publications. *La rebeldía sexual de la juventud* is one such publication (albeit not one of her most overtly political texts). Her falling out with socialism came in September 1932, when *El Socialista* supported Azorín in some local Madrid elections, rather than Antonio Zozaya* who was favoured by republicans (Guzmán, 1977b: 15). Zozaya was a translator and publisher, who in 1880 had founded the Biblioteca Económica Filosófica [Economic Philosophical Library], with emphasis on translations of philosophy, and was also writer of popular novels in series such as La novela mundial, La novela semanal [The World Novelette, The Weekly Novelette]. Two features of Zozaya as a writer are likely to account for why Hildegart supported him rather than the other contender, Azorín. The style of Zozaya's non-fictional publications on philosophy, sociology, issues of freedom and the law, would have been in the style of reading enabled by the library of Aurora's father, added to which his writing of fiction in popular series was something in which Hildegart herself was about to participate, with her contribution to La novela proletaria [The Proletarian Novelette] in September 1932, and was one in which the author addressed a popular rather than an elite public. More significant still than Zozaya's chosen styles of writing is the fact that he was one of the founding members of the Liga, and thus a companion-in-arms in an organization to which Hildegart was completely committed.

When Hildegart first writes to Ellis she tells him of her membership of the Socialist Party, and about how much time she spends speaking at political meetings (2 December 1931). But it is noticeable that she tells him little more about her political activity and political publications. Most specifically she omits to tell him of her resignation from activities associated with socialism (as announced by her at the end of ¿Se equivocó Marx . . . ?).

With her resignation from official socialist organizations (the UGT, the Federación Nacional de Juventudes Socialistas [National Federation of Socialist Youth], and the Agrupación Socialista Madrileña [Madrid Socialist Group]) Hildegart did not sever her relations with organized politics: she became affiliated to the Partido Republicano Federal [Federal Republican Party]. It was in this context that she came to know Abel Velilla, the young man whose relationship with her according to some accounts, but not that of Aurora, was at the base of the murder. She evidently did not regard herself as having given up Socialism, but rather that she had become detached from a particular form of it.

The Limits of Eugenic Tolerance

There was considerable overlap in Spain between the interests of eugenicists and sex reformers. A source of tension, however, was the question of homosexuality. The eugenic agenda, concerned with best breeding practice for the improvement of the race focused on 'proper' masculinity and 'proper' femininity, because breeding had to be from good stock. In its 'Latin' form in Spain, eugenics took on a role of general vigilance about how to procure optimum conditions for the process of procreation. The sex reform agenda, as summarized in the ten planks of the WLSR (see Chapter One), had many interests in common with eugenics. It advocated 'conscious parenthood', and thus control of conception, it supported eugenics, and set out to protect various vulnerable parties, namely the (unmarried) woman and her child, and those who would be affected by prostitution and the dangers of venereal disease. It believed in systematic sex education. But the sex reform agenda had other planks that fell into a grey area and that were not obviously going to be easy to accept in Spain. The aims of political, economic and sexual equality for men and women were possible within the eugenics framework, but in the event the emphasis on woman's maternal function held the possibility of inequalities (holding that the sexes were equal but different could lead to restriction and discrimination). The freeing up of the institution of marriage and divorce was an area where eugenics and sex reform might agree, but where their actual approach to marriage might be rather different. But the two planks that dealt with sexual variation (planks 8 and 9) were much less readily going to find favour within Spain. Sex reformers generally supported the idea that sexual variation (described – even in the WLSR planks – as 'disturbances') should be thought of as the result of pathology, and not deemed to be criminal or sinful. The consequential plank, that viewed sexual acts as criminal only if they infringed the sexual rights of another, logically called for their support. But the idea encapsulated in the plank 9, that 'Sexual acts between responsible adults, undertaken by mutual consent, to be regarded as the private concern of those adults' was for some a step too far in recognition of sexual inclinations and practices. In addition this plank was not directly compatible with the agenda of eugenics, which was, after all, concerned with breeding, and not with tolerance of sexual variation. Not all Liga members would necessarily be behind the planks with implications for homosexuality. Among others Marañón had theorized the 'intersex' state in *La evolución de la sexualidad y los estados intersexuales*, Vital Aza held strong views on 'proper' sexuality, and the dissent caused by these planks at the foundation meeting of the Liga demonstrates that this was a difficult area. Hildegart's role in that meeting was twofold, to try to see the planks through the meeting, and to arrive at consensus. Consequently she appears to be in favour of those planks that aimed at the toleration of homosexuality. Yet close perusal of her attitude to the subject (expressed at different points) suggests that she was rather less tolerant than is implied in the position she adopted at the Liga meeting.[10]

Homosexuality is not obviously prominent in Hildegart's public output, but it is strikingly at odds with her private views. She touches on it briefly in the concluding section of *La rebeldía sexual de la juventud*. Listing those who, because of their dedication to their profession, will have an abstemious sexual life, she suddenly utters a puritanical warning: 'Quien viva sólo por el sexo y para el sexo se atendrá a sus consecuencias' [He who lives only by and for sex must abide by the consequences]. Homosexual relations are mentioned in the final part of the list: 'Quien tenga relaciones con individuos de su mismo sexo no será penado ni castigado. Son muy libres de hacerlo siempre que cuenten con el asentimiento y no se impongan con la violencia' [If someone has relations with individuals of the same sex he will not be subject to any punishment. They are free to do this providing it is with the free consent of the other and not imposed by force] (1931d: 253). Two attitudes are discernible here. First, there is the Biblical style of discourse as she adopts the high moral ground of one who disapproves of sexual activity as an end in itself. It could be classed as that of a hard-line eugenicist who believes that the point of sexual activity is procreation, and nothing more. But it also carries a remarkable resemblance to the way that Aurora spoke both at her trial and in her interviews with psychiatrists at Ciempozuelos. At the same time the public rehearsal of tolerance for homosexuality is in a discourse borrowed directly from the WLSR planks.

Elsewhere, however, Hildegart's attitude to homosexuality is distinctly more troubled, and it emerges in her third letter to Ellis (5 January 1932) when she is clearly in a disturbed state. The letter is long, agitated and gossipy, and came with a number of photographs of Spanish politicians.[11] Its overriding concern is with homosexuality. In a postscript Hildegart tells Ellis of her current lecture programme, which is all about Christ, in which He is read as a physiological and mental oddity, the lectures being

'¿Did Jesuscrist Exist?', '¿Herence and Physiologie Of Jesus', 'The Intelligence And The Delirium Of Jesus', 'The Amorality Of Jesus', and 'Diagnostic Of Jesus Madness'. She sent two cuttings to Ellis related to this, one of an interview in which she expressed enthusiasm for a work she planned on 'Casos patológicos de perversión sexual' [Pathological cases of Sexual Perversion], in which she planned to look at people in Spanish public life (Coca, 1931), and a report on 'La inteligencia y el delirio de Jesús' [The Intelligence and Delirium of Jesus] from *El Socialista* (identified as 16 January 1932).[12] A further cutting (from *El Noroeste* of Gijón of 27 March 1932) refers to a lecture on 'Homosexualismo' [Homosexuality] (anon, 1932). Hildegart is reported as declaring that homosexuality has affinity with artistic tendencies, citing Leonardo da Vinci, Miguel Angel, Oscar Wilde and Christ as examples. She refers to the concept within Ancient Greece of homosexuality as the 'prototipo de la masculinidad' [prototype of masculinity] and the training in China of adolescent youths who are then procured by the rich. Her understanding of homosexuality appears to be based, *pace* Lombroso, on physical characteristics, and seeing it as a degenerate condition which threatens the political health of the country: the homosexual can be identified by his hands, by the lack of 'manly' features in his face and other signs that are 'virtually infallible'. But she did not stop here, and added that the greater part of rivalries in politics could be attributed to homosexual desire. She called on men and women to make sure that in future men were truly men and women truly women. Here Hildegart's equation of homosexuality with narcissism, or with the physical signs of degeneration, speaks more of suspicion than of a detached preparedness to live and let live in relation to sexual preferences other than heterosexuality.

¿Quo Vadis, Burguesía?

This last appeal, that men should be men, and women should be women, is a preoccupation that dominates Hildegart's thought through 1932. Specifically, as she outlines in the body of the letter of 5 January 1932, her concern is with an absence of 'proper' sexuality in politics. Her covert views about sexuality and politics become evident not only in this letter but through *¿Quo vadis, burguesía?*, a short novel in the series La novela proletaria (no. 22) (probably in September 1932),[13] a copy of which she sent to Ellis and which illustrates her emotional reaction to homosexuality.

It was by no means unusual for members of Spain's intellectual elite to write popular novels, and other founding members of the Liga did so, including Bravo, Juarros, Saldaña, Cansinos-Assens, González Blanco*, Hernández Catá, Ortiz de Pinedo and Zozaya. Current politics could obviously be given some coverage in this medium, and the title of ¿*Quo vadis, burguesía?* suggests it should be read in this way. The combination, however, of what Hildegart tells Ellis about the novel and her agitated commentary upon the principals of a political drama suggests that this is more than mere political commentary.

The novel tells of a political scandal resulting from the relationship between Don Pascual de Zarzamora, traditional in politics and religious belief, and Luis Ogral, an *obrero* imprisoned for his political activity. The two of them, because of a change in government, find themselves in the same prison. Ogral decides to send a letter to Zarzamora (using a go-between with the nickname of 'Princesita' [little Princess]), since the two of them are apparently in prison for similar reasons, and slowly a relationship between them is established. Zarzamora and his wife decide to do what they can to help Ogral, and she goes to visit him. Eventually, when the two are released, Ogral is welcomed in Zarzamora's household, and with the passing of time becomes more and more accustomed to a superior lifestyle, being supported by Zarzamora in his legal difficulties. When famine affects the workers, Ogral finds his sympathies not with them, but with his new bourgeois companion. In a final confused scene crowds attack the house where the two of them are to be found. The press reports that Zarzamora has been killed, and that Ogral dies after being subjected to horrific mutilation. The final cry is of '¡Muera el traidor!' [Death to the Traitor!].

The plot pursues Hildegart's idea that the linking of passion and politics is particularly suspect when homosexuality is involved. Zarzamora is the cause of his wife's frustration and irritation, leading her to seek solace elsewhere, and he is not the father of his children. He is grotesquely feminized, a textbook case of failed sexual identity: 'De grandes ojos inexpresivos, cejas muy móviles, frente carente de las viriles entradas, cabellos rizosos y rubios, boca gordezuela, dilatada casi siempre por repulsiva sonrisa' [With great expressionless eyes, mobile eyebrows, his face lacking manliness, curly blond hair, plump mouth, almost always widened into a repulsive smile] (Hildegart, 1932d: 4).[14] Ogral, meanwhile, consonant with the habitual characterization of the pueblo, is all man: he exudes confidence, virility, decisiveness, his features conveying his masculinity. Seen through the eyes of Zarzamora's wife, there is no doubt that she has the 'real' thing here. With her experience of men she fully appreciates him: 'Era éste un hombre maduro. Tenía unos ojos azules, claros, fríos, acerados; el pelo rubio también, pero sobriamente alisado; la boca cortada como una herida roja en la palidez del semblante . . . las facciones acusadas y enérgicas' [Here was a mature man. His eyes were blue, clear, cold, steely; his hair blond also, but smoothed down in sober manner; his mouth slashed like a red wound in the pallor of his face . . . his features sharp-cut and energetic] (Hildegart, 1932d: 7–8).

The plot is not just, or perhaps not even primarily, a political one. The surface line of the corruption of honest politics as practised by workers has running beneath it, with a strong note of disapproval and repulsion, a plot of sexual seduction. This displays all the dangers of sex that will be summarized in Aurora's comments on sexuality when interviewed in Ciempozuelos, and that are fleetingly glimpsed in the highminded pompous pronouncement of Hildegart in *La rebeldía sexual* cited earlier. Meanwhile, strong messages about appropriate sexuality are sent out. The relationship is (properly) initiated by the masculine Ogral – as a worker he is 'naturally' the epitome of virility – while the bourgeois Zarzamora has been degraded. The degenerate bourgeois then turns the relationship from a gesture of political fraternalism into a personally driven relationship, while retaining the façade of political support. No explicit sexual relationship is detailed, but all the dynamic of the seduction of Ogral by the needy yet powerful Zarzamora is imbued with the initial strong signals about the different sexuality of each as established at the start.

Hildegart left Ellis in no doubt about what the novel meant. The dedication she wrote (in longhand) on the copy of *¿Quo vadis, burguesía?* she sent to Ellis was explicit about how to decode it. Zarzamora represented the president of the Republic, Alcalá Zamora*, and Ogral was Largo Caballero*. As she points out, 'You read Ogral backwards, and you will see'.

The letter of 5 January 1932 is far more explicit, and expands on Hildegart's suspicion that the greater part of political rivalries had homosexuality at their base. She expresses distinct unease about a number of figures in public life she presumes to be involved in homosexual relations: Largo Caballero, Alcalá Zamora, Azaña*, Casares Quiroga*, Zulueta* and Rivas Cherif*. She recounts a story about a 'suspicious' meeting of the first two of these in a prison cell (as will be elaborated in her novel). If anything, she is even more concerned about homosexuality in women, and cites Victoria Kent*, Julia Iruretagoyena* and Clara Campoamor*. Her general tone in this letter is a mixture of salacious gossip and scandal, with adjectives such as 'monstrous' and 'strange' peppering her account. Her conclusion suggests the extremity of her views: 'This will explain to you that our political situation is too so infirm, and that there happen so bloody facts between us. There are neither true men nor true women directing our country, so we can expect no more of them'. The echo of the lecture on 'Homosexualismo' is proof of the underlying track of her thought, but also of what at this point amounts to an obsession. She promises to send Ellis newspaper cuttings and photographs so that 'you can judge of the true of my opinions over our political'. These cuttings and photographs, preserved in the British Library collection and annotated by Hildegart include, for example, 'Mr Azaña. Actually First Minister. ¿Isn't he ugly? His "relationship" with his brother in law, with Casares Quiroga, Zulueta, Marcelino Domingo* and . . . several others', and, on the back of the page, 'all gouvernment. I suppose that you will know all off them by the small portraits I include. See how few are the normal men in the group'. In her letter she confesses herself puzzled.[15]

A mixture of things occurs in this letter. Hildegart spills over with obsessive concern about supposed homosexuality in politicians (for which there seems to be little evidence, if any), but she also asks Ellis for help, saying she has read his book on 'Sexual Inversion' to try to understand. Almost simultaneously she shows herself determined to pursue her discussion of homosexuality, affirming that 'when I have these cases finished I will tell you in several letters some of the small things that I judge decisive to know the character of these men and women'. Her use of 'cases' flags up her intention to be seen as 'examining' them as would a doctor or lawyer. The relative caution of *La rebeldía* is set aside in her eagerness to give more examples, and as she tries to engage Ellis in her reaction ('¿Isn't he ugly?', 'See how few . . .', '¿Don't you think it strange . . . ?', 'when I have these cases finished I will tell you in several letters . . .'). The extremity of feeling expressed in this letter suggests that Hildegart, perhaps at the prompting of Aurora, has been driven to a level of panic about the prevalence of what elsewhere she has claimed to be a characteristic of degeneration.

Ellis, it would appear, responded with some calming comments, since when Hildegart writes back on 19 March 1932 she explains about her pamphlet on 'The Eugenic Problem', adding that she was very young at the time and asking for further guidance. Nonetheless, Ellis evidently thought there was some basis for her allegations of the extent of homosexuality in the Spanish government, and put a postscript to a letter to Norman Haire, dated 14 January 1932 (and thus written as soon as he had received her letter of 5 January 1932):

> Did you know that many of the leading figures in the new Republican regime in Spain are homosexual? So at least I hear from a remarkable young Spanish girl lawyer in Madrid.

Though prompt, Haire's response was characteristically guarded. In a letter of 15 January 1932 he commented: 'Your news about the Spanish Statesman is interesting. I had not heard anything of it'.[16]

Possibly Ellis's response to Hildegart had some effect although *¿Quo vadis, burguesía?* came out that September. We might view as a further result of the exchange the more flexible view of homosexuality that emerges in Hildegart's article in the February 1933 number of the *Gaceta Médica Española*. It appears that originally this article was to have been called 'Algunos comentarios en torno al problema de la intersexualidad' (see n. 4). The disappearance of the word 'intersexualidad' probably indicates Hildegart's public detachment from Marañón, whose ideas she criticizes, with some accuracy and force. A further article, 'La influencia de las pasiones homosexuales en los acontecimientos políticos' [Influence of Homosexual Passions on Political Events], never came out. If, as seems likely, it relates to *¿Quo vadis, burguesía?* and to the suspicions Hildegart airs in her letter to Ellis on 5 January 1932, it may not have been accepted for publication.

A further dimension lies behind this mobility (or confusion) on the question of homosexuality in Hildegart's mind, namely Aurora's views which came out in no uncertain manner in her time in Ciempozuelos. Aurora was shocked by what she saw as the homosexuality of staff and inmates of the prison where she had been interned originally, the staff because they tolerated homosexuality in the inmates, and the inmates because almost all were involved in homosexual practices (Rendueles, 1989: 15). Her account of her family (summarized in Chapter Two) expresses strong disgust, and virtually no measure. The question inevitably arises of whether Aurora is in fact defending herself against a sense of suppressed lesbianism in herself. With such complications as a background, it is scarcely surprising that there is confusion and internal conflict in Hildegart's views on the subject.

In further exchanges between Ellis and Hildegart after the flurry of concern about homosexuality in her letters to him it is possible she came to be more independent of Aurora. She mentions homosexuality in 'Endocrinología, delincuencia y eugenesia' [Endocrinology, Delinquency and Eugenics], her article in the first number of *Sexus* (1932a) where she follows the line of Marañón, by which endocrinology explains homosexuality, and urges acceptance of the idea of the 'intersex' state as one which allows for it. While she writes with some measure and compassion, it is worth noting that she is concerned, as are various other theorists, to categorize: the idea of variability, of a spectrum of choice and behaviour that might move across categories, and thus be a flow that was not subject to taxonomy and control, is something to be avoided. In her later article in the *Gaceta Médica Española* in which she critiqued the ideas of Marañón, her views on homosexuality had become patently more flexible, a sign perhaps of her increasing detachment from the ideas of Aurora (Hildegart, 1933b).[17]

A consequence of taxonomy is the enhanced authority of the taxonomist, whether doctor or lawyer. An awareness of this authority is part of Hildegart's second article in *Sexus* (1933), 'Ensayos en torno a la criminología sexual' [Essays on Sexual Criminology] where she promotes the standing of the doctor, who 'más competente que ninguno, tiene el deber de hablar, y muy alto, para ilustrar a la opinión y al legislador' [more competent than anyone else, has the right to speak, and to do so loudly, to enlighten public opinion and the legislator] (Hildegart, 1933a: 49). Drawing on the theories of Freud for a sexual explanation of various acts she argues for a series of crimes to be removed from the penal code, since they represent not crime but (sexual or physiological) disorder. But if Hildegart includes homosexuality in this, she nonetheless thought homosexuals should be required to undergo treatment if it was thought they represented a threat to the community (Hildegart, 1933a: 59).

The articles in *Sexus* constitute the most public showcase for one involved with the Liga, and with the WLSR outside Spain, given that this was the title of the international journal of the WLSR (Dose, 2003: 2).[18] By their dates these articles show that Hildegart was learning to tread her own path on homosexuality, particularly as shown in her critique of the ideas of Marañón. If this is so, it had come about within a space of months and arguably through the exchanges with Ellis.

NOTES

[1] The emphasis would fall on parents, seen as the educators of children in sex, particularly on the mother, something which would be revolutionary in social terms (Vázquez García and Moreno Mengíbar, 1997: 155).
[2] Other articles in *Revista de Occidente* in the period 1923–36 promoted a generally traditional view of gender roles in society. These articles included translations of Simmel, Kretschmer, Jung, Keyserling and pieces by Marañón and Pittaluga (Sinclair, forthcoming).
[3] This was reviewed in the *Eugenics Review* (April 1932).
[4] One source of confusion is that Cal may have drawn on the list of Hildegart's publications printed at the end of *Venus ante el Derecho*. This list stated that Hildegart published an essay in February 1933 in the *Gaceta Médica* ('Algunos comentarios en torno al problema de la intersexualidad') [Some Comments on the Problem of Intersexuality] and that a further one, 'La influencia de las pasiones homosexuales en los acontecimientos políticos' [The Influence of Homosexual Passion on Political Events] would appear in the *Gaceta Médica* in May 1933. The *Gaceta Médica* is in fact the *Gaceta Médica Española*. The first of these articles appeared, but under the title, 'Sugestiones en torno al problema de la bisexualidad' [Suggestions on the Problem of Bisexuality].
[5] Cal refers to Hildegart's works as 'escritos' [writings] and lists from 1929 to 1933. Clearly some works go through various forms, so that *El problema eugénico: punto de vista de una mujer moderna* (published by *El Socialista* in Madrid) is the same as, or related to, *Una mujer moderna*

ante el problema eugénico (Madrid 1929, listed by Cal as the first edition), which in its turn is *El problema eugénico: Una mujer moderna*. See Cal, 1991a: 193–5.

6   This will reappear in a modern edition as *Medios para evitar el embarazo. Paternidad voluntaria* [How to Avoid Pregnancy. Voluntary Fatherhood] (Zaragoza: Guara, 1978). This edition, however, states that its first edition was brought out by Ediciones Orto, Mataró in 1938, to coincide with the first move to set up the Federación Española de Planificación Familiar [Spanish Federation for Family Planning].

7   Cal lists this as being published in the collection La novela proletaria. Given the size of the work, this seems unlikely, unless her reference is to a brief popular version of the work.

8   These works are listed by Cal (1991a: 195). With the exception of *Venus ante el derecho* these works have disappeared from public view. They are listed, however, at the end of *Venus ante el derecho*. See note 4.

9   From the list of future publications given by Hildegart at the end of *Venus ante el Derecho*.

10 The complexities regarding public attitudes to homosexuality, and indeed the forms that homosexuality took in early twentieth-century Spain, are tracked in full detail by Cleminson and Vázquez García (2007: Chapters One and Two). Their discussion provides a full context in which to see the attitude of Hildegart and others towards homosexuality, and the provisions proposed regarding homosexuality in documents of reform.

11 The photographs are in the British Library archive, and are annotated by Hildegart.

12 According to Hildegart's ideas in the *El Socialista* 16 January 1932, Jesus was a homosexual, and being surrounded by men to whom he was an object of attraction, believed himself to be the centre of creation. See also in this collection *El Noroeste* (Gijón, 27 March 1932) where the report on Hildegart's lecture on 'Homosexualismo' (not the announced topic, which had been on 'La sobre población y la crisis mundial' [Over-Population and the Third World Crisis]) includes Jesus in a list of homosexuals.

13 This was a vigorous left-wing series directed by Augusto Vivero that ran to twenty-seven titles in 1932. Eduardo de Guzmán, who would be favoured by Aurora for writing up the events of Hildegart's life and death, produced *El confidente* in this series as no. 8.

14 In this pen-portrait of an invert (as in some of her commentaries on homosexuality in the letters to Ellis), Hildegart subscribes to the turn-of-the-century view that homosexuals could be identified by feminine traits. See the discussion of the beliefs about anatomical characteristics in Cleminson and Váquez García (2007: Chapter Two).

15 There is a lack of clear evidence to support what Hildegart is saying here. Nonetheless, there was at least one published work that alleged the (passive) homosexuality of Azaña (Carlavilla, 1956).

16 Both letters from the Haire correspondence with Ellis, Sydney University Library, 3.16.
17 Hildegart also translated a brief article by Ellis for the first number of *Sexus*, in which Ellis argued that homosexuality had always been part of human existence, and was just one natural intersexual condition in the range of variation (Ellis, 1932). The article was reprinted in the anarchist journal *Orto* in 1933.
18 Dose details the difficulties of publication of the various versions of *Sexus*.

Chapter Five

Hildegart's 'child', the Spanish Liga

Our League will march beautifully, and you will always know that it is because your[1] anwsered my first letter that I became interested and charmed with the proposition of doing some practical work in Spain. (Hildegart to Ellis, 30 March 1932)

Before any Commitee had been named, the League was only mine. I was his only supporter and propulsor. Now, and it must be soo and I am happy for it, all the elected for the Commitee have a part in their ideas and in their love for our League and I am but one more. It seems as if I have had a child with great efforts, and seen afterwards being born, I had to give it to a nurse, for I could not give him the milk of my breast, though I know that the presence of the nurse is necessary to save the life of the child. I hope you can understand me, and you will know how I am writing this letter so happy, so happy and yet a bit sorry. (Hildegart to Ellis, 1 May 1932)

That is the saddest part of all. People would be interested. But the first workmen are not. They have not said 'no', but they are moving slowly and yet more slowly, with a drowsy movement. I don't mind to work and work hard for the League if only they will help me. (Hildegart to Ellis, 25 June 1932)

Hildegart's involvement with the Liga, indeed the life of the Liga itself, occupies a narrow window of time, from its foundation in March 1932 to a short time after her death in June 1933. Not surprisingly, as the evidence of her letters to Ellis demonstrates, her relationship with the Liga was central and intense, full of close and emotional personal commitment. This chapter will take that relationship as its focus, examining Hildegart's role in the founding of the Liga, and the evidence of discord in the organization. Some of the tensions derived from professional differences between members, but the underlying major issues would relate to the promotion of eugenic issues on the one hand with the drive for sexual reform on the other.

As evidenced in her major 1931 works *La rebeldía sexual de la juventud* and *El problema sexual tratado por una mujer española*, Hildegart has an interest in both areas, and while much of her writing falls under the broad umbrella of eugenics, her activity in the Liga foundation meeting at least shows her as espousing the more revolutionary aspects of the WLSR. In *La rebeldía sexual* she presents it as the solution to a series of problems relating to marriage, sex, prostitution and sex education that have been outlined in previous chapters, its remit being broader than matters of sex education and the spreading of information about contraception. Her definition of the WLSR and its aims is drawn virtually verbatim from Saldaña, *La sexología* (1930: 22–3), although without acknowledging him:

> Vino al mundo para contribuir a que la cuestión sexual no sea la denominada 'cuestión tabú' por excelencia, sino que quede sometida en todos sus aspectos al término científico, pero al propio tiempo tratado con toda publicidad. (Hildegart, 1931d: 145)
>
> [It came into the world in order to ensure that the sexual question should not be automatically referred to as the 'taboo question', but rather should be considered according to the definitions of science, while being given maximum publicity.]

Again, following Saldaña, Hildegart speaks of 'redemption', in terms of redeeming humanity from its prejudices in sexual matters, a redemption to be brought about by the study of sociology and ethics (the disciplines that Saldaña cites) (Hildegart, 1931d: 145). She already has a clear idea of who will form the Spanish chapter and names as possible supporters Marañón, Madrazo, Nóvoa Santos, Vital Aza, Otaola, Jiménez Asúa, Saldaña, Torrubiano Ripoll, Ruiz Funes and Noguera. All would become founding members of the Liga.[2]

Setting up the Liga

Hildegart uses her correspondence with Ellis to pursue questions about the founding of the Spanish chapter of the WLSR, but her first letter is very much a bid to be recognized as a fellow-reformer. She tells Ellis how much she has read, including his work the *Psychology of Sex*,[3] along with the writings of Spaniards of her time such as Marañón, Jiménez Asúa and Vital Aza, and then sets herself apart, declaring that she considers both Marañón and Jiménez de Asúa to take a 'reactionary' attitude to the psychology of sex (presumably in comparison with Ellis himself) (23 October 1931). Having established her position she makes her direct appeal to him to 'explain me the creation and accord taken by that Ligue of Sexual Reform, of which you are president in England's name', a request she follows up in her second letter when she asks how the WLSR was 'born' (2 December 1931).

It is characteristic of the way that Hildegart will regard the Liga that she puts her question in terms of birth, and it is also not entirely coincidental that her next letter (5 January 1932) is about sex rather than the practicalities of setting up the League in Spain. As outlined in Chapter Four, it is full of gossip about the sexual lives of prominent politicians of the Republic, and we could read her intimations of the lack of 'proper men and women' as a fear that the conditions for 'proper birth' are lacking in public life. A few weeks later she tells Ellis that plans to set up a chapter in Spain are well advanced, and that the Liga's structure has been decided. There are to be seven sections: sex education, feminism and marriage, birth control, eugenics, prostitution and prevention of VD, a rational attitude to sexual inversion and a section composed of lawyers. Her own position, she hopes, will be that of secretary (8 February 1932).

There are two questions to look at here. First, how far can we infer that Hildegart has been the prime instrument in setting up the Liga? An immediate response is that it seems hard to believe that she alone should have set it up, and one wonders whether she simply decided to take an independent line of enquiry on the subject, one that was no more than background to the activity of others. It should be pointed out that there was already a route through which Spaniards could belong to the international activities of the WLSR. It was announced, for example, in *España Médica* (1 August 1930) that the fourth congress of the WLSR would take place in Vienna (an event at which Freud, George Bernard Shaw and Stefan Zweig were to figure) and that Spaniards who wanted to attend should contact the Spanish member on the WLSR committee, Dr Fernán Pérez.[4] Yet the level of her activity and involvement in the Liga from this point is both considerable and significant. The figure of thirty-three interested persons she cites in this letter is close to the total of forty-one (excluding regional representatives) that she will give in her official summary of the foundation meeting. That a girl of seventeen should reach this position suggests two possibilities: that she was exceptional and had already been accepted as such, or that the Liga itself was exceptional in placing its secretarial matters in the hands of such a young woman.

The second question concerns how far the Liga that Hildegart presents to Ellis correlates with the organization that actually came into being. Close reading of the foundation document reveals the degree to which there was a gap between what she had hoped and planned for, and what in the event was feasible. Thus is it important to compare the structure of the Liga as she initially describes it to Ellis, with what appears to have been the eventual public statement of its aims that the Liga would make in the first number of *Sexus*.

The foundation meeting of the Liga took place on 3 March 1932. The copious report sent by Hildegart to Ellis of this meeting is important because it reveals which aspects of sexual reform and the WLSR's platform were specific to or particularly significant for the Spanish context. The document names the objectors to different planks in the platform and thus clarifies the positions on sexual reform held by prominent men of medicine, law and public life in Spain.[5] But this document is also significant because it demonstrates Hildegart's (self-reported) role in the situation. She appears from her account to operate not merely as a recording secretary but as the chair of a difficult and complex group (which it no doubt was).

A further complexity derives from the form of the document. The greater part of it comprises Hildegart's detailed notes for the meeting, reflecting (or implying) discussions that have gone on beforehand about the WLSR's planks of belief, and the objections of various members to aspects of those planks. What we see then is her campaign of preparation. An appendix to the document summarizes points that were made at the meeting, in which her responses to initial objections to individual planks were further discussed, and decisions taken on the planks concerned.

Hildegart prefaces her report with a summary of recent sexual reform activities involving Spaniards, citing among other things the 1928 Eugenics Conference and attendance of both Dr Sánchez Gómez (as official representative) and Dr Gregorio Marañón (as an independent delegate) at the 1929 Congress of the WLSR. The coming of the Second Republic in 1931 then prompted the WLSR to see Spain as ripe for further sexual reforms. It was an 'excelente campo de experimentación' [excellent site for experiment], a phrase that suggests Spain as object rather than agent of its own destiny, and that indicates an uncertain dynamic by which it is difficult to see how far Spain's reforms were coming from within, and how far they were prompted from outside. Hildegart then signals her own activity that has brought the Liga to its present point, her correspondence with Ellis, Leunbach, Haire and Hirschfeld and her role in gathering together some forty persons, in addition to a number of regional representatives to found the organization. In a disarming phrase she alludes to her activity: 'Me comprometí a hacer las gestiones que se estimaran precisas' [I took it upon myself to set the necessary measures in motion]. Throughout Hildegart's report on the Liga (drafted for the record, but also for Ellis to read) we become conscious of the possibility that there is some doubly-oriented speech so that in recording the proceedings she is also possibly covertly addressing Ellis, overemphasizing her own power and importance, as this phrasing of the last quotation implies. A key point she makes is a distinction between other countries where the League grew out of a fusion of groups with aims in common, and Spain where what is happening is a top-down development. To some degree this paves the way for her to deal with dissent, in that she will advance the view that the different sections might act as interest groups loosely bound in federation.

Founding Members

To give some sense of the dynamic between professions we need simply refer to Hildegart's list of members. Her listing of these members (with some slips of the pen) suggests a hierarchy of importance. They are:

Recaséns
Ramón y Cajal
Cossío*
Marañón
Jiménez de Asúa
Saldaña
Morata
Juarros
Huerta
Haro
Noguera
Sanchis Banús
Nóvoa Santos
Macau
Sánchez Covisa
Vital Aza
Bugallo
Otaola
Sacristán
Sánchez Taboada
Navarro Fernández
Rocamora[6]
Barrio de Medina*
Bravo (D. Julio)
Ruis Funes[7]
Zozaya
Hernández Catá
Hernández Alfonso*
Lafora[8]
Torrubiano y Ripoll
Varela Radio*
Pittaluga
Amador Pereira[9]
Cansinos Assens
Ortiz de Pinedo
Sánchez de Rivera
Dantin Cereceda[10]
Edmundo Gónzalez Blanco*
López Ureña*
Pedro Cifuentes*
Sainz de Aja

In addition to these a number of provincial members are listed separately by location: Bilbao: Dr Gardo;[11] Santander: Dr Madrazo; Zaragoza: Dr Oriol y Anguera; Salamanca: Dr Barcia Goyanes*; Almería: Dr Campoy Ibáñez; Cádiz: Dr Alacalá Santaella*; Valencia: Marín Civera and Dr Roberto Remartínez*. Hildegart anticipated that, given the amount of support locally, a section of the Liga would be formed in Valencia, and that there was also reason to set up a subsidiary section in Barcelona: a Liga Catalana, that would include the four provinces, was being established. Her contacts here were Pi y Suñer* and Carrasco Formiguera.[12]

Some twenty-eight of these were from the field of medicine, and only about eight from law, the remainder coming from other areas of public life, including journalism and education. The imbalance between professions is evident from the start, and might account for the energetic contributions of the lawyers in particular.

The first three names on the list are of elder statesmen acknowledged by Hildegart as having given signal public support. The next seventeen, down to Navarro Fernández, can be regarded as prime movers in the Liga. They are cited with some frequency in the correspondence with Ellis, or figure significantly in Hildegart's life. Further down the list, the ostensible importance of members within the workings of the Liga diminishes, while some, such as Lafora, Torrubiano y Ripoll and Pittaluga are evidently of importance outside the bounds of the Liga. Towards the end of the list there are those who will be significant in education (such as Dantín Cereceda) or in the literary world, such as Cansinos Assens and González Blanco.

The Decalogue and Dissidence

Much of the foundation meeting was occupied by discussion of the WLSR's ten planks. Curiously they are referred to as the 'Decalogue', a term replete with Biblical associations, contrasting with the secular term 'planks' used in the WLSR 1928 congress.[13] The advance objections of members of the Liga to various parts of the Decalogue show clearly how they voiced the concerns of their particular professions or areas of expertise. No less interesting are Hildegart's pre-prepared responses, showing that she not only recorded the discussion but was also braced to challenge the arguments of various delegates. What comes through is her initial determination to secure acceptance of the planks, and what emerges from the document (or rather from the section that is formed by her initial notes) is an impression that her outlook extends beyond that of some of the experts in the different sections. Her notes, however, are the first word rather than the last, and the appendix points towards the compromises that will eventually be adopted. She takes the planks in order, and her wording shows that she uses the 1928 Copenhagen version.

The conservative doctor Nóvoa Santos made his presence felt by his objection to plank 1, 'Political, economic and sexual equality of men and women'. One wonders whether Hildegart conveyed any irony with her tone when observing that his objection is based on his 'radical feminismo' [radical feminism].[14] The skill of her plan consists, however, in keeping this conservative member on board by pointing out the multiplicity of slots available for members to be active.

Plank 2, 'Separation of marriage (and especially divorce) from the tyranny of Church and State', brought a different range of objections. Sanchis Banús had made an objection on the basis of his socialism, declaring that the State could and should be prepared to intervene in the life of the individual. This nicely crystallizes one of the issues of eugenics and sexual reform, and highlights an inbuilt conflict about how far private activity could and should be legislated for when part of the agenda for reform was the improvement of the race. Hildegart's (planned) response was that the communist dictatorship of Soviet Russia had been among the first to recognize secular unions and to guarantee the rights of the children produced from them. The position expressed in this plank, for her, was the need to defend private activity so long as it did not impinge negatively on the community. The discussion recorded in the appendix shows that this was not sufficient as an argument in response, and this plank on marriage stimulated vigorous debate. Marañón, summing up and smoothing over, suggested that it would be imprudent to go against public opinion in a way that would damage much of the work of the Liga, so that it would be preferable to suppress this plank.

Losing support for one of the early planks could be seen as the way the Liga would be set on a path towards a significantly diluted version of the WLSR agenda, and it would be followed by strong objections to the sixth, eighth and ninth planks. Intervening planks on controlling conception (plank 3), on improving the race through eugenics (plank 4) and protecting the unmarried mother and her child (plank 5) were less problematic. Plank 6, however, predictably did cause difficulties. Its formulation, 'A rational attitude towards sexually abnormal persons, and especially to homosexuals', prompted a vigorous response from Saldaña. In general Saldaña makes up for his minority position as lawyer (and possibly also for a minority position of one who is conservative in matters of reform) by the frequency of his interventions. Given his conservative approach in his essays on sexology, and yet his centrality to the movement, his (perhaps self-appointed) role appears to be that of guarantor of standards, always with an eye to the legal. His main issue was with how far the State should hold back on regulation of perversions. He believed that there was a need to ensure that allowing tolerance did not lead to public scandal, and that the action on homosexuality should perhaps be limited to legislative pressure so that appropriate education would avoid such 'deviations'.[15] Marañón took a diplomatic line on this, suggesting that the word 'homosexuality' could be removed since the underlying principle was observed in planks 8 and 9. In the event, however, his final suggestion was that it would be best to suppress this plank as well.

The plank on prevention of prostitution and venereal disease (plank 7) and the plank proposing that disturbances of the sexual impulse should be regarded as more or less pathological phenomena and not 'as crimes, vices or sins' (plank 8) did not cause particular difficulty.[16] Plank 9, however, drew an interesting comment from Haro, who suggested that the word 'sexual' could be removed from the ninth plank, in order to protect the rights of the unborn child (who could be born damaged even if the act leading to its conception was by mutual consent). His broadening of the issues of the planks here is noteworthy, and conceivably deflected attention from one of Hildegart's initial points by which, through swift sleight of hand she referred to 'actos sexuales entre adultos responsables – normales – ' [sexual acts between responsible – normal – adults]. Plank 10, on 'Systematic sexual education', was approved without difficulty.

The resulting collection, the 'Octologue' (minus the planks on the separation of marriage from Church and State, and on working towards a rational attitude in relation to 'sexually abnormal persons, and especially to homosexuals') was approved. But after all this, when the aims of the Liga were finally published six months later in the first number of *Sexus* (October/November 1932), they had been considerably altered; what appeared now was a set of six bland recommendations in which much of the force of the original planks was lost, although a higher profile was given to 'authority'.

The Decalogue was thus translated into the following declared aims of the Liga:

1. Orientar los problemas de la ética y la sociología sexual con arreglo a principios biológicos.
2. Servir de medio de unión entre las organizaciones e individuos que compartan su punto de vista.
3. Divulgar el conocimiento científico de los temas sexuales.
4. Combatir aquellos prejuicios que impidan la creación de una actitud racional frente a las cuestiones del sexo.
5. Recabar de los Poderes públicos la máxima atención a estos temas, juzgándolos como problemas vitales para el porvenir de la raza, que deben interesar por igual a todos los Gobiernos, del matiz político que sean.
6. Solicitar de los Poderes públicos la promulgación de leyes y modificación de las existentes que aseguren y garanticen un cambio favorable a la comprensión legítima de estos problemas sexuales.[17]

[1. To consider problems of ethics and sexual sociology in accord with biological principles.
2. To serve as a means of contact between organizations and individuals that share its views.
3. To disseminate scientific knowledge on sexual matters.
4. To work against prejudices that stand in the way of the creation of a rational attitude to sexual matters.
5. To secure maximum attention from public authority to these matters, in the belief that they are problems vital for the future of the race, and of equal interest for all governments, regardless of political persuasion.
6. To seek from public authority the promulgation of new laws and modification of existing ones in order to secure

and guarantee change that will be favourable to the legitimate understanding of these sexual problems.]

The first number of *Sexus* appeared in October/November 1932, some months after the foundation meeting, and after the signs of discord that Hildegart had reported to Ellis in her letters. That the statement of the Liga's aims abandons the ten planks, and does not even consist of the eight that according to Marañón would have been feasible, is arguably a sign of real difficulty. A further simplification can be observed in the sections. Instead of the seven originally envisaged by Hildegart, five were formed: eugenics (Haro, Otaola, Sacristán), feminism and marriage (Vital Aza, Macau, Carmen de Burgos), sex education (Huerta, Blanco, Bugallo Sánchez), prostitution and prevention of venereal disease (Sánchez Covisa, César Juarros, Sáinz de Aja), legislation (Ruiz Funes, Saldaña, Torrubiano) (*Sexus* 1 (1): 124–5). The two sections that were suppressed between the foundation meeting and the *Sexus* list were the sections on birth control, and 'deviations of the sexual instinct'. The organization of the Eugenics Conference for the following year would highlight presentations aimed at education and science, and would to a large degree steer clear of those areas of belief within the WLSR that were contentious.

The Liga and Internal Strife

A newspaper article in the Ellis collection, signed by Alfonso Cernadas, gives evidence of a curious tension between the public status of the Liga and that of Hildegart herself. The main title is 'CHARLANDO CON HILDEGART' [CONVERSING WITH HILDEGART] whereas the mention of the Liga is consigned to a sub-heading in smaller type. The article, whose source is unidentified, was evidently written after the meeting on 3 March 1932 which had set up the constitution of the League, and after a lecture tour in Asturias that Hildegart tells Ellis about in her letter of 19 March 1932. Despite the fact that the Liga is now launched, the article starts by introducing Hildegart in her public persona, adding that one of her latest activities is to 'organize' the Liga. It refers to her as 'secretaria y fundadora' [secretary and foundress], and reports her publications, *Limitación de la prole, Educación sexual, Sexo y amor, Revolución sexual, Rebeldía sexual de la juventud,* and *Paternidad voluntaria*. The account she gives in this interview highlights the significance of Ellis, and cites him as the person who had interested her in setting up the Spanish chapter of the WLSR. Ellis was, in her view, the 'father' of the Liga. He was, however, as the correspondence indicates, a father that she had sought out. This could be seen as an unconscious echo of her mother's activity in seeking a suitable father for her child, although another possibility is that it was an approach made at her mother's prompting.[18] Whatever the history, Hildegart (who was not listed as an organizing member of any of the sections) makes it plain that her role was central. Inspired by Ellis, by her mother, and by Marañón, whose *Tres ensayos* she found to be a 'spark' from outside, she presents herself as the Liga's chief administrator, the instigator of its activities.

At the end of Cernadas's article there are two comments that warn of the difficulties that lay ahead for Hildegart and the Liga. Hildegart is credited with saying that H. G. Wells had singled her out for recognition: 'Usted, como española, puede ser, por su talento y por su juventud, "el lazo de unión de los sectores internacionales"' [As a Spanish woman, and with your talent and youth, you could be the 'link between international sectors']. The confidence with which Hildegart relays this to the interviewer could with hindsight be construed as a naive and ingenuous view of herself that takes no account of the envy or resentment that it might inspire. Yet she also alludes to the difficulties. She declares that she is satisfied with her work (and presumably with her role in the Liga) but complains about squabbling among the Liga's members: 'Me molestan únicamente esas pequeñas rencillas, esas ambiciones que quieren salir a la luz no noblemente y disputando el puesto, sino reptando' [The only things that bother me are the petty squabbles, signs of ambition that surface not fairly and openly because people want to fight for their positions, but crawling into view].[19]

In a letter dated 19 March 1932 Hildegart writes of her frustrations with Marañón (who, it would seem, did not want to move forwards as rapidly as she did in the work of the Liga), and of a 'small fight' she had with Dr Sanchis Banús. She goes on to comment 'It is very disagreeable to fight with the ignorance and the stupidity of a great deal of persons, but I don't break down'. In subsequent letters she goes on to report something much more specific, namely difficulties in her relationship with Dr Francisco

Haro, treasurer of the Liga and one of the three members involved in the section on eugenics. She first mentions him on 22 April 1932 as 'one of the younger but most intelligent doctors', and a pupil of Marañón.[20]

In a letter dated 18 July 1932 there was a further issue with Haro, namely the fear that he might take charge of *Sexus*, the Liga's planned review. Hildegart was scathing, not least because of Haro's lack of linguistic ability: 'he does not know language well, and besides he cannot write to any of you, by the same reason. I think that you will have seen how he calls you in his book. He writes your name as: "Havellok Hellis"'.

Hildegart's fears about Haro, however, went beyond her concern that he might want to take over the review, and the letter of 18 July 1932 shows how she believes him to be at the root of manoeuvres to remove her from her position as secretary (see Chapter Seven). One can only speculate about Haro's intentions. He might well have objected to Hildegart's strong proprietary attitudes towards the Liga, attitudes evident in some of the interviews and letters discussed so far. Such attitudes might also have alienated other members of the Liga, in addition to which it is clear that Hildegart was all set to embrace the ten planks of the WLSR while significant members of the 'Liga-to-be' had reservations about some of them. It is possible Haro was opposing Hildegart on a more general issue, namely whether doctors or lawyers should have the whip hand in the direction of the Liga. Doctors were prominent in public life. Alternatively, he might have objected to Hildegart's youth or gender. Stronger than any of this, on eugenic grounds, might have been issues of parentage: Hildegart's father was unknown, and her mother, Aurora, was observably odd if not at that time identifiably mad.[21]

Several months pass before Hildegart writes again to Ellis about how the squabbles in the Liga were affecting her. But on 6 October 1932 she notes that the Spanish Liga was 'passing a very bad time', and on 22 October elaborates on that remark in ways that suggest not just her distress but her belief that all within the Liga, including Marañón, may be against her: 'Perhaps you will be astonished by this but you can't imagine what a hard work it has been for me to manage and move the League until now, and what a coarse fighting has taken place some time ago'.

Hildegart's difficulties did not escape the thoughtful attention of Ellis. In a letter to Margaret Sanger of 30 January 1933 he advised caution in entrusting Hildegart with the organization of an international conference on birth control in Madrid in 1933. Not only did he see her as 'so young and inexperienced in conference organization', but perhaps more crucially commented (presumably in the light of the chequered history of the Liga) that 'her youth & success arouses jealousies, especially among some of the men'.[22] Despite these difficulties, however, it is not clear that Hildegart's link with the Liga came to the early end suggested by Cal who traces problems back to Aurora's insistence on the strategy of temporary sterilization of all men reversing it for a period of three years judged optimal for eugenic purposes (Cal, 1991a: 89).[23] Hildegart's letters to Ellis, while continuing to report difficulties in the Liga, do so in general terms rather than with reference to her own difficulties with it (6 and 22 October 1932). On 10 April 1933, two months before her death, she writes about 'exceptional activity' in the Liga, preparatory to the Eugenics Conference and the publication of the second number of *Sexus*. In addition to this, in the report made by *El Debate* on 9 June 1933 of the murder, we are told that Hildegart 'actualmente desempeñaba la secretaría de la Liga de Reforma Sexual' [was currently secretary of the League of Sexual Reform] (cited by Álvarez Peláez and Huertas, 1987: 103). This appears to support more general evidence that Hildegart continued activity within the Liga into 1933, as indeed her prominent role in the second number of *Sexus* attests, although it must be said that this report seems to be the exception rather than the norm.

What Hildegart does not do in the letters is give any indication that her mother was a cause of the problems in the Liga. Possibly she edited out of her letters references to difficulties in which her mother might have had a part. Yet the evidence gained retrospectively, and specifically through the psychiatric report at Aurora's trial, suggests that her mother was not only prominent in the Liga, but was a major source of discord. Indeed, one might almost think that the report afforded the opportunity for the expression of a backlog of resentment towards Aurora. Given that it was dated 20 September 1933, it was written just four months after the appearance of the second number of *Sexus*, which in its turn came out a bare month before the murder of Hildegart. This compression of events makes even-handedness less likely than otherwise. The report leaves no doubt about the degree to which there was resentment at the way in which Aurora attempted to influence decisions in the Liga, and asserts without reservation that Aurora was a problem from the outset. Shortly before the murder, it relates, there were events in the organization of the Liga 'que le producen grandes disgustos y contrariedades al no ver triunfar su criterio tanto en la elección de personas como en la aceptación de sus principios' [that profoundly upset her, as those she favoured were not chosen nor were her principles accepted] (Rendueles, 1987: 208). More than this, however, she wanted to have her view prevail: 'a todo trance pretendía prevaleciera su criterio personal en abierta oposición con el mantenido en otras partes en asociaciones similares' [At all costs she tried to have her views hold sway, in opposition to the position adopted in similar organizations elsewhere] (Rendueles, 1989: 206). Aurora's paranoia was manifest, she was hostile to the men of science within the Liga, and she caused disruption: 'Llegó a tener violentas discusiones con alguno de ellos y creía ver en determinados familiares de ésos actitudes semejantes. Su suspicacia llegó a interpretar arbitrariamente en este sentido incluso las frases más corrientes y usuales' [She eventually had violent arguments with one of them and thought she perceived similar attitudes in those connected with them. Her suspiciousness led her to make arbitrary readings in some cases of the most ordinary and habitual phrases] (Rendueles, 1989: 209). There is no hard and fast evidence that Aurora accompanied Hildegart in all her dealings with the Liga, but there is every probability that she was a prominent presence. Certainly Aurora appeared to have been with her throughout her studies. An observation made by Julián Besteiro places a focus upon a troubling closeness: 'ir tan pegada a su madre, me evoca la imagen de una cría de canguro encapsulada en bolsa invisible y con el cordón umbilical intacto, canal de una hipertrofia comunicativa gigante en dirección única' [the way she goes along so close to her mother's side makes me think of a kangaroo's joey inside an invisible bag and with the umbilical cord still uncut, a great one-way primitive communication route] (Cal, 1991a: 85). And, as fleetingly revealed in the letter of 25 June 1932 to Ellis, Aurora was evidently not just a constant counsellor for Hildegart, but one who thought her views should be taken into account. Thus commenting on how action might be taken forward on the abolition of prostitution, Hildegart observed to Ellis that 'We thought that these measures ought to be known in public – when I say we, I speak of my mother'.

The conflicts outlined so far provide a troubled background to the successful publication of the two issues of the Liga's review, *Sexus*, in which Hildegart plays a major role. The chequered life of *Sexus* is discussed in the following chapter.

NOTES

1. i.e. 'you'.
2. The WLSR is also referenced in *El problema sexual*, where there is a report of the Vienna Congress, attended by Marañón and Sánchez Gómez (Hildegart, 1931b: 192).
3. Havelock Ellis, *Studies in the Psychology of Sex*. Originally published in 1897, revised and reprinted in 6 vols (Philadelphia: Davis), 1920–8). It seems likely that this is the edition to which she refers.
4. See the extensive article on the Asociación Española de Médicos Escritores y Artistas, set up in 1928, at www.medicosescritores yartistas.com/abajo01_a.htm.
5. The position of some of those Hildegart mentions in her letters is detailed by Glick (2003), namely Marañón, Jiménez Asúa, Sanchis Banús, César Juarros, Nóvoa Santos. See also Glick (1981, 1982).
6. It seems likely that this is either R.S. Rocamora (b. 1880), or Jaime Peyri Rocamora.
7. i.e. Mariano Ruiz Funes.
8. i.e. Gonzalo Rodríguez Lafora.
9. From the Liga document itself it would appear Amador Pereira is not part of the medical profession, since he is referred to as 'Sr Pereira'. His intervention in the meeting to set up the Liga, in which he cites a case of a family with five abnormal children, suggests that his interest is in social provisions, and is conceivably a lawyer.
10. i.e. Juan Dantín Cereceda.
11. This is possibly José Gardo Sanjuan, a mercantile administrator (1892–1963).
12. i.e. Manuel Carrasco i Formiguera.
13. See Crozier (2003) and Dose (2003) for detail of the phrasing of the planks. The Biblical phrasing was conceivably in deference to the theological tendencies of Torrubiano Ripoll and Saldaña.
14. The evidence of Nóvoa Santos's position from *La mujer, nuestro sexto sentido*, for example, is that 'radical' equates with conservative, in that his view of woman is of a being undeveloped in relation to man.
15. See this discussion in the light of the emphasis by Cleminson and Vázquez García (2007), who observe that because 'the medicalization of homosexuality in Spain did not respond to a campaign for the decriminalization of same-sex acts, there was less emphasis on the sexual aspects of the question'.
16. See Cleminson and Vázquez García (2007, Chapter Two) on how

from the 1870s discussions around sodomy and pederasty did not take place in the field of mental illness, but in the field of criminality. Saldaña proposed that 'vices or sins' be removed from this plank. Hildegart argued for the general acceptance of 'sin' as indicating what was against the natural law of the reproduction of the species, and that 'vices' referred to 'defect, bad condition, error, damage'. Two things might be recalled here: the connotations of 'vicio' are different from 'vice' in English, the translation suggesting something that is either innate or an accident. Secondly, Cleminson and Vázquez García, referring to Quirós and Llanas Aguilaniedo (1901: 260–1), emphasize the typical Mediterranean distinction between 'active' and 'passive' in the context of homosexuality. They point out that 'those males that practised the insertive role, including "pederasts" and those "impassioned by children" were not real inverts but pseudo-inverts and their practices were more the result of vice than of their specific nature' (2007: Chapter Two), which suggests that 'vice' in this case relates to some form of intention, rather than resulting from an innate condition.

17 These are the aims of the Liga as published in *Sexus* 1 (1) (October/November 1932), 118–19. An interesting intermediate stage can be detected from A.V. de la V. (1932) where mention of the State is omitted from the second plank and the sixth plank, 'A rational attitude towards sexually abnormal persons, and especially to homosexuals', is omitted entirely. Otherwise the planks are as discussed at the foundation meeting, and closer to the WLSR formulation than the bland final version published in *Sexus*.

18 Lafora, in his series of articles published after Aurora's trial asserts that Hildegart founded the Liga 'por consejo de su madre' [on her mother's advice] (Lafora, 1934e).

19 While the article does not elaborate upon Hildegart's reference to the internal squabbles 'pequeñas rencillas', her correspondence with Ellis does provide additional information on them. These are examined in Chapter Seven with a particular view to the complex dynamic between Hildegart and Aurora, and between the two of them and members of the Liga.

20 In this letter, Marañón is listed as president, César Juarros and Ruiz Funes as vice-presidents, Haro as treasurer, and Hildegart as secretary. It is interesting to note the respective esteem given to Haro and Marañón in the foreign press. The *Eugenics Review* 24 (1) (April 1932), 53–4, published C. Wicksteed Armstrong's long and enthusiastic review of Haro's book *Eugenesia y matrimonio* (Madrid, 1932), which contained a foreword by Marañón. A year later the same journal (*Eugenics Review* 25 (1) (April 1933), 54) published Esmé Gilroy's short and less than complimentary review of Marañón's *La evolución de la sexualidad* translated by Warren B. Wells as *The Evolution of Sex and Intersexual Conditions* (London, 1932).

21 See Haro in Noguera and Huerta (1934: 310–66) for the discussion of recessive genes in heredity.

22 Ellis to Margaret, 30 January 1933 (Margaret Sanger Papers, Library

of Congress (Washington, 1977), reel 134, frame 366), cited in 'Sanger and the "Red Virgin"', *The Margaret Sanger Papers Newsletter* 30, Spring 2002 (*www.nyu.edu/projects/sanger/sanger_and_red_virgin. htm*).

23 The Liga is relatively lacking in prominence in Cal (1991a). This may be because Cal draws substantially on Guzmán's account of Aurora (written in 1933 after Aurora had invited him to visit her in prison) and which also gives a limited treatment to the Liga. Aurora was excluded from the decision-making of the Liga at all stages and her downplaying of the Liga to Guzmán is arguably prompted by the distress this exclusion caused.

Chapter Six

The Liga Speaks

But now, everything is going on well. I have not visitied Dr. Haro since that day in which I called him by telephone. And I am going to play him a bad game. He is interested in his directing the Review that will appear on October. I am going to oppose him. And if he is angry, I am going to say him several things that will get him angrier yet. I will say that our Review needs each time, one or two contributions from the membrs of W. L. S. R. He cannot translate them, for he does not know languages well, and besides he cannot write to any of you, by the same reason. I think that you will have seen how he calls you in his book. He writes your name as: "Havellok Hellis". You see, he has not read neither the spanish translation of your books, where your name is rightly spelled. Don't think that many of the members of the League know it. But they are modest, they don't want to have an international relations, and they are not to be blamed. But he must know. Besides, I have other sensible reasons. All the members and future contributor have a great deal of things to do. I will have to be always over them, visiting or calling on them by telephone to have their papers in order to be edited in the Review. They won't deny their presence to a woman, by Spanish gallantry, and to a friend. But they will get sorely bored if Dr. Haro had to do this same thing. So that, the commitee of Redaction of the Review wil be formed by the Executive Commitee, but I will be too the Secretary and so indirectly the Director of the Review. I think he will get angry. But I don't mind him.

And now a special pray. I NEED a contribution of you for the first number of our Review. You can write it in English. I will translate it for you, and I am sure you will not find yourself saying absurd things that you have never thought. I know how to translate. ¿Can we depend upon your contribution? Please say yes. It should be a real, real pleasure for me. (Hildegart to Ellis, 18 July 1932)

Imagined and Imaginary Communities

Movements of reform in Spain in the late 1920s were characterized by their fragility and short life, and the history of the Liga, as outlined in the preceding chapter, was singularly beset by difficulties. Not all of them came from outside pressure. Nonetheless, while coming into being in the early years of the Republic might have seemed ideal for a new organization, the Republic brought its own problems: intense debate about issues and difficulties failed to result in the bringing forward of practical measures that might impact on those issues.

Just as the community of nation is formed by print culture (Anderson, 1983), so too the liveliness and viability of movements, whether political, social, educational or – in this case – bent upon reform in eugenics and sexual matters, are reliant upon an effective means of creating a communal culture. Navarro Fernández's Hygiene Campaign demonstrates it: weekly meetings in cinemas and other public venues might have reached one audience, but another (broader) audience was envisaged in the publication of *Sexualidad* which carried accounts of the meetings and further literature to extend the discussion of matters of eugenics and hygiene. In like manner the vibrancy of the eugenics activity of the anarchists in eastern Spain was without doubt not only evidenced by the reviews published, but was itself enhanced by that publishing activity.[1]

Self-creation through publication is a key feature that distinguishes specialist reviews such as *Sexualidad* from more general press activity. There is a concentrated aim not only of carrying news about the society represented in a journal, but also of presenting a public view of that society. The construction of a group image, with all its facets, is fundamental to movements such as eugenics and sex reform, and the importance of the review is crucial to the sense of perceived public image.[2] It is the shift from the margins to the centre, constituting the distinction between the move of Michel de Certeau's tactician which 'insinuates itself into the other's place, fragmentarily, without taking it over in its entirety, without being able to keep it at a distance' and the establishment of an institution, which, operating through 'strategy', 'assumes a place that can be circumscribed as *proper (propre)* and thus serve as the basis for generating relations with an exterior distinct from it (competitors, adversaries, "clientèles", "targets", or "objects" of research' (Certeau, 1984: xix).

Publication – as illustrated by countless ephemeral periodicals – is a route through to subversion, but also to acceptance. It is of little worth to have ideas if no one but a small circle of intimates can share them. But there is a distinction to be made between publication that spreads views from the margins, and the bid being made in print by a body seeking to establish itself as a contender with others, a body that seeks Certeau's idea of a 'proper' place. The publications of eugenicists and those associated with the sex reform movement thus engage in a double operation. They carry an awareness that the views they print are going to be read as novel (and indeed must be so). At the same time, there is a need to establish an ethos of a movement, an internal respectability that at the same time is one that allows the movement to be compared and associated with others.

The publication of *Sexus* needs to be seen in this light of the need to establish a movement. It needs to be remembered that it was not simply the production of the Spanish chapter of the WLSR, and by a similar token the eventual demise of the journal, and of the organization it represented, was not restricted to Spain. As Dose points out (2003: 2) the WLSR made various attempts to establish an international journal that would be called *Sexus*, first in Vienna and then in Berlin, but without success. The publication of *Sexus* in Spain, as with that of *Le Problème Sexuel* in France, was an act of association with the international WLSR. In this situation we can see how it engaged in a multiply-oriented discourse, on the one hand establishing itself as the organ for the Spanish movement (with a view to being recognized by the international movement) and on the other setting out to engage a Spanish public in issues of eugenics and sex reform. These two agendas account for some of the oddities in balance and presentation.

Sexus and the Balance of Power

It is evident from a survey of the differing reactions at the foundation meeting of the Liga that there were tensions within the organization not just of belief, but between different professional groups. The foundation meeting provides evidence of

Hildegart's attempt to foresee problems, and of Marañón's activity (as the chair of the meeting) to judge a tactical path in relation to the planks that would ensure the survival of the group. But the tensions did not go away, and in the act of making the activities of the group public they inevitably resurfaced. The internal differences between members can be seen from the changing structure of *Sexus*, and to some degree through the balance and content of the articles.

There were two numbers of *Sexus*: Oct/Nov 1932, and April/May 1933. The publication of the second number overlapped with the Primeras Jornadas Eugénicas Españolas [First Spanish Eugenics Conference] which took place between 21 April and 10 May 1933, and the opening speech given for the conference by Noguera, President of the Liga by this time, are reprinted in this number.

Publication as a Balancing Act

The editorial board of *Sexus* 1 contains

Dr Vital Aza   Sr D Jiménez Asúa
Dr Haro García   Sr D Gregorio Marañón
Sr D Luis Huerta   Dr D José María Otaola
Dr César Juarros   Sr D Mariano Ruiz Funes
                Dr D José Sánchez Covisa

Alphabetical ordering removes a sense of hierarchy, so that both Jiménez Asúa and Marañón (powerful in other contexts) are simply part of a list. There seems to be an attempt also to smooth out the possible rivalry between professions. Of the nine listed five are given the title of doctor, and four the lay title of Señor. Marañón, meanwhile, who in other contexts will be referred to by the title of Dr, for some reason here has been deprived of his qualification. Hildegart is listed as 'Secretaria de Redacción', and is referred to as Srta. Hildegart. The message is of calm, democracy, lack of rivalry, consonant with the face that the Liga wants to present to the world.

The inner reality was far from this calm balance. From the end of Chapter Five it will have been clear that the issue of containing Aurora exacerbated the already complicated task of balancing interdisciplinary and interprofessional tension within the Liga. In the case of *Sexus* (the public face that the Liga presented to the world) the problem of Aurora is not evident, but the tensions between professions remain. There is no doubt that the question of Hildegart's place in the structure must have been a delicate one – the more so since there is every sign that she was absolutely central to the review seeing the light. The problems of maintaining an internal balance (that would also constitute the balance of the face of the Liga as presented to the outside world) can be read through the actual contributions to the two numbers of *Sexus*.

The internal structuring and content of the first number of *Sexus* are carefully designed to fit the idea of the Liga as a movement concerned with 'sexual reform on a scientific basis'. Science is thus deliberately well to the fore in the articles, the first three of which are by doctors, Juarros, Otaola and Vital Aza. The next is by one occupying a sort of middle ground, Havelock Ellis, the man whose medical qualifications were gained via the Society of Apothecaries, and a man who did not practice medicine. His contribution is followed by one from Saldaña (who had been more prominent than perhaps anyone else in the debates at the foundation meeting), and one by Hildegart, with a focus on science. Two more 'neutral' articles follow: an interview with Magnus Hirschfeld (going, as it were, to external authority, in speaking to a founder-member of the League), and one on Beacon Hill School (no author is given, but the probability is that it was penned by Hildegart). The rest of the number contains matter pertinent to the World League of Sexual Reform, including the statutes of the Liga and the WLSR's programme of action.

The way the articles are presented shows the high level of professional self-awareness within the Liga, and each contributor is designated according to his or her professional field. Thus Juarros is given his credentials as psychiatrist, as academic, and his offices (within medicine and criminology) are listed. This contrasts with Otaola, who is simply listed as gynaecologist and president of the section of eugenics. In the case of Otaola, however, we can see a different bid for authority in the body of his article, one that will be echoed in the contribution of Saldaña. Both use Latin to establish their position.[3] Otaola simply gives his title in Latin, 'De re eugénica y euthénica' [On eugenics and euthenics], and opens with a Latin tag quoted from William

Temple, thus citing an exotic (and thus authoritative) authority. Saldaña goes much further. His epigraph consists of a quotation in Latin from *Casti connubii* [Of Human Marriage][4] (and thus restricted in its readership) and is literally stiff with detailed papal and Biblical references, not to mention formal rhetorical structure. Vital Aza, with his deliberately technical title of 'Algunos comentarios clínicos y sexuales sobre la fecundación artificial' [Some Clinical and Sexual Commentaries on Artificial Insemination], has a different strategy for making his mark, leading with exotic references, and impressing by the length of his opening sentence, some eleven lines long.

Sexus 1: Calibrating Content

Although the articles in *Sexus* 1 carry the signs of science and medicine (crucial to the ideals of the Liga as an organization that wants to promote a 'rational' and scientific approach to sexuality) they are in fact not scientific papers. There is, however, a discourse that moves from birth to youth, and in so doing it is suggestive of the 'natural' progression of the arguments to be deployed. In this way, the self-promotion of the Liga is one of normality, of speaking as if its voice were coming not from the margins, but from the centre of experience. Thus the Liga is the child of the WLSR, and the publication in hand as one that 'viene a luz' [comes into the world] (*Sexus* 1 1932: 5). In related manner, the article by Juarros on 'Normas básicas de la educación sexual' [Basic Norms of Sex Education] is focused towards normality, but also suggesting that normality includes being calm about sexuality – an idea to be passed on to the child. This is a cautious act of eugenic self-presentation, in that passion and desire are implied as absent. This 'naturalness' of the body in eugenics, a topic returned to with frequency, is thus a feature of how the body might be experienced as less troubling in the absence of either curiosity or repressed desire. What is being presented is the acceptable face of eugenics, in which more disturbing aspects of sexuality (in the form of 'aberrations') are minimalized.

That said, it has to be noted that the papers are not universally non-threatening. Otaola's offering 'De re eugénica y euthénica', is of hard-line eugenics, full of details on the inheritance of physical and mental defects. The tone is exhortatory, and the paper asserts the authority of the doctor (viewed as the one who may or may not 'authorize' the procreation of a series of infected and disabled beings). But this authority is supported by being set in the context of external influence: the London Eugenics Society is cited (Otaola, 1932: 25), a singling out of influence that reinforces the conclusion that in this area of social belief there was a particularly strong link between Spain and England.

Vital Aza's article on artificial insemination treads an interesting line. His scientific approach to the reasons that might justify artificial insemination argues that male disorders might give just cause for its use while female ones do not (since, he claims, the latter can be corrected). His fundamental argument is that what matters most of all is the act of fertilization, so that the desire for a child can be satisfied, and it would appear that sexual satisfaction is not relevant to his reasoning. The main thing is to ensure motherhood.

These three articles operate as a type of warm-up for the reader, taking us through discussions that are on the surface scientific, calm, rational, even if they contain attitudes to eugenics and sexuality that are far from bland. The gloves are (almost) off, and the following article by Ellis, 'El infierno de la patología sexual' [The Hell of Sexual Pathology] suggests by its title that he is entering the ring with the hard-liners. Ellis's attitude to having the gloves off, however, is to broach subjects that others in this number have failed to do. That is, they have remained within eugenics, a field better known in Spain at the time, and – in its emphasis on parenting, health and procreation – not obviously problematic. Ellis takes up the sex reform line, clearly a more sensitive area. His approach is to avoid the idea of pathology and to think of human interaction. The question, he says, is not whether an act is abnormal but whether it causes harm. His perspective on sexuality is wider than that of Juarros, and has a greater sense of distance. More importantly, he is the writer who now broaches homosexuality – something that was sidestepped at the foundation meeting as a tactical move to ensure general acceptance of the aims of the Liga. Ellis proposes the view (consistent with the WLSR planks) that homosexuality exists on a scale of variation, and is the result of hereditary factors. Far from making this, or any other aspects of sexuality, a cause for strong reaction (as implied by the 'infierno' of the title) his effect is de facto one of calming. What happens here, then, is that the authority from outside Spain is used to deal with those issues that at the foundation meeting had been thought too controversial to write into the planks of belief. Ellis's article simultaneously advertises the international nature of the Liga and – by coming from the margins – is able to speak more freely than those from the inside.

The following article, by Saldaña, moves discussion away from the body into religion and the law (in relation to marriage). His is the only paper in this collection not related directly to the body and sexuality, except in his concern to avoid the 'contaminations' resulting from inappropriate unions. Saldaña is a prime example of the high-mindedness and self-confidence of the eugenicist in full flow, well set to put in place the legislation that would protect the race.

Finally, we have the curious offering of Hildegart. The apprenticeship with Ellis that we can surmise to have taken place through their correspondence does not seem to soften her approach here. Her article sweeps across the fields of the body (endocrinology), crime (delinquency) and the desire for a better race (eugenics), and in many ways she is as hard-line as her compatriots. Indeed, looked at as a whole, the collection of articles in this number (by contrast with the publication of the proceedings of the Eugenics Conference) is less 'Latin' than Stepan's definition would suggest (see Chapter One).

If one sees *Sexus* 1 as the presentation of the public face of the Liga, it is hard to overlook the slightly troubling prominence of Hildegart as writer and general organizer – a feature that may or may not have been a problem. If the Liga was Hildegart's child, *Sexus* seems even more so. She translates Ellis's paper; she is implied as being the interviewer of Magnus Hirschfeld, founder of the WLSR; and, although not named as the author of the article on Beacon Hill School, could be deduced as such. By her own admission she is author of the 'Historia del movimiento internacional y español de Reforma Sexual' [History of the International and Spanish Movements of Sexual Reform]. In addition to this, given her position as secretary, she presumably penned the whole of the 'Información' [Information] section, containing the statutes of the Liga, reports on the sections and WLSR congresses. By this, she accounts for sixty-two pages out of a total of the 126 pages of the first number (this is without including her translation of Ellis's article, of twelve pages). If she feels that she has a major role in the production of the review, it is with some justification.

Sexus 2: a Different Type of Struggle

By *Sexus* 2 there is a shift between the professions and their representation. Three people have been removed, César Juarros, Marañón and Jiménez de Asúa, that is, one doctor, one lawyer, and one (Marañón) who – for the purposes of this board – had had his medical qualification made invisible. A further three are added, producing a distinct majority of medical qualification, and reducing the total number on the board to eight so that the new layout is:

Dr Vital Aza
Dr Barrio de Medina
Dr Haro García
Dr D Juan Noguera

Dr D José María Otaola
Sr D Mariano Ruiz Funes
Dr D José Sánchez Covisa
Sr D Rodolfo Tomás Samper*

Those who are not medically qualified are now in a distinct minority of two. Luis Huerta has moved to be a co-secretary of the publication, alongside Hildegart, and his name precedes hers. There is one new name, the educationalist Tomás Samper. This addition (with the move of Huertas to the co-secretaryship) suggests that the review – guided by its medical authorities – is now working towards a self-presentation as a community, and is doing so via those best suited to working for change, those in the profession of teaching. The other feature of the new editorial board is the notable absence of those who had participated in the discussion of the **WLSR** planks at the Liga foundation meeting: Saldaña, Nóvoa Santos, Torrubiano Ripoll. Sanchis Banús, also absent from both editorial boards, had died in June 1932, but having made his contribution to the Eugenics Conference. Conflict has been edited away.

The move between the two numbers of the journal shows an ironing-out of the original professional competitiveness between members of the Liga, and what seems to be a hardening of the line on eugenics. The other factor in the dynamic of the journal is that by the second number (April/May 1933), the Eugenics Conference which ran from 21 April to 10 May 1933 was clearly occupying many of those in the Liga. Of the new names strengthening *Sexus II*, Barrio de Medina, Juan Noguera, Rodolfo Tomás Samper and Luis Huerta, all but Barrio de Medina appear on the organizing committee of the conference, all of which is strongly medical.

Behind the shift in the secretarial arrangements there is the complex and fraught tale of Haro's interventions, outlined in Chapter Five. The shift to a two-secretary solution (mooted for the Liga, by which Hildegart as lawyer and not-yet doctor is moved sideways by one doctor with support from another) is one that appears to have been applied to *Sexus* as well. The other shift to be noted is that of the Liga's presidency, now in the person of Dr Juan Noguera, director of the *Gaceta Médica Española*.

The contents of *Sexus* 2 also indicate further alterations in Hildegart's position. In some ways she is as prominent as ever, given that she translates no fewer than six out of the ten pieces in that number, including an article in Norwegian on the Vinderen laboratory in Oslo. This also points to a further shift in the second number, towards foreign experts.

It has to be said that the composition of the second number of *Sexus* is more disparate than the first one. Being produced alongside the proceedings of the conference it is perhaps suddenly the poor relation, and if it has widened its net in terms of items from significant international contributors such as Kehl, Haire and Ellis, they are in fact part of Hildegart's immediate circle. This does not apply to all international contributions. Almerindo Lessa*, for example, is at this point at the outset of his career. Hildegart has been fortunate in securing Haire, in Spain for the Eugenics Conference (and at the same time it appears that he had been asked by Ellis to see if Hildegart was well – and she writes on 16 May 1933 to reassure Ellis that she was indeed well). As for Almerindo Lessa, there is no evidence that she knew him, and his article, 'Problemas de Psicología Sexual: El amor' [Problems of Sexual Psychology: Love], fragmented and disorganized, praising incoherence and the development of the sentiments, sits oddly in the publication of an organization that proclaims a scientific basis for its investigations into sex. It would on the other hand not have been out of place in Navarro Fernández's Hygiene Campaign. Finally, Noguera and Huerta, the other two contributors to this number, are the editors of the proceedings of the Eugenics Conference, and are respectively president and co-secretary of the Liga. The whole package on the surface looks like a production of wider international scope, but there is a strong element of the parochial and the opportunist in the articles commissioned or received for it.

Despite (or conceivably because of) the make-up of the cast of contributors to *Sexus* 2, there is something both more hard-line and more outspoken about this number. The lead article, after Noguera's brief speech for the opening of the Eugenics Conference, comes from Kehl, who comes over as less than conciliatory on eugenic measures. His paper, laced with statistics on crime and degeneration, argues that improving social conditions can only really have an effect on the generation whose conditions are improved, and does not impact on degeneration. His language also (which we must remember is translated by Hildegart) refers to 'los indeseables que sobreviven para sufrir y para sobrecargar los elementos útiles y productivos' [undesirables who survive only to suffer and to overload those who are useful and productive] (Kehl, 1933: 13). He speaks (in terms stronger than those of Ortega in his 1931 essay on *La rebelión de las masas* [The Rebellion of the Masses]) of the fate of the elite, 'amenazada de exterminio' [threatened with extermination] (Kehl, 1933: 17).

Huerta's article on prostitution does two things.[5] It foregrounds the issue of prostitution (the abolition of which had been fought for with energy by Juarros) and it produces a survey of social developments in Russia since the revolution. Soviet Russia had been a source of fascination for Spaniards through the 1920s, and the interest – while including curiosity about 'free love' and new concepts of marriage – had involved considerable doses of idealism.[6] Huerta's work thus illustrates how Russia was seen by many in Spain as an example of how sex reform (rather than eugenics) might come to be a social reality. He draws on the work of Llopis, Álvarez del Vayo and others, including Riazanov, whose *Comunismo y matrimonio* [Communism and Marriage] would appear in an edition with Hildegart's *¿Se equivocó Marx?* in the series Manuales de Cultura Marxista [Manuals of Marxist Culture], published in Buenos Aires by the review *Claridad* (founded 1922). Like many reformers, Huerta is profoundly elitist, looking at the plight of the masses from the conviction that they are not able to guide or fend for themselves. His imagery is as florid as that of Ortega or indeed of Baroja (1904), whose terminology in *Mala hierba* [Weeds] is – perhaps unconsciously – taken up in passing:

> El roturar los cerebros de las masas requiere un previo descuaje de las malas hierbas de prejuicios, de las rutinas y del empirismo grosero mezclado con el fanatismo más ciego. En almas adultas, de función mental polarizada, esto constituye una empresa más temible y arriesgada que luchar con las fieras en la selva virgen o defenderse con una pistola de una espantosa nube de mosquitos. (Huerta, 1933a: 25)
>
> [Before ploughing the brains of the masses one must first clear them of the weeds of prejudice, routine and coarse empiricism mixed with blind fanaticism. In adult souls, where the mental function is concentrated, this is an enterprise that is more risky and fearful than fighting with wild animals in the virgin forest or defending yourself against a terrible cloud of mosquitoes with a pistol.]

The contrast Huertas makes between pre- and post- revolutionary Russia idealizes the latter, by implication suggesting that there could be a similar style of development away from oppressive sexual mores in Spain. His news is that Russia is advanced in this respect: prostitution in Russia is now illegal, whereas in 1910 there had been an estimated 50,000 prostitutes in St Petersburg.[7] The willed logic, veiling the idealism of Huerta's view of post-revolutionary Russia, mutates into naive and sentimental idealism in the final section on the future in which he sees 'el sentimiento' [feeling] as the element in man that can be educated for a better purpose. The cry of '¡EXCELSIOR! ¡EUGENESIA! ¡ERGOLOGÍA' [EXCELSIOR! EUGENICS! ERGOLOGY!] (Huerta, 1933a: 33) says it all.[8]

Haire makes two appearances in *Sexus* 2, each designed to bring Spain into a sharpened awareness of the international climate of eugenics. In his article 'En qué consiste la Reforma Sexual' he argues strongly that there cannot be absolutes in accepted sexual behaviour, with the conclusion that there is a need for a new legal code that will reflect modern sexual morality (Haire, 1933: 41–2). While stating (misleadingly) that he is English, and bases what he has to say on English sexual life, Haire avoids dogma, and more tellingly, avoids the emotionalism of writers such as Kehl and Huerta in this number. His position is that of encouraging from the sidelines, as indicated by his final words, 'yo os deseo sinceramente que tengáis todavía valor y SIEMPRE valor' [my sincere wish for you is that you should continue to have courage, ALWAYS have courage] (Haire, 1933: 47).

Haire's other appearance is in the form of an interview conducted by Hildegart. In the course of it he makes two statements that are both startling and strongly out of keeping with any myth of a prevailing Catholic morality. What is most striking is the way that he relays – as an outsider – certain assumptions he has noted. He observes that it appears to be assumed to be natural for all men in Spain to go to the brothel at some point in their life, and he adds that in similar manner it is expected that the entire population, at some point in their life, will have a venereal disease. These observations are left without further comment.[9]

If we think of this in terms of *Sexus* being used as the vehicle for the Liga to create its public image, the international element is being used tellingly for the transmission of difficult information. The markedly international character of the second number, demonstrating how the Liga is involved in a movement that is wider than the Spanish domestic scene, participates in the Liga's self-construction in a way that allows observations of Spanish life to have the impartiality of the outside observer. The self-construction of the Liga thus comes both from the inside and the outside, from those who choose these contributions and those who step in to 'help' with the revolutionary content of the review.

Meanwhile Hildegart, the discreet interviewer of Haire, writes in her own article on legislation and those offences linked to sex and sexuality. This gives us a brief view of the concentrated and energetic output of Hildegart. Her article, substantial, well-referenced, is the more impressive when we realize that it appears at the same time as she is giving four lectures on birth control for the Eugenics Conference. Here she is speaking as a lawyer, and presenting herself as a liberal one. Thus contrasting with the list of sexual offences given by Wulfflen, whose survey of 'sexual crimes' included fetishism, crimes associated with sadism and masochism, 'homosexual crimes' and widespread crimes of abuse, including the activity of pimping, she presents a restricted range: exhibitionism, 'homicidio voluptuoso' [voluptuous homicide], injury resulting from sadism or masochism, theft associated with fetishism, the abuse of youngsters, and 'anti-natural' crimes such as necrophilia.[10] What is more striking, however, is her excursion into sexual aspects of crimes such as kleptomania, and types of homicide which have sexual associations. Hildegart does not draw explicitly on Freud (although this connection suggests itself) but makes a strong case for considering a wide range of crimes as suitable for treatment rather than punishment, because of the way in which they are linked to sexuality, or derive from sexual problems that in their turn might be caused by hormonal disturbances. Her view is that there should not be provision in the legal code for 'sexual crimes' but that the law should take sex into account as a factor.[11] Some companion views are more sinister. Homosexuality, for example, is a condition to be treated rather than to be permitted (the line of 'hard' eugenecists, not of sex reformers) (Hildegart, 1933a: 57, 59).

In sum, the act of self-construction for the Liga that *Sexus* carries out is energetic and curious. The character of *Sexus* 2 has a strong bias towards social and legal reform (contrasting with the greater emphasis on the body in *Sexus* 1). While its editorial board has taken on a markedly medical slant, the 'medicalized' approach is, if anything, downplayed in favour of legislative reform. What we may see here is a mixture between local survival tendencies for the group as a whole (which meant that for the Liga to survive, there was a need to have medical personnel on board, arguably to professionalize its activities) and the spirit of legal reform that was more possible in the days of the Republic than under Primo. Cast in the framework of Certeau, the juggling with personnel we can regard as local tactics, whereas the legal drive of some of the content of *Sexus* 2 signals that what is in mind is the shift to strategy, by which the Liga would be instrumental in legislative change within the State.

Planning and Execution of the Eugenics Conference and its Proceedings

If *Sexus* is the specialized review of the Liga, in which issues between the professions are played out, albeit with an increasing sense of communication to the outside world, the Eugenics Conference operates at a different level of making the concerns of eugenics public. Mounting a large event of public lectures (rather than addressing a specific audience who would obtain the review through subscription) is an act of placing a group centre stage in the public eye, and subsequently publishing its proceedings the act of making that group's self-constructed identity memorable. If *Sexus* shows some the attempt on the part of the Liga to move from tactics to strategy, the Eugenics Conference – perhaps significantly because it was not labelled as the organ of the Liga – is the venture that gives a firm and strategic basis for eugenics activity to be remembered in Spain. Paradoxically, however, it appears that in the event tactics held more vigour.

The Eugenics Conference was a major event for Spain, arguably the culmination of the work of two or three decades. Its function was to make public and *available* knowledge about sexuality and procreation fundamental to the belief in change through eugenics. All of this, we should recall, was in the context of recent memory, namely that of the banned Eugenics Conference of 1928. This time there would not be the outcome of being banned by decree; nonetheless, the difference between the planned programme of the conference and the published proceedings that eventually emerged in 1934 indicates that there were other problems of a purely practical nature.

From the printed programme for the conference printed in *Sexus* 2 it is quite clear that the organization of the conference comes from a series of medical bodies: the Asociación Profesional de Estudiantes de Medicina [Professional Association of Medical Students], the *Gaceta Médica Española* and the Liga.[12] The members of the organizing committee of the conference are presented without title, just with their affiliation to the organizations they represent, providing some sense of democracy and neutrality. This is somewhat lost in the cover page of the proceedings, where the directors, Enrique Noguera and Luis Huerta, appear side by side – or perhaps shoulder to shoulder – each with their attributions of authority, although what is noted is the expertise of each in the field of the other. Noguera is cited as a doctor, but formerly of the Teacher Training College of Barcelona, while Huerta is cited as a primary school teacher, formerly of the Faculty of Paidology in Brussels. Both have their link with the *Gaceta Médica Española* noted.

By any standards, this was meant to be a major gathering, and far more ambitious than the 1928 conference. Some eighty-nine lectures were billed in the programme, besides the presentations related to the opening and closing sessions of the event. Although the members of the organizing committee were associated with medicine, it is obvious that the intention of the event was to give broad coverage to the topic of eugenics. A series of 'technical courses' would cover genetics, anthropology, ecology, biological and social selection, birth control, prostitution (and abolitionism), the pathology of work and poverty, puericulture and 'maternology', obstetrics and gynaecology. There was also a series of sections to consider eugenics in relation to a variety of topics. These ranged from the medical to the broadly cultural: syphilis, tuberculosis, cancer, endocrinology, haematology, neurology and psychiatry, psychoanalysis, hygiene, pedagogy, law, history, literature and politics. Many of these technical sections were evidently a planner's ideal, and are announced as still being organized: the two courses of biological and social selection, puericulture and 'maternología', and the sections on cancer, endocrinology, haematology, neurology and psychiatry.

There is, of course, a discrepancy between what was announced as the programme of the conference, the papers that were in fact given, and those that were published in 1934. Such a discrepancy is likely for any major event, but what the difference between the programme and the proceedings represents here is the step from the imagined self-presentation of this group in their major conference, and the version that would be passed down to posterity.

Of those who were billed to speak, and either did not do so, or did not complete their papers for publication, some were evidently outside the Liga and its eugenic affiliates, and their inclusion was undoubtedly intended to broaden the public view of the field, involving some figures of obvious prestige – a step towards strategic stability. Such is the case of Zubiri, the philosopher, and Azaña, president of the Republican government. Similarly, Américo Castro, due to speak in the section on 'History and Eugenics' (but announcing his lecture as 'El amor en el romanticismo' [Love in Romanticism]) provided a strong link with the Residencia and the Centro de Estudios Históricos [Centre for Historical Studies]. Others, such as the philosopher Fernando Valera, had links with eugenics (in his case through publishing in the Cuadernos de la Cultura in Valencia, where numerous eugenicists and sex reformers also published).[13] Oliver Pascual was billed to step outside his field of working on the digestion to speak on the inheritance of acquired characteristics and the 'degenerate constitution', while in the section of ecology Enrique Rioja was to remain, broadly, within his field of biology and the environment, as was Téllez Plasencia, the physicist.[14] There is no record of who had set up the section on 'Literature and Eugenics', but they had clearly chosen prominent names associated with the Residencia and the *Revista de Occidente*: Salinas, Espina, Jarnés, Bergamín, Lorca and Alberti. Their number also included Alfredo Cabello, whose book *El libro del cine* came out in 1933, and who was due to speak on 'El amor en el cine' [Love in the cinema]. In the section on politics and eugenics, those who were in the initial programme and who did not appear subsequently were the communist César Falcón and Romero Otazo (known for his study on democratic thought in Saint Thomas Aquinas published in 1930), neither of whom had announced a topic, the prolific Marxist Wenceslao Roces, due to speak on 'Proletariado y procreación' [Proletariat and Procreation] and Luis Bello, best known for his concentrated attention to schools in Spain, and his tours of inspection to document standards. The absence of Méndez Bejarano and Sánchez Covisa (both due to lecture on syphilis) is more surprising given their links with the Liga.

A number of the technical sections originally included to broaden the scope of the conference sank virtually without trace, and unsurprisingly these were the very ones that had been announced in the programme as being at the planning stage only. By contrast, two other sessions on literature and eugenics and on politics and eugenics had been well organized, with seven and five speakers respectively, but failed to materialize. One paper from each of them (Jarnés on love in the theatre and Reyes on politics and eugenics) was actually given.

The final conference not only omitted lectures from the original one, but also brought in new ones, and here we can see a shift back to the Liga. In structural terms this could be seen as the original broad outreach of the event having been abandoned (through lack of support, perhaps), and numbers were then boosted by staunch Liga supporters. This meant that the profile of the conference became more emphatically and more precisely eugenic. The new participants include Madrazo, with a paper on the 'optimistic concept of life' and a number of strongly established supporters from the inner circle: Recaséns, Jiménez de Asúa, Sanchis Banús and the two Noguera brothers, all of whom produced mainstream and uncontroversial pieces. Recaséns, organizer of the 1928 conference, reprinted his 1928 lecture on eugenics and procreation; Jiménez de Asúa spoke on legal aspects of conscious motherhood; Sanchis Banús on mental illness provoked by excessive or pathological procreation in a context of poverty; Enrique Noguera on how the Eugenics Conference came into being; his brother Joaquín Noguera spoke on maternity and infanticide in the context of the law.

What do these changes signify? At a banal level we could interpret them as constituting nothing more or less than the result of over-optimism at the planning stage of an event, and that the final programme results from realism and pragmatism. But it is noticeable that the attempts to include people from outside the inner circles of eugenics and sex reform, attempts made with the best of intentions, and the desire to make this activity one of wide scope and broad appeal, largely remained on the drawing board. What fills the conference proceedings in the end is a range of papers with a clear focus on the title of the event, 'Genética, eugenesía y pedagogía sexual' [Genetics, eugenics and sexual education]. Yet despite the trimming of the technical courses, there is a distinct openness and range about the publication, contrasting with the second number of *Sexus*, published at virtually the same time. The attempt to draw in new blood to the team of those interested in eugenics, and who had engaged with the Liga (despite its somewhat different agenda of sexual reform) was not entirely successful, and the final bolstering up of numbers for the 1933 conference was achieved primarily through the Liga and its contacts. In broad terms, therefore, the Eugenics Conference, while not representing the Liga, actually gives the most prominent representation to the works and interests of the Liga. If the Eugenics Conference represents the strategic establishment of a group, it is born of a complex desire, by which a broader cultural and social base (conceived of as a more stable and recognized act of communication) comes to resemble strongly, almost without intention, the marginal and tactical concerns of those involved in the Liga.

NOTES

[1] See Cleminson (2000) for detailed discussion of the anarchist reviews *Salud y Fuerza* (1904–14), *Generación Consciente* (1923–9), and *Estudios* (1929–36).

2   An example of this is the way Freud defended the psychoanalytical journals associated with him, and eventually insisted on the detachment of Adler from the Zentralblatt für Psychoanalyse.
3   For the connotations of this see the tradition of pastoral theology where Latin was used for 'difficult' or sexually explicit material, the language acting as a barrier to all but an elite inner circle who would be able to read this material (Sinclair, 2005: 107–12).
4   The papal encyclical on marital chastity brought out by Pius XI in December 1930; called *Casti Connubii* (Of human marriage), the encyclical reasserted the church's authority in the sphere of the family, marriage, and sexuality, and prohibited birth control, abortion, sterilization, and eugenics as violations of Catholic principles.
5   The article appears to form a group with two articles on prostitution Huertas had published in the *Gaceta Médica Española* (1933b, 1933c).
6   See Sinclair (2004b) on the idea of Spain's 'love affair' with Russia.
7   Huerta does not cite figures for Spain. Lafora in 1933 estimated some 40,000 prostitutes in Madrid and Barcelona, and in 1931, according to Recaséns, there were 70,000 in Barcelona alone (Guereña, 2003: 392).
8   'Ergología' is a neologism, presumably indicating the study of proper occupation.
9   In the interview Haire gave Hildegart in *La Libertad*, 11 May 1933, he estimated that between 50 and 60% of Spaniards suffered from venereal disease, compared with between 7 and 10% in England (Hildegart, 1933c).
10 Hildegart's departure from Wulfflen is in part a separation from Saldaña. See Mike Richards (2004: 843), who notes that Saldaña in *La sexología* (Madrid: n.p. 1930), 234, praises the analysis of Wulffen whose 'profundo análisis de la fémina, iluminado por paradigmas eligidos entre los más radiantes de esencialidad – la mujer espía, la furia revolucionaria, la sufragista, la envenenadora, etc – conduce directo y, mejor, arroja rápido a la evidencia de estados anormales de la vida sexual en la mujer' [profound analysis of woman, illustrated by some of the most outstanding paradigms of her essence – the spy, the revolutionary Fury, the sufragette, the poisoner, etc. – leads directly, or even precipitately into the evidence of abnormal states of sexual life in woman].
11 This is an approach that could with profit and interest, albeit with some difficulty, have been applied to Aurora's trial. For a broader view of this see Cleminson and Vázquez García (2007: Chapter Two) on earlier approaches in Spain to sexual perversions.
12 Eladio Suils and Francisco Acebes represented the Asociación Profesional de Estudiantes de Medicina, Luis Huerta and Enrique Noguera represented the *Gaceta Médica Española*, and Juan Noguera and Rodolfo Tomás Samper represented the Liga.
13 He published *Liberalismo* [Liberalism] and *Introducción a la filosofía* [Introduction to Philosophy] in this series in 1930.
14 Both of these were Republicans who would go into exile as a result of the Civil War.

Chapter Seven

Writing to the 'fairy god'

Mr. Henry Havelock Ellis.

I know that you read with special interest all letters of youths, and though this be perhaps a little longer than others we receive, I beg of you most sincerely to lend it a bit of your attention, for I am a girl, my age is sixteen years old, and I am spanish, three things which I expose first as my only racommandation to you. (Hildegart to Ellis, 23 October 1931)

I am glad you like my portrait. In every one I do of myself, I appear very mature, but it is not my fault you know. But if I don't photo my face but my body also, effect is perhaps worst. Imagine yourself what I told you in past letter. I am nearly a meter and seventy centimeters hight, and I weigh seventy eight kilograms. So that I appear as a splendend woman. If it were not for my hair, my corsckrewes[1] are much longer than most in the portrait appear and we can only use this combing here until we are twenty years old, people would not judgue of my age, save in my conversation and manners, and perhaps in my little experience of life. If it were not for my Munmy, I confide in everybody and that, as you know is always perilous.

You cannot imagine what a pleasure we have had when we received your photo. You look so nice in it. . . . . in this last one although so small, to see your figure so arrogant and virile and your white hairs, is a pleasure for sight. I have shown it to my particular friends and all are charmed of you. I will put it in my writing table, with a beautiful picture frame. (Hildegart to Ellis, 5 January 1932)

Well, dear Dr. Havelock a great deal of thanks for your lovely present, for your remembers in the newspaper, and for everything in which you have been so wonderfully good for me. You are some sort of fairy god for all of us. (Hildegart to Ellis, 19 March, 1932)

I was so charmed to receive your letter. It was for me such a great pleasure to hear from you since such a long time you hadn't written that I could not help reading it with my Munmy three or four times (Hildegart to Ellis, August 1932)

I suppose the postman knows already your letters, for when one of them arrives, the penny I give him for every one he brings, and they are quite a lot I assure you, is even more graciously offered. Your last one was a delicious long letter, and I spent a lot of time in commenting it with Munmy, so you see it was a rest in my work. (Hildegart to Ellis, 6 November 1932)

The story of the sexual reform movement in Spain and Hildegart's place in it, traced in the preceding chapters, is one of remarkable and complex flowering, at times despite, and at other times because of evident currents and conflicts through the first three decades of the twentieth century. But the private life of Hildegart is itself exceptional, a life caused and complicated by the desires of her mother Aurora. The source that tells us most clearly about this is Hildegart's two-year correspondence with Havelock Ellis. This chapter looks at that correspondence in detail, using it as a tool to gain access to that side of Hildegart not evident through her published works, and in particular examining it for the evidence it gives us about the nature of her relationship with her mother. The letters are an extraordinary testimony to Hildegart's life, with all its fears, ambitions and ingenuousness mixed with premature maturity. It is here that we find a wholly new voice for her, and a window onto the private life lying behind her busy and complex public life. For this reason the letters are transcribed in their entirety in Appendix I. As the above extracts reveal, the relationship from Hildegart's side was warm, friendly, ingenuous and touching.

There are some twenty letters in the British Library collection, a number of them extremely long.[2] The collection also contains occasional postcards, photographs, and some notes by Ellis, press cuttings concerning Hildegart, and a number of letters to Ellis about Hildegart after her death. The length and nature of the letters suggest that for Hildegart the relationship with Ellis was a significant element in the last two years of her life. They relate aspects of her public activity, including her publishing plans and negotiations she is involved in to publish various works by Ellis, and, most of all, her activity in the World League for Sexual Reform.

The letters from Ellis to Hildegart have unfortunately disappeared without trace, and we can only deduce or intuit their possible content. Letters from Ellis to others such as Haire which make brief reference to Hildegart, do, however, give us some sense of his view of her. Further light on Ellis's view of Hildegart is cast by his article 'The Red Virgin' published in the *The Adelphi* in 1933. It was the arrival of this article in the post which, according to Cal (1991a: 107–8) and according to the statement of Aurora herself as included in the psychiatric report on her by José Sacristán y Gutiérrez and Miguel Prados y Such, 20 September 1933 (entire report reprinted in Rendueles, pp. 199–229, p. 211ff), triggered the shooting of Hildegart the next night. In addition to this, Ellis's view of Spanish woman portrayed in *The Soul of Spain* (1908) gives a more general context for his reaction to Hildegart, particularly his idea of the strength of Spanish women. Haire, the Australian psychiatrist who had become prominent in the world of sexual reform in Britain, would be a crucial final witness to the state of Hildegart just prior to her death, and a link between Ellis and subsequent events.

The pairing of Hildegart and Ellis in correspondence is remarkable, crossing as it does the generations and national barriers. When she first wrote to Ellis from Madrid in 1931 Hildegart was sixteen, and Ellis (born in 1859) some fifty years her senior. Hildegart was unknown in England at this point, though she would later have contact with H. G. Wells and Haire.[3] By this date, as will have been evident from earlier chapters, Hildegart was well known in Spain, a prominent figure in the press, a popular lecturer, and fully recognized as a major contributor to the movement for sexual reform in Spain. Ellis, meanwhile, had made his name in the field of sexology some forty years earlier, with *Man and Woman* (1894). With the seven volumes of *Studies in the Psychology of Sex* (1897–1928) he further secured his name in the field, not only in England but – in this case more significantly – in Spain. The frequent references to Ellis in the works of those concerned with sexual reform and eugenics attest to this, and Hildegart refers to having read his works on the

Psychology of Sex, adding that she finds that 'your assurances are all true' (Hildegart to Ellis, 23 October 1931).

The role of Ellis in Hildegart's life has been predominantly the subject of surmise. Brief references are made to there being a 'lively correspondence' between Hildegart and Ellis and H. G. Wells by Rosa Montero (1995: 188), although Fajardo (1987a: 133; 1987b: 132) alludes to the influence of H. G. Wells on Hildegart, but not of Ellis. Rendueles mentions both Wells and Ellis, but does so primarily in order to illustrate the paranoid fantasies of Hildegart's mother that the two men were agents of the British Secret Service. Rendueles also speaks of how Wells visited Spain, and how Hildegart, who acted as his interpreter, was given several 'cartas elogiosas' [laudatory letters] from Ellis (Rendueles, 1989: 132). Grosskurth's biography of Ellis also makes brief reference to a correspondence (Grosskurth, 1980: 434–5) while the article by Anne Summers on the correspondents of Ellis (1991) sets the Hildegart correspondence with Ellis in a broader context.

The letters of Hildegart to Ellis cannot be considered a simple testimony of fact. Yet because of their private nature, they allow us to see a side of Hildegart that is special, the side she chooses to reveal to Ellis, a man with whom she develops a close emotional bond. At the same time we need to remember that the self that she projects in the letters to Ellis is a self she wishes him to see. This sense of Ellis as interlocutor, as one who can be treated as ideal confidant, and yet as one whose respect she wishes to retain, is one that needs to colour our reading of the letters throughout.

A Pen of her Own?

Hildegart's public writings as outlined in earlier chapters are such that they would clearly have won Ellis's interest and respect, and it is with reason that she draws his attention to her publications at the outset. It is clear that she has gone well beyond the initial background for her work of late nineteenth-century socialist utopians (a background particularly evident in *¿Se equivocó Marx...?*), works which would have been part of her grandfather's library, and thus part of Aurora's own autodidact education, and by extension that of her daughter. Some of her publications have a mass of contemporary references, particularly in the areas of law and psychology, a surprising number of which are American. And by the time she writes to Ellis she is proclaiming her independence from her Hispanic background. She sees herself – and in terms of her areas of interest it is with some justification – as an international figure. Ellis was not, however, blind to her shortcomings. In 'The Red Virgin', he points out that her published works, remarkable though they are, and being 'clear and vigorous, showing a wide knowledge of literature and of social movements in other lands', also contain 'misinformations, extravagancies, and youthful weaknesses of style'. He adds that there is a lack of coherence in her lectures on Jesus, where 'she sets forth alike the mythical theory and the pathological theory, and they are opposed' (Ellis, 1933: 177).

For many writers, the early stage of writing is where one most clearly detects influence, something from which the writer's 'own voice' will eventually emerge. In the case of Hildegart there is a complication. Her range of reference displays increasingly wide reading and awareness of the work of others, and arguably her own line of thought that becomes more firm. But there is the issue of the unacknowledged influence of her mother. Aurora's presence is in one sense not hidden: the dedication of *Venus ante el derecho* (1933) in which she gives such generous acknowledgement of her mother makes this clear. But after Hildegart's death Aurora's presence in her daughter's voice would become a matter of heightened speculation.

In the letter of 5 January 1932, we have the evidence of Ellis's positive view of Aurora's nature: 'You tell me that my mother is wonderful', and in 'The Red Virgin', published some two years later, it seems that he continued to hold this positive opinion, presenting Aurora as someone who 'is evidently herself a remarkable woman, and already among what I call the "New Mothers" of today' (Ellis 1933: 175). Throughout the letters there is a sense of Aurora as always in the background, as Hildegart habitually signs off with kind regards sent from her mother as well as herself.

The murder inevitably changed Ellis's perception not just of Aurora at the end, but of Aurora as she must have been. In a letter to Haire of 23 June 1933 he comments on how he has been sent cuttings about the murder by 'my Spanish lawyer friend in Barcelona', and having noted that the material contains little of importance, and 'various contradictions', he comments 'It is not clear who the father was', and adds 'Some say H.'s life with her mother was a martyrdom'.[4] A postscript to the letter, written up the left-hand margin, adds his further thoughts about Aurora, in which he seeks to reassure himself that the correspondence with Hildegart had been fundamentally a private one: 'I think I am right in understanding from you that H.'s mother did not know English. So she could not have supervised H.'s English letters', adding 'H. usually wrote to me in English'.[5]

Aurora's influence on Hildegart was described in starker detail in a letter written to Ellis on 1 July 1933, after Hildegart's death, by Mrs Gillett-Gatty who presents Hildegart as constituting the mouthpiece for her mother.[6] She recounts the concern she had felt at the way Aurora did not manage to express her own self and views. Sadly, it appears in retrospect that she expressed concern for the wrong one in this fated pair:

> I was so anxious, so fearfully anxious, (& here I knew I could not possibly be mistaken) as to the future of Doña Aurora. What, I used to say to her, 'What on earth will you do, if Hildegart dies, or marries, or disagrees with you, before you die yourself? Do at long last, make the necessary efforts to write your own books & go & stand up & deliver your own speeches &, at all events, cease to live a life as if you were the unborn embryo in Hildegart's uterus!' Hildegart would hear this & smile & agree & say to me in her pretty English (rather like an educated Indian's) 'That is ver-y true. I wish you could make Mummy speak her-self. But she will not, ev-er'.[7]

When focusing on the relationship between mother and daughter, Mrs Gillett-Gatty had no doubts about where the power lay:

> I wonder if you now realise, not that Hildegart was a Trilby to Doña Aurora's Svengali, but that until Hildegart was got hold of by the Federalist Party, she was a perfectly intelligent human dictaphone, into which her mother spoke & Hildegart subsequently wrote, or uttered, the message?

Her most telling comparison, which picks up that age uncertainty that we can see in Hildegart's letters, was to compare her manner of delivering speeches to that of children of six to eight who are asked by adults to recite, and who do so standing on a dining-room chair.

Ellis would almost certainly have been disturbed by a later letter from Mrs Gillett-Gatty. She wrote on 21 June 1933, having visited Aurora in prison. Her letter passed on a request from Aurora for books to be sent to her. Evidently Ellis asked for more detail on the sort of books that could be sent, and was assured in a letter of 11 August 1933 that Aurora was able to read both English and French (with a dictionary). This would have undermined his belief, expressed to Haire, in the confidentiality of Hildegart's letters to him.

The 'fairy god'

Why did Hildegart write to Ellis? This question relates to content and to the identity of the recipient. In relation to the former, Hildegart wanted to make contact with an expert, she wanted to learn, and to ask his advice on how to set up a branch of the League in Spain. As for the latter, we need to ask two subsidiary questions. Why, as Anne Summers has observed, was Ellis important in his own time – particularly to women – given that his thinking was woolly and his theories clearly at odds with feminism (Summers, 1991: 169)? Secondly, why should Hildegart write to Ellis and not – if her interest was in the field of sexuality, as she declares in her first letter – to Freud? To frame the second question like this is to underestimate what might be inferred as the answer to the first question. Ellis's patience and responsiveness as friend and correspondent were renowned, whatever the eccentricities of his ideas. And to ask why Hildegart did not write to Freud instead of Ellis is to work from the erroneous assumption that in matters of sex at this period in Spain Freud would be the obvious point of reference. The relative prominence of Freud and Ellis in Spain was discussed in Chapter One. In addition to the general significance of the two, there is the relative lack of prominence of Freud in the circles of the international sex reform movement. Thus Herbert, reviewing the *Proceedings of the Third Congress of the World-League for Sexual Reform, London 1930* in the *Eugenics Review* in 1931, noted with regret the low level of awareness of Freud, and commented: 'It is a pity that the psychoanalytical views of the Freudian school, which are of such vast importance in their epoch-making discoveries, have not found more frequent expression in the Congress' (Herbert, 1931: 168).

Closer to Hildegart, and possibly more significant in her decision to approach Ellis was Saldaña, lawyer, sexologist, and the director of her doctoral thesis on law. His 1930 essays on sexology, studded with international references, but with marked biblical underpinning, suggest that here is the clearest source for Hildegart's initial interest in Ellis who is referenced frequently, and given virtually the same weight as Freud. Saldaña cites him, for example, as the definitive author on secondary sexual differences in *Man and Woman* (1894), a work he subsequently refers to as Ellis's *summa sexualis* (Saldaña 1930: 66, 71). In the light of this it is noteworthy that Hildegart appears to have treated Saldaña with some high-handedness in the Liga foundation meeting. It is also of interest that when she writes to Ellis she cites not Saldaña but Marañón, Jiménez de Asúa and Vital Aza as those whose works on sexology she has already read. This may reflect her apprehension by this stage that Saldaña (like other senior members of the Liga) was less open to progressive ideas on the sexes than she might have wished. Saldaña was one of those prominent in the review *Sexualidad*, in which Hildegart's very early articles appeared: his esteem for Ellis is reflected by two other contributors, E. Gómez Sebastián, and Jaime Torrubiano Ripoll.

As the correspondence develops, however, it becomes clear that there is more than a simple meeting of minds or exchange of ideas. The exchanges of photographs, Hildegart's comments on her own appearance, and on that of Ellis, indicate a relationship that from her side at least grows in intensity and subtlety of feeling. In response to Ellis's request that she should tell him about herself she sends a photograph (with comments on it) in the letter of 5 January 1932. She also evidently received a photograph from Ellis. Three letters later, 19 March 1932, at the end of an enthusiastic and optimistic letter she mentions that she has been reading Sanger's *My Fight for Birth Control*, and clearly picking up from this declares that 'You are some sort of fairy god for all of us'. By this – knowingly or unknowingly – she places herself in the position of other women admirers of Ellis, notably Sanger herself and his companion Françoise Cyon, and in which an appreciation of Ellis's gentleness is combined with a reaction to his person that verges on wonder. Sanger had been impressed by Ellis's appearance at their first meeting: 'His tall, straight slender figure, his great shock of white hair, his massive head, his well-kept though straggling, shaggy beard, his wide, expressive mouth – that of a faun – all combined to give one the impression that here indeed was a veritable god' (Sanger, 1932: 99).[8] Hildegart does not go so far, but her comment, 'to see your figure so arrogant and virile and your white hairs, is a pleasure for sight', encapsulates in quaint fashion a eugenicist's esteem, timorous politeness and yet a strange forwardness. Ellis becomes Hildegart's confidant, and at the end of the long letter of 18 March in which she pours her heart out about the goings-on in the Liga and the machinations of Haro, she refers to two photographs of him that she has on display in her workroom, declaring that 'I like to look at them, and have them looked on'. She thus conveys not only that this is a relationship for her, but – in the spirit of doubly-oriented speech – the presence of these photographs in her workroom is a type of message for others. The summer passes, full of occupation, and then Ellis sends a book. Hildegart reproaches him (22 October 1932) for not having written in it (clearly part of her own practice, evidenced by the annotations on the photo she sends him, and on assorted other press clippings): 'as I love as much the book as your writing I was very sorry that you had written nothing in it. I won't pardon you for that forgetfulness', but she softens the blow with a valedictory 'Thanks for all'. The reproach is friendly, affectionate, and communicates Hildegart's humour, responsiveness and lively emotion. By 18 February 1933, two letters before the end of the correspondence, there is some intensity in her attitude, conveyed again through the subject matter of photographs: 'I want a photo of yours. I have only a very, very small one, but not a nice one where you appear just as you are. I think I deserve one', her reason being that she wants it 'always beside me'.

Hildegart's Languages: Public and Private

Whatever the doubts about the possible mixes of authorship in the public works of Hildegart, the language used in them (with the exception of her novel, *¿Quo vadis, burguesía?* which uses the idiom of the popular novelette, with all its excesses) is relatively unremarkable. The letters to Ellis provide a broader spectrum of discourse, the more personal levels of which he refers to in 'The Red Virgin'. With Ellis, Hildegart is the professional young woman who addresses him as a professional mentor, but she is also an ingenuous and insecure person who, like so many other women, identified him as a receptive listener, in her case an interlocutor who was never there in direct contact with her. With the exception of one letter, she writes to Ellis in English, a language over which she has a reasonable command rather than a quasi-native fluency. Yet her communicative abilities allow us to read emotional levels and areas of difficulty, notwithstanding or conceivably heightened by the struggle of expression of the self in a foreign language. Early on Ellis has clearly suggested to her that she might write less, but on 8 January 1932, she adds a postscript to a letter written on the 5th, and adds 'Although it is against regulations, I cannot be silent. So I had to write the so few words. ¿Do you pardon me . . .? If not I will cry a bit, but I can't help it. It is superior to my energies'.[9] Hildegart's response to his suggestion is emotional, almost flirtatious, certainly not the cool detached phrasing of the young intellectual who writes to consult a potential intellectual mentor. It says much of the varied nature of the relationship from her side, something that did not pass unperceived by Ellis: as he observed in 'The Red Virgin', 'Hildegart remains girlish in spirit as the tone, though not the matter, of her letters always shews' (Ellis, 1933: 178–9).

Above all what we find in Hildegart's letters to Ellis is that she viewed him as the desired and ideal interlocutor as formulated by Martín Gaite (1973). A form of the interlocutor is embedded in Freud's concept of transference, and is played out with insistence through the course of the correspondence. But Martín Gaite's model spells out nicely, and with less negative implication, the desires fundamental to the relationship we have with those to whom we speak. She outlines the way in which we all wish to be able to tell our story to an interlocutor who will hear it as we wish to tell it, emphasizing therefore not the relationship with the interlocutor as a type of transference, a pathology that will need to be analysed in order to be dispelled, but rather as a relationship that springs from the desire and the vulnerability of the speaker. Her model is significant because it emphasizes the sheer desire that we have to be heard as we wish to be heard. She speaks of how we all have a 'latent narrative capacity' that can find a satisfactory coming into being through conversation with others. But we cannot produce this narrative that defines us without the required interlocutor (1973: 21). Mattingly, writing in a medical context (1998: 6–14), without speaking of the interlocutor as such, emphasizes appositely how the narrator *performs*: 'Narratives mean to be provocative. They request a different response from the audience than denotative prose. Narrative offers meaning through evocation, image, the mystery of the unsaid. It persuades by seducing the listener into the world it portrays, unfolding events in a suspense-laden time in which one wonders what will happen next' (1998: 8).

The desired interlocutor is not the only one present in the letters, however. There is an implied interlocutor (the one the speaker seeks) and an 'inferred interlocutor' (the one a third party may be able to infer). The latter returns us to Freud, in that the obvious transferential relationship that runs through the letters is that of writing to an absent father. Ellis as a source of knowledge, understanding, support and responsiveness, fills the paternal void in Hildegart's life. In the light of this we become aware of a perceptible gap between the way Hildegart regarded her relationship with Ellis (as her interlocutor) and the way the reader of the letters, as if reading a psychiatric narrative, can interpret that relationship. The fact that the letters are (with one exception) written in a language not her own (arguably a protective device), and are directed to a man who is perceived as a father-figure who, at a distance, can act as the ultimate silent therapist, lends weight to this interpretation.[10]

When Hildegart first writes to Ellis on 23 October 1931, her initial words are direct, and, in their clear vulnerability and unpretentiousness, make a claim upon his paternal protection. Her initial disarming sally is designed to catch attention, as she presents herself to him as he might see her, according to her gender, age and nationality. At the same time, viewed retrospectively, her statement about herself and its simplicity of syntax ('I am a girl, my age is sixteen years old, and I am spanish'), have a striking and slightly unnerving resemblance to the bald and simple statements of Aurora about herself at her trial.

How can we interpret Hildegart's approach to Ellis? Presenting herself as one interested in his field of expertise could be construed as a relatively standard academic or professional approach. But her manner of so doing, her confident display of knowledge and determination that he should see her as an exceptional woman brings with it a sense of excess. It is clear that Hildegart believed herself to be exceptional. Whatever the grounds for this (her impressive list of publications) her actual manner of self-presentation indicates the degree to which she had absorbed her mother's vision of her. Thus on 2 December 1931, when she responds to Ellis's request that she write in her own language, it is striking that the self she presents is the one that was constructed by her mother, a recital of 'truths' that she has been told about herself, and her early childhood, bearing out the commentary of Mrs Gillett-Gatty referred to earlier.

Hildegart's subsequent reversion to English for the remainder of her letters to Ellis suggests an ongoing attempt to construct her self in a manner separate from the construction imposed by her mother. She is determined to present herself on Ellis's linguistic ground although her English, while serviceable, is not wholly fluent. Choosing the language to be spoken always carries an element of power. In the circumstances it is noteworthy that Hildegart uses English despite the fact that it is not fluent, and there is thus an element of over-determination in her choice. An element here is arguably her desire not to succumb to the self-narrative with which her mother had provided her.

The first letter Hildegart writes to Ellis is in English and the opening is direct, striking, outlining some of her activities, approaching him as one liberal revolutionary to another, and asking him for advice about setting up the Liga. It would appear that Ellis's reply quite cannily makes enquiry about Hildegart's *self*, that is, the self she has not yet revealed to him. It would appear he also suggested she write in Spanish, since this is what she then does, and it will be the only occasion. The second letter is notable not only for its language, but for the presentation she now gives: not as the active public mover for sexual reform, but as the daughter of her mother. Her first words on her *self* define herself, but as the object created by her mother. She is an 'hija eugénica' [eugenic child], born a year after her mother's father had died. She thus places herself in the family genealogy. But she also makes herself agent of the birth, saying that 'deliberadamente vine yo al mundo' [I chose to come into the world].

She states that she is 1 metre 70 (*c.* 5'7" and weighs 80 kilos (12 stone 11 lb), a detail that might be casual were it not for an ongoing emphasis in the letters on her size and physical appearance. Curiously, in her last letter to Ellis, Hildegart will reply to what seems to have been his concern about her health (perhaps prompted by his friend Dr Norman Haire having seen her). Assuring him that he has no need for concern, she reiterates her height and weight (now down to 77 kilos), adding that 'Munmy besides cares greatly of me'.[11] She fills in some of the detail of her precocious development (she walked as soon as she was put in a position to, at eleven months – a detail that sounds remarkably like her mother's version of her infancy). In outlining her education, conducted at home by her mother, she passes in the second sentence to detailing her *sexual* education, with the anecdote noted in Chapter Two about the consequences of learning at the age of three about the sexual nature of the rose, and relaying that knowledge to a somewhat elderly maid. Again she claims Ellis's attention to her advanced position as a child who had known about and been able to discuss sex.

It is in the third letter, 5 January 1932, that Hildegart's mother is introduced (again prompted by a comment of Ellis). There are no blemishes in the positive portrait offered to him, but there is a disturbing final remark: 'She goes with me everywhere, and is my full and absolute companion'. In her tracing of her maternal origins Hildegart mixes in awareness of the nature of her upbringing (her mother has educated her about sex), and the theory that has produced it (she is 'the product of a "matriarcado" following perhaps the "Mutter-recht" de Bachofen'). She is fully and solely the product of Aurora: 'nothing but her influence has been felt by me, and I am absolutely a complete work of herself'.

The third letter also amplifies Hildegart's physical vision of herself, with now some touches that show some self-awareness, but also the previously noted mixture of precociousness and innocence. So she refers back to her height and weight, in a phrasing that has little or no understanding of social conventions of distance:

> I am glad you like my portrait. In every one I do of myself, I appear very mature, but it is not my fault you know. But if I don't photo my face but my body also, effect is perhaps worst. Imagine yourself what I told you in past letter. I am nearly a meter and seventy centimeters hight, and I weigh seventy eight kilograms. So that I appear as a splendent woman.

She also appears to intuit her uncertain location in any known social age:

> If it were not for my hair, my corsckrewes are much longer than most in the portrait appear and we can only use this combing here until we are twenty years old, people would not judgue of my age, save in my conversation and manners, and perhaps in my little experience of life.

In a parting shot that is disarming, and simultaneously defensive and seductive, she adds:

> If it were not for my Munmy, I confide in everybody and that, as you know is always perilous.

Pathologies of Motherhood

On the face of it, the presence of Aurora in the correspondence is benign. The view of her that can be construed from the above is that of a constant companion, always supportive, always there. Her function is that of a shadowy third in the correspondence; she is regularly present in Hildegart's valedictions, and whether or not she actually read Ellis's letters to her daughter, she appears as a regular implied reader. But the letters contain a series of unconscious communications that belie such an interpretation.

The pathologies inherent in the situation between Aurora and Hildegart derive from Aurora's dominance. The whole manner in which Hildegart was conceived and then educated was precisely engineered (and confirmed in Aurora's statements at her trial). In both a material sense and in the psychoanalytic understanding of the term, she was the 'object' created by her mother. It has been observed that Aurora came to the creation of her daughter with a history of displaced attentions. Pointing out that Hildegart was conceived after the death of Aurora's father (he died in February of 1914, and Hildegart was born in December of that year), Rendueles suggests that she was a replacement object (Rendueles, 1989: 79). What is not clear is whether this object was to replace Pepito (her sister's child that she had reared, and who was taken from her) or Aurora's father. The idea of Aurora being caught up in a 'family romance' (Freud, 1909) has also been advanced (Fajardo, 1987a: 131–2; Rendueles, 1989: 49–66). The form this would have taken in relation to Pepito is that Aurora, having taken care of her sister's child and then being deprived of him, embarked on a more grandiose project, that of having a child all of her own. Fajardo emphasizes the nature of the eugenic project that underlay this, suggesting that if she had been able to transform Pepito, the product of an 'impure union' into a prodigy, she imagined she might achieve yet more if she had a child whose conception would be free of passion, and all hers to bring up (Fajardo, 1987a: 133).[12]

Rendueles takes up the idea that Hildegart represents an object to replace Aurora's father. In relation to this he argues that there is evidence for a split in Aurora's mind between an idealized father and a mother who was both frivolous and rejecting of Aurora herself, a mother alleged to have had a lover in common with the sister. Aurora was to recall having seen, at the age of three, her mother kissing a man (Fajardo, 1987a: 132). This background led, according to Rendueles (1989: 52–3), to a basic family split, in which Aurora's father was ranged with herself on one side, and her mother and sister on the other: good versus evil. Rendueles implies, but does not overtly state, that within this framework there was a forbidden oedipal love on Aurora's part for her father (1989: 57). He suggests that the identity of the man Aurora saw kissing her mother is that he was no stranger, but her own father. The transformation of the identity of the man in Aurora's mind would thus have resulted from the infantile rejection of the idea of sexual activity between the parents. Into this fraught world of thwarted desires, the 'object' created by Aurora, Hildegart, was to be a perfect being who would solve everything. Hildegart was thus the 'repression of her mother's desire', and when Hildegart, in her growing fame and independence, seemed to be slipping out of her mother's control, she had to be killed.

There is a further interesting disparity of detail, fascinating for what it reveals of the interpenetration of Aurora and her daughter. On 19 May 1933, a month before she was killed, Hildegart published an article in *La Tierra*, 'Caín y Abel', in which she interpreted Cain as a symbol of progress. The article, reprinted by Rosa Cal (1991a: 199–201), is however understood by Rendueles as being authored by Aurora, no doubt because of the way the article is referred to in the clinical case-notes of Aurora (1989: 135). Despite the public attribution of the article to Hildegart, Rendueles fuses or confuses the two (Rendueles, 1989: 122). This is analogous with the way that the clinical notes from Ciempozuelos refer to the article as 'su' [hers], in a manner that could be understood as though it were Aurora's (that is written by her), rather than as the article she possesses.[13]

A slightly different interpretation of the Aurora/Hildegart relationship is that offered by the Lacanian analyst Pilar Dasí. According to this reading, Hildegart represents the 'lack' of her mother, a lack that will lead finally to her destructive act. Essentially the interpretation of Dasí is similar to that of Rendueles, but with the clarification that Hildegart is an unrecognized, unarticulated extension of her mother's repressed desire which threatens to be made an actual lack, or deprivation, by Hildegart's proposed journey to England. In Dasí's interpretation there is a joint occupation of the world of the Real by Aurora and her object-daughter. On the threat of Hildegart to become a subject she had to be annihilated. The evidence of the letters does not necessarily contradict this bold interpretation.

Decoding Conflict

Earlier interpretations regarding the pathology of Aurora (and its possible effects on her daughter) already discussed have not benefited from access to the correspondence of Hildegart with Ellis. Yet the pathology of Aurora, and indeed other disruptive elements in Hildegart's world, is borne out by numerous subtexts of the letters. Well before the tragic event of the murder, the letters convey – albeit unconsciously – evidence that all was not well for Hildegart. This emerges in her comments in relation not to her mother, but to others about her. Specifically we can track the disturbance in two areas: when she writes to Ellis about homosexuality (the details of which were discussed in Chapter Four), and when she details the atmosphere of paranoia and conflict in the Liga.

Internal Dissent in the Liga: Trauma and Transference

Only a month after Hildegart writes about the Liga being set up in February 1932 a dynamic comes to light in the form of a vacillation between her manic euphoric excitement at how well it is going, and what seem to be equally manic commentaries on the difficulties that are occurring. From June 1932 onwards there is moreover a strong sense of paranoia and isolation in relation to the others involved in the Liga. Within the framework of paranoia two people are singled out as bad objects: Marañón, a source of increasing disappointment, perceived as womanish and hysterical, and Haro, committed to trying to oust her from her position as secretary to the Liga.

A further crucial element, not consciously acknowledged, is the presence of Aurora. As would become evident in June 1933, Hildegart's mother was not simply unusual and independent, but murderous. In the letters she is apparently a benign person in the background who sends greetings to Ellis, but a number of comments and interventions can be understood in more sinister ways than might at first appear justified. Read retrospectively, her opinions, and above all her suspiciousness, may have been behind the outburst of gossip about homosexuality in public life that preceded Hildegart's account in the correspondence of the setting up of the Liga, and are a significant hidden presence behind the conflicts within the Liga.

In the spring of 1932, when the Liga was founded, it is clear that Hildegart had a strong proprietorial relationship to it. On 1 May 1932 she writes of her distress at surrendering control of the Liga to others. As she expresses it to Ellis:

> It seems as if I have had a child with great efforts, and seen afterwards being born, I had to give it to a nurse, for I could not give him the milk of my breast, though I know that the presence of the nurse is necessary to save the life of the child. I hope you can understand me, and you will know how I am writing this letter so happy, so happy and yet a bit sorry.

Not only does Hildegart give the impression that the Liga is her business rather than that of Marañón, but she is increasingly negative and dismissive. On 6 November 1932, it appears that Ellis has said something positive about Marañón and that she feels it necessary to set the record straight, albeit with a profession of sympathy:

> I find that you are somewhat mistaken in thinking that Dr. Marañon has a great reputation. He is in the descending point of his life... people don't respect him as they did, they generally mock at him, he is generally called 'Gorgonio', and even the journalists laugh between themselves – I know this last thing for I am now a journalist like them, and I work too in their professional meetings – of Gorgonio's ridicule own doings. Between the medical class he had – that is the truth – a great many envies. Now, no. They all pity him, for his loss has been a rapid one. I too am sorry for him.

In the following months there are difficulties within the Liga, and Marañón emerges as a shadow image of Aurora. In August 1932,[14]

Hildegart refers to Marañón fondly as 'our dear D. Gregorio', and the letter contains further images of affection, with references to her outsize teddy bear, constant companion and comfort (with more than a slight hint of him as substitute emotional object, (perhaps as the guardian-father). But suddenly, three letters later on 7 September 1932, something has happened. Marañón has become ill and, in Hildegart's discourse, he has become feminized. He is now a jealous woman, a female figure unable to tolerate her success, and disturbingly close to Aurora in his attributes:

> He is in the 'menopausic' period, he has a horrible 'impetigo' all over his body; the doctors order him to be away from all active work, he is loosing memory and faculties; in fact he is not the same Dr. Marañón he was, though his great will will maintain him up perhaps some more years. Besides, unfortunately for him, he is like a good woman, very jealous of me and of the name I have already in Spain

What stands out is the image of Marañón being jealous *as a woman*, an image that particularly calls up the sexual jealousy that Haire would see at the root of Aurora's killing of her daughter.

There is a great deal of confusion in this letter, in which we can discuss the stresses of one who knows about coping with the unpredictability and prickliness of a person who is ill, and to whom one is closely bound. This person, figuring here under the name of Marañón, has links with the figure of Aurora. The point of clarity in all this is Hildegart's address to Ellis as a sympathetic listener and, perhaps, as father-figure, a type of arbiter amid the confusion. Later Hildegart makes this evident in her relating of these troubling details, adding: 'as you are for me like a father I tell you all the truth'. In talking of Marañón, it is as if some of that discourse of eugenics and degeneration unconsciously creeps in. While it was he who had theorized a phase in men which corresponded to the menopause in woman, there is something more than that here, and something that is amiss. Hildegart's characterization of him is decidedly in the field of the feminine. She moves from referring to him as a 'menopausic' woman, to 'a bright little girl of six (6 November 1932).[15] Her emphasis on the feminine here signals Marañón's abnormality (in his own terms): what he had outlined as the characteristics of the 'critical age' for man was the tendency to become heavier and more hirsute with advancing years (Marañón 1925, chapter 25).

In the letter of 18 February of 1933, we go beyond uncertainties about gender, and fear has entered the arena, expressed in the context of the Liga, with Marañón as enemy. In this screen presentation roles are reversed, so that Hildegart regards Marañón as considering her his enemy, rather than the reverse. In reading her account of those who are for or against Marañón, there is the possibility that it is also a dislocation of what are arguably growing tensions between herself and her mother (who will kill her four months later). She emphasizes that since she (unlike others) has economic independence she is free to be critical of Marañón. This could be construed in the literal manner she intends it, or alternatively as a sign of her awareness of potential independence from her mother (whose own economic independence had left her free to pursue her aim of creating a eugenic child).

In the early letters, and as shown in Chapter Four, Hildegart spills out naively and questioningly her doubts and suspicions about homosexuals in Spanish public life (views that could be her own, or those of Aurora transferred to her). In the later letters screen presentations allow us to intuit some of the complications going on in the life of Hildegart and the mother, who is to kill her. Aurora is thus presented in the form of a man, Marañón (consistent with the 'hombruna' features she undoubtedly had): a man who starts as the great masculine inspiration and the patriarchal figurehead necessary to bring into being Hildegart's 'child', the Liga. Marañón then comes to embody both her mother (the jealous, menopausal woman), and then simply the being who is dangerous because no enemy is too small for it.

In the structure of perversion, it is customary to give emphasis to the *active* player in the drama. The *object*, or the *agent* of the perversion is relegated, even in discussion, to simply that, without regard to the experience of being object or required agent.[16] In the structure of abuse, more weight is given to the victim, although in the exploration of potential victim pathology a problem arises in that the victim is then subject to a second objectification as the abuse is explored (see Forrester, 1990: 62–88). We might regard Hildegart as the perverse object of her mother's desire (and one who came to threaten to eclipse the mother who had caused her to be). In more sinister fashion – in terms of the level of control and influence to which she was subjected – we might consider her to be the victim of her mother's abuse. Her murder relegated the pains of the secondary objectification to the area of her reputation. Whether object of perversion or abuse, however, the pressures on Hildegart add urgency to her communications with Ellis, as the one who might hear and understand.

What develops subsequently in the correspondence is a pattern of extremes, a splitting between what in Object Relations would be termed good objects and bad objects, with Aurora as a barely perceptible but highly significant underlying presence. Ellis throughout is a good object, the good father, the perfect interlocutor. The position of bad object is occupied first by Haro, then by Marañón. According to the account in the letters, Haro is outwitted, and Marañón suffers loss of health and public esteem. When Hildegart writes of these bad objects, her tone becomes more distressed, her judgements lose balance, and the account of plotting is such that one is inclined to query its veracity. When she is not focussed upon these two bad objects, the tone is open, friendly, and the letters are full of her doings and hopes. In Object Relations terms, the vacillation is between the paranoid–schizoid position on the one hand, with high levels of paranoia and exaggeration, and where good and bad objects are sharply separated, and on the other the depressive position, characterized by humour, acceptance and tolerance.

On the surface Aurora gradually emerges as another reader of Ellis's letters, and indeed as co-respondent to them. Tracking it shows other things. On 19 March 1932, Hildegart opens, 'you cannot imagine how happy I was and my mother too when *we read* what you spoke of Spain and of me' (in response to an article Ellis had sent, emphasis mine) and in a postscript: 'My mother too wishes you a happy year'. This is innocent enough, but in the rest of the letter the first doubts about Marañón appear, and Hildegart reports her 'small fight' with Dr Sanchis Banús, commenting in a manner that conveys her self-enclosure, and sense of superiority (attitudes shown consistently by Aurora at her trial): 'It is very disagreeable to fight with the ignorance and the stupidness of a great deal of persons, but I don't break down'.

Aurora is then absent from the letters until May 1932, and in her absence Hildegart makes a number of positive comments about others in the Liga, including Marañón as 'an ideal president' (30 March 1932), and Haro, the man appointed treasurer (22 April 1932), who she notes is 'one of the younger but most intelligent doctors'. Placing herself in relation to them she observes that the three of them will make a 'good triangle for directing the League'. In the event this will form a strange oedipal triangle, with Marañón eventually as the mother-figure, Haro as the father-figure who disrupts the relationship of Marañón and Hildegart, and Hildegart as the proto-son who makes a bid for power, and risks castration by Haro.

Hildegart's mother returns implicitly to the correspondence as the source of her daughter's sense of self on 1 May 1932 where Hildegart speaks of mixed feelings at handing over the Liga to others, declaring that 'I am glad because I have accomplished the first part of my work', the phrase speaking of the destiny her mother had for her. At her trial Aurora would make this explicit, saying that she had created 'un ser, una mujer, que representara la bandera de la libertad' [a being, a woman, who would represent the flag of liberty], one whose task would be to educate through her speech and writing (Pérez Sanz and Bru Ripoll, 1987 II: 71).

In the next two letters, paranoia and distress abound, and at first (25 June 1932) Hildegart's disturbance derives from the fact that others in the Liga do not work as she does to further its cause. A revealing insertion is made in her longhand (the rest of the letters always being in typescript) where she refers to Marañón as a woman 'not as a normal woman, but as a hysterical one'. Then, speaking of the laws relating to prostitution, Hildegart suddenly says: 'We thought that these measures ought to be known in public – *when I say we, I speak of my mother . . .*' (emphasis mine). Ellis is thus presented with two women who see him as interlocutor, and indeed is made aware of the mother's presence within the Liga, a presence confirmed in the psychiatric report of Sacristán and Prados (Rendueles, 1989: 206).

Haro then comes centre stage as bad object, and Hildegart writes to Ellis (18 July 1932) about his machinations to remove her from her position as secretary. A blow by blow account, increasingly novelistic in tone, depicts her wandering the streets weeping. Mysteriously she shifts from having her mother with her to appearing alone:

My head was really topsy-turvy. ¿What had happened..? Thanks that I am of a very resistent nature, and that Munmy was with me. But when I came to the outside, I could not decide myself to go to see Marañón immediately. I must wait. I went roaming by the nearest streets, crying, not to lose my place as a secretary – you see it only means work for me – but to find myself thrust so, and without any motive whatever.

Haro had proposed there should be two secretaries: a 'social' one (Hildegart) and a 'scientific' one, who would be a doctor. This manoeuvre, which would curtail Hildegart's power, might have been to ensure that doctors had the whip-hand in the direction of the Liga, or simply to side-line the intrusive and difficult Aurora. Hildegart's interpretation, however, is that this is a plot against herself, and the atmosphere of paranoia intensifies. She speaks of numerous telephone calls and letters warning her that her prime enemy was on the inside of the Liga (references which might in fact have been to her mother).

By October Marañón has become the bad object (a weak one, rather than a malicious one), and the place of the good object has come to be occupied by Juarros. The letters of 10 October and 6 November are full of gossip and the surprisingly intemperate tone that characterized the letter about Haro. Hildegart casts aspersions on Marañón's work, alleging that all his work is copied from German publications. Evidently Ellis wrote (perhaps countering some of her points) in response to this in October, since on 6 November Hildegart (in her unconsciously dual persona) says 'I spent a lot of time in commenting it with Munmy'. Hildegart, however, expresses regret for Marañón's state: her comment expresses a desire to make that state public while wishing to 'maintain me aside from all the many factors that have led him to this state of disgrace'.

Ellis was undeniably an interlocutor who understood rather more than Hildegart intended, and had read her distress. He appears to have said something to that effect because on 16 May 1933, in what would be her last letter to him, she assures him, 'You must not be worried about my health. I am quite healthy'. Clearly she interprets his concern as being with her physical health rather than her mental state. What transpires between this letter and her death less than a month later is not clear, but there does seem to be a case for believing that if Aurora became in some manner deranged, Hildegart also by now was in a state that was not entirely stable.

NOTES

1. 'corkscrews', i.e. ringlets.
2. This figure includes the letter to Ellen Key drafted at the same time as the first letter to Ellis.
3. Hackl's novelistic account (1990: 85) suggests that the chronology is that Hildegart knew Wells before Ellis, and that Wells organized an introduction to Ellis.
4. Haire correspondence with Ellis, Sydney University Library, 3.16. The ink for these two sentences is darker than in the preceding sentence, indicating, perhaps, that there was pause for thought before these last two comments.
5. It is striking that Ellis tried to protect himself from the thought of Aurora's intrusiveness despite evidence to the contrary.
6. This is part of the British Library Ellis archive. Katharine Gillett-Gatty had trained as a nurse in the early 1920s, and came joint third in an optional test paper taken after a post-graduate week at the General Lying In Hospital in London (*British Journal of Nursing Supplement*, 3 June 1922, 360, in a section focussed on obstetrics and maternity care). How she came to know Hildegart is a matter of speculation. She wrote to Ellis from Paris, and then Denmark, but appears to have continued to have contact with Spain after the outbreak of the Civil War. See her letter to Rozika Schwimmer of 20 February 1937 referring to her war experience (Margaret McFadden, 2004: 263).
7. The passing reference to Aurora being like the embryo in Hildegart's uterus is a fascinating reversal, by which Hildegart was (potentially) the mother to Aurora in her unfulfilled being. The image also indicates the primitive physical suggestions that this pair made.
8. Françoise Lafitte-Cyon (Delisle), Ellis's companion in the years Hildegart wrote to him, habitually referred to him as 'Faun', or 'Pan' (see Delisle, 1946: 284, 308).
9. In 'The Red Virgin' Ellis refers briefly to the fact that he wrote to her 'that she must not too often waste her precious time and strength in letters to me' (Ellis, 1933: 178).
10. It would possibly be a step too far to suggest that Hildegart here engages in Freud's concept of 'family romance' by which the adolescent fantasizes that their 'real' parents are not the ones who have brought them up (and are found wanting) (Freud, 1909). But the fact of being a 'eugenic child' and of having a father whose identity was kept unknown would fuel the possibilities for engaging in such fantasies.
11. This strange misspelling of 'Mummy' is retained throughout the correspondence.

12 The argument that Hildegart was literally her mother's object is supported by accounts of Aurora's behaviour in the asylum, where she took to making dolls, eventually producing in 1942 one of lifesize, complete with erect penis. On this topic there is a disparity between Fajardo's initial 'flier' article which draws on the work of Rendueles and states that when the nuns in charge of Aurora at the asylum burned the dolls, she became an elective mute, a rejection of language which she maintained until her death (Fajardo, 1987b: 133), and the more sober account of this final stage given by Rendueles in which the reference is to a single life-size doll being destroyed (Rendueles, 1989: 194).

13 '2-2-36. – Nos trae *La Tierra*, y nos muestra un artículo y un comentario de ella: "Caín y Abel; Injusticias." Todas las palabras del texto tienen su significado si se sabe comprender e interpretar. Nos promete traernos un comentario *de su artículo* hecho por ella y en el que nos explicará párrafo por párrafo y palabra por palabra' [2-2-36. – She brings us *La Tierra*, and shows us an article and her commentary: 'Cain and Abel: injustices'. All the words of the text have a meaning if one knows how to understand and interpret. She promises to bring us a commentary *of her article* which she has done and which she will explain to us paragraph by paragraph and word by word] (Rendueles, 1989: 38, emphasis mine). *La Tierra* was a publication in which Hildegart figured prominently at the end of her life. It is notable in its warm and empathic response to Hildegart's death, retaining a sense of admiration for Aurora as mother. The assertion about the authorship of the article on Cain and Abel appears, however, not in *La Tierra* but in other publications: Lafora, in *Luz*, 21 June 1934, will attribute the article to Aurora; Juan de Toga in *El Liberal*, 25 May 1934, also gives this attribution. This is despite the internal sense of the article which points to Hildegart's understanding of the dangerous and creative role of the rebel. If the article were by Aurora, then the evidence of her exaltation and mania would be strengthened.

14 The date of this letter is in the hand of neither Ellis nor Hildegart, and was presumably inserted by an archivist.

15 The age of six is, incidentally, that suggested by Mrs Gillett-Gatty for Hildegart in her image of her speaking as if she were a child reciting.

16 See Freud's three 1905 essays on the theory of sexuality, 'The Sexual Aberrations,' 'Character and Anal Erotism' (1908b), 'A Special Type of Choice of Object Made by Men' (1910) and 'Fetishism' (1927).

Chapter Eight

Filicide: Perfection and Eugenic Death

Yet each man kills the thing he loves, by each let this be heard, some do it with a bitter look, some with a flattering word. The coward does it with a kiss, the brave man with a sword! (Oscar Wilde, 'The Ballad of Reading Gaol', 1898)

... The two explained it next day in political press saying that gouverment had intended to apply Mr. Alcalá Zamora the tragical 'ley de fugas' – do you know what this is?, to say that the prisoner has intented to escape although it is not true and kill him by the back. (Hildegart to Ellis, 5 January 1932)

I have just had a letter from a Final-year medical student who was present at the post mortem examination. He says there were two bullet wounds in the head, one in the left breast and one 'au sexe'. So it evidently was sexual crime. (Haire to Ellis, 16 June 1933)

– Creo que no se ha inventado nada más hermoso que la vida, y que a ésta en la tierra debemos encomendar nuestro entusiasmo.

– Creo que el problema de la vida está en gozarla con la mayor intensidad y con la mayor extensión. (Hildegart, 'Oración de la Eugenesia' [Eugenic prayer])[1]

[I believe that nothing has been invented that is more beautiful than life, and that on earth it is to this that we should devote our enthusiasm.

I believe that the issue of life is to enjoy it as much as possible and with the greatest intensity possible.]

DIAGNÓSTICO: ¿Paranoia? ¿Esquizofrenia paranoica?
[DIAGNOSIS: Paranoia? Paranoid schizophrenia?]
(Diagnosis of Aurora, 24 December 1935)

La muerte de la señorita Hildegart a manos de su propia madre, que, enamorada de su obra hasta el paroxismo, la destruye antes que verla desvirtuada por el influjo extraño de un amor no previsto, es un tema rico en sugestiones, que plantea varios problemas interesantes para la psiquiatría y la ciencia penal modernas. Y, sin embargo, trátase en el fondo de un drama bien antiguo que tiene sus antecedentes en la moral espartana, tan en desuso desde que la mayoría del mundo civilizado empezó a regirse por los postulados del cristianismo. (*Heraldo de Madrid*, 9 June 1933)

[The death of Hildegart at the hands of her own mother, who, loving her creation to extremity, destroys her rather than seeing her spoiled by the influence of a love affair that had not been foreseen, is a theme rich in suggestions, and one that poses a number of interesting questions for modern psychiatry and penology. And yet, in the end, it is an ancient drama that has its roots in Spartan morality, now well out of use since most of the civilized world has taken to being governed by the postulates of Christianity.]

... Hildegart and her mother had set themselves an ideal of superhuman achievement which threw them off their balance. I suppose it often happens that heroic enthusiasm is paid for in neurosis while the more 'cabbagey' people rest solidly on their stalks. (Richard Rees to Havelock Ellis, 17 June 1933)[2]

Hildegart Eclipsed

On 9 June 1933 Aurora Rodríguez shot Hildegart four times with a revolver as she lay in bed, bringing her life to a violent and untimely conclusion. Aurora freely admitted her act, and was strident in her claim to have had full responsibility in committing it. After the murder she went straight away to the house of the lawyer Juan Botella Asensi, and announced what she had done. She continued to affirm her culpability for the crime throughout her trial, so that the issue was never whether or not she had killed her daughter, but simply why, and whether or not she could be held responsible. Aurora was tried for murder in 1934, initially being sent to prison with twenty-six years to serve. She was transferred on Christmas Eve 1935 to the women's asylum at Ciempozuelos where she remained until her death on 28 December 1955 (Fajardo, 1987b: 133).

Hildegart's violent end did more than destroy her considerable potential. It caused a notable distortion in the public memory of her life, and most significantly it deflected interest from her reputation as a social activist and sexual reformer. Her murder attracted considerable attention in the press, both in Spain and elsewhere in Europe, but with the murder trial the focus rapidly shifted, and Aurora came to the fore. This eclipsing of Hildegart by Aurora continued, and is expressed in the former's relegation to a parenthesis at the end of a subtitle in Cal's book, *A mí no me doblega nadie: Aurora Rodríguez: Su vida y su obra (Hildegart)* [No one Breaks Me: Aurora Rodríguez: her Life and Work (Hildegart)]. Two accounts track Aurora's life around and after the trial, Rendueles (1989), and the excellent close analysis of issues in the trial by Álvarez Peláez and Huertas (1987).[3] All the accounts deal with the life of Hildegart as well, and Cal in particular traces her life and activities in the press, but the emphasis is still on the murder, on Aurora and her motivation.

Reports in the press show the diversity of public 'knowledge' about the event, and the cuttings collected by Ellis include items from the *Daily Herald*, the *Sunday Chronicle*, the *Sunday Referee*, the *Daily Express* and *The People*, with an unidentified newspaper cutting in Swedish about the book by Guzmán and Endériz. In these Hildegart is variously referred to as a 'scientific child' killed by her mother (*Daily Express*, August 1933), a 'Trilby' (*Daily Express*, 25 May 1934), a ' "eugenic" daughter' (*Daily Herald*, 28 May 1934). Even here, however, the preoccupation was not with Hildegart's life, but rather her death, and – as the story of Aurora's eugenic planning of her daughter's conception emerged – with the identity of her father.

Immediate reaction in the foreign press to Hildegart's death paid attention to a series of images that portrayed in grotesque manner how Aurora was believed to have shaped and controlled her daughter. Some details were frankly grotesque. Thus the Reuter report published in the *Sunday Referee*, 10 September 1933, suggested that Aurora had produced a freak: 'From the moment that Hildegart was born, her mother moulded her to her own ideals. She gave her a special diet which developed her brain and made her abnormally huge, and later chose all her reading'. This detail was reiterated by the *Daily Express*, 25 May 1934, during the trial, in 1934: 'She never left the child alone a moment, watching every step of her education, and providing special diet to develop the brain and physique too', adding that 'The girl – who passed brilliant examinations – became a mere intellectual puppet whose every word and gesture were dictated by the mother'. Curiously, despite this fixation with Hildegart's size (something which to some degree she shared, reassuring Ellis about her height and weight) or perhaps because of it, some newspapers chose to present a physical image that glamorized Hildegart and bore little or no resemblance to the pictures normally circulated. *Crónica* of 18 June 1933 had a full front page with a photograph of Hildegart with short curly hair, one that it reprinted in its account of the trial the following year on 3 June 1934. Perhaps significantly, the less flattering photograph produced in *Luz*, on 24 May 1934, is one that has never appeared elsewhere. More glamorous pictures captured the eye of the press after the murder, particularly the foreign press. The *Daily Herald* on 28 May 1934, the day after Aurora was sentenced to twenty-six years in prison printed two photographs: that of Aurora emphasizes her mannishness and heavy features, while that of Hildegart is of a glamorous vamp (a photograph also used in *The People*, 27 May 1934). In the drama of mother and daughter, polarization between murderess and victim was maintained, so that Hildegart was not tarnished with her mother's masculinity. Contrasting with these images of extremes, the photograph sent to Ellis by Hildegart is refreshingly natural (see book jacket).

In one of her earliest published works, Hildegart had commented on child mortality (presumably including deaths by infanticide), deeming more 'horrible' than the prospect of infant deaths that of infant lives spared only to live 'como anormales, como degenerados' [as abnormal and degenerate beings] (Hildegart, 1930b: 35). Her strong eugenic line, which did not emphasize the survival of the fittest so much as the iniquity of enabling the survival of the less fit was to be twisted in the motivation of Aurora for murdering her.

Why did Aurora kill Hildegart? Here there is no simple view, since Aurora's statements were presented to different interlocutors, and mediated according to particular interpretations. In the trial Aurora had a performance to mount, and did so with dedication. In the interviews with Guzmán and Endériz she had a special performance: they were her chosen interlocutors (in the sense in which Ellis was the chosen interlocutor of Hildegart), picked by her to draft *her* version of events, something that has influenced biographers towards using it as a source. In the interviews with psychiatrists, both for the psychiatric report for the trial and in the asylum of Ciempozuelos, there was also an element of performance. And in all of these instances, there was necessarily interpretation by those writing up Aurora's statements about her self and her actions, so that the information reaches us through a filter. Her statement at the trial, an event at which there were numerous witnesses, could conceivably be construed as the most 'truthful' of the accounts, but it too has to be read as much for its manner of presentation as for its content. Her intention was to leave the judge and jury in no doubt, an intention that is itself a statement. We need therefore to wrestle with possibilities of credibility between these accounts, while remembering that no account will ever be exact.

At the time of the trial, plausible story-lines were mixed with fantastic ones. The overall summary offered by the prosecutor was that Hildegart wanted her independence (and to 'recover her personality'), had fallen in love, and wanted to become more involved in politics (Toga, 1934b). Aurora's first explanation to Botella Asensi, the lawyer she went to see, was that she had killed her daughter because she was so beautiful (report in *La Libertad*, 10 June 1933). She had killed Hildegart to 'protect' her, to protect her purity from future soiling and degeneration: 'yo no quise que nadie me la quitara ni por amor ni por ideas políticas, porque había sido siempre sumisa y dócil a todos mis mandatos, y antes que nadie me la quitara me adelanté yo' [I didn't want anyone to take her from me either for love or political ideas, because she had always been submissive and acquiescent to all my orders, and before anyone could take her from me I acted first] (Dubois, 1934a). She stated that she had, as it were, helped Hildegart to commit suicide, in that – she said – Hildegart had begged her repeatedly to kill her, and that while her response had been that she should be brave and kill herself, Hildegart had said that she lacked the necessary decision, and begged her mother to carry out the deed (Massa, 1934).[4] Aurora alleged that the ultimate reason for killing Hildegart was that she had created her to work for peace, and that she could see that she was heading towards espionage and war (Toga, 1934a).

Judging Aurora: Madness and Badness

Aurora's reasons, cited above, have a type of sequential logic. The central drama of judging Aurora was the issue of whether she was to be thought mad and consequently not responsible for her actions, or to be thought sane but bad, a criminal. Views on her mental state came from two quarters, each represented by prominent medical authorities. Bearing witness for the defence were Sacristán and Prados (the first of these having been one of the founder members of the Liga). Sacristán was at this point director of the asylum for women at Ciempozuelos and Prados was director of the San José psychiatric hospital in Malaga. Lafora had been approached to serve for the psychiatric assessment for the prosecution (alongside Vallejo) but declined as he was preparing for public examinations (Álvarez Peláez and Huertas, 1987: 114).[5] This was perhaps a convenient response. He would find the time to write no fewer than twelve articles published between 20 June and 27 July 1934, in which he discussed clinical issues arising from Aurora's case. The doctor who would produce the assessment for the prosecution with Vallejo was Piga.

The strategy of the defence was to argue that Aurora's ideas made her identifiably mad. Álvarez Peláez and Huertas note that Sacristán and Prados made unreasonable inferences about the sanity of Aurora with respect to ideas that were in fact widespread at the time (1987: 97). There is a nuance to be seen in this understanding by the defence, however. Prados referred to 'el concepto que de la eugenesia tenía la procesada' [the concept the accused had of eugenics], which suggests not a devaluation of eugenics as an idea but rather a comment on Aurora's eccentric and extreme approach to it (Grau, 1934b). Nonetheless these doctors distanced themselves from ideas, some of which – in the case of Sacristán – could not have been entirely foreign: he at least had belonged to the Liga.[6] The underlying complications here relate to issues of membership and diversity, and tell us as much about the disparity of those interested in eugenics and sex reform as it does about the effect that Aurora might have had on the Liga. What is curious is the apparent attitude of those examining Aurora for the defence. Given their memory of her interference in the Liga, one might have expected them to be more critical when listening to her testimony.

The psychiatric statement for the prosecution by Vallejo was at pains to present Aurora not as the victim of madness or delirium, but as a person in touch with her circumstances, albeit with a range of ideas and reactions that were somewhat strange. The defence had suggested that a number of features of Aurora's life, and certainly of her ideas, were signs that she was exceptional. Vallejo took some of these features and presented them as life events that could be interpreted as normal. He listed Aurora's experience as a single mother, her adherence to a range of beliefs that fell outside central social norms, other aspects of her pregnancy and decisions affecting the upbringing of her daughter. He took a strong line in affirming that Aurora suffered no mental illness. If she was of difficult temperament she was still responsible for her actions (Toga, 1934b).

But Aurora was a force to be reckoned with, even during the trial: 'A veces, no sabíamos quién interrogaba a quién: tal era la destreza de la procesada al contestar a las preguntas' [At times we did not know who was interrogating whom: such was the skill of the accused in answering questions] (Grau, 1934a). Vallejo commented that Aurora's aim with the experts had been to 'deslumbrarnos con su talento' [dazzle us with her talent] (Dubois, 1934c). The point was that for Vallejo this display of virtuosity might show that she had a paranoid character, but it did not prove that she came into the category of the 'delirious', which would have made her 'mad' rather than 'bad'. The irony of the difference between the defence and the prosecution was that the former, containing a member of the Liga, had set the beliefs of eugenics and sex reform into the area of 'mad' belief (not least framing it as the belief that a woman might have 'indulged' in). The prosecution took the line that what Aurora had believed in was 'normal', and that she was responsible. The planks of the Liga defended sexual abnormality, and held that it should not be deemed criminal, consistent with the final conclusion of the testimony for the defence. The difficulty of the defence lies in the route that their discourse took in order to make their conclusion persuasive: they set aside their own view that eugenic and reformist beliefs might be normal in order to ensure that Aurora was classed as 'abnormal'. The prosecution, meanwhile, presented a view of Aurora's beliefs so normalized as to fail to be realistic or to convey their extremity.

Rereading Aurora: Sex and Death

A letter from Haire to Ellis written 16 June 1933, a week after Hildegart's murder, contained disturbing detail about the nature of the killing. A medical student who had attended the post-mortem stated that there had been four shots, two to the head, one to the left breast, and one, as he put it, 'au sexe'. Haire added 'So it evidently was sexual crime'. Haire's speculation was, however, fairly simple in terms of what a 'sexual crime' might have meant, in that he added 'It is believed that the motive was jealously [sic] of a lover – some people say a male lover and some say a female'.[7]

When we unpack Haire's conclusion, it is far less simple than might appear at first sight. A sexual crime implies that Aurora's action went further than being consistent with Oscar Wilde's chilling observation in 'The Ballad of Reading Gaol' that 'each man kills the thing he loves' (1898), even though Wilde's example was of a man killing a woman. Closer to home, it seems consistent with the idea of a murder prompted by jealousy, expressed by Hildegart's former teacher: 'un amante prefiere la muerte de su amada, si no ha de ser para él, antes que verla feliz en brazos de otro' [a lover will prefer the death of his beloved, if she is not to be his, rather than see her happy in the arms of another] (Saldaña, 1929: 30). What complicates the issue is the fact that the jealousy for possession of Hildegart was felt by her mother, not by another lover.

If Aurora was jealous of a lover, accounts agree that the 'lover' in question was Abel Velilla.[8] But not all agreed that there was a lover, and *La Tierra* on 12 June 1933 published a letter from Velilla in which he stated that he had never spoken of love to Hildegart, nor visited her at home, and that his only feelings for her had been of admiration for her talent and gratitude for her work in politics. The idea that Aurora might have killed through jealousy was dismissed as improbable in an obituary by Federica Montseny. She emphasizes the degree to which Hildegart was under her mother's control, and speaks with passion and empathy about Hildegart's plight, suggesting that the degree of separation that would have allowed for jealousy was missing.[9] Hildegart throughout her life, according to Montseny, had been nothing but the prisoner of her mother, a 'masculine' manager who required her to work non-stop. For her, Hildegart was a plant forced to grow in unnatural circumstances and that bore its fruit prematurely, and at a high cost (Montseny, 1933).[10] Lafora however, in his articles in *Luz* would draw on Freud's sexual theory of paranoia, and his note of how humanitarian activity could come from the sublimation of repressed homosexuality. Noting that from the outset there had been hints in the press of homosexual jealousy as a motive (although it has to be said such hints are not particularly evident in the press) he elaborated the idea that homosexual love had prompted the killing (Lafora, 1934i, 1934j).[11]

That Aurora might have been jealous of a lover implies the idea that somehow Hildegart, rather than being simply a daughter, was a desired sexual object – or even a 'possession' experienced as a sexual object. The reaction of Aurora is thus, according to the suggestion of Haire, a reaction to being deprived of her sexual object.

It can be regarded either as a curious irony or a type of insight that Hildegart's essay in the second number of *Sexus* on 'Criminología sexual' shows an element of prescience about what was to befall her. Her view that a wide range of crimes derived from sexual problems, and that these in their turn might derive from hormonal problems, has an uncanny resonance with what was to be her situation. The suggestion that Aurora had hormonal problems was never made, but her mannish appearance and instability could be considered consonant with them. Hildegart's close study of endocrinology for her article in the first number of *Sexus* might have suggested potential for speculation about the effect of endocrinal disturbance, but it seems not to have been entertained by others.

Filicide most frequently takes the form of infanticide, an act commented upon by eugenicists, including Hildegart, as one undertaken either through desperation (too many mouths to feed) or in the perception that the child was sickly and unlikely to survive. Modern research on filicide estimates that some 56 per cent of cases can be attributed to 'altruistic' reasons, and that many murders 'committed out of love', often associated with suicide, have the motivation of protecting the child from imagined or real suffering. Stanton cites Harder's view that there may be an excessive love for the child that is in fact a type of reaction-formation against hostility towards the child. Moreover a cause of filicide may have at its root resentment towards the way the murderer was treated by their own parent (Stanton and Simpson, 2002: 10, citing Feinstein, 1964).

Weldon presents the most sustained argument for the complexities behind filicide by a mother, arguing for it to be understood as a type of female perversion. In men perversion is typically directed against others (viewed as part-objects), but in women, Weldon argues, the perverse act is directed either against themselves, or the objects they see as their creation: their babies (Weldon, 1988: 8). This idea of the child as the object of the mother's creation clearly fits Hildegart and Aurora in a particularly specific way, and the idea of the *creation* is one claimed strenuously by Aurora, who discounted as far as possible the role of Hildegart's father. The role of a girl baby for a perverse mother is one that sits in a broader family context. Weldon observes, as did Feinstein, that the mother's own mother is part of the structure, and that the way the mother feels about her mother influences the way she feels about her own daughter (Weldon, 1988: 52–3; Feinstein cited in Stanton and Simpson, 2002: 10). Referring to Winnicott's idea of the 'transitional object', Weldon outlines how the infant girl comes to be used by the mother: 'to be invented, manipulated, used and abused, ravaged and discarded, cherished and idealized, symbiotically identified with and deanimated all at once'. The infant thus (in the classic terms used to define fetishism) comes to be the missing phallus for the mother, and then becomes her 'toy' or 'thing' (Weldon, 1988: 72). The case history cited by Weldon in which a patient suddenly became the 'exclusive object of her [mother's] dedication and devotion' has strong resonance with Hildegart's case, not least the detail that the mother became the 'constant witness' of all her daughter's actions. Other features of Aurora's situation are syntonic with the definitions of perverse motherhood as delineated by Weldon and others. Aurora's conflicted relationship with her own mother emerges both from the clinical record of Ciempozuelos and from the assessment for the defence by Sacristán and Prados. The clinical record, in so far as some of it appears to be *verbatim*, is more outspoken, less processed. Hence we have Aurora's comment of 3 November 1936 about her mother that 'Tenía más sexo que seso' [She had more sex than brains]. A woman who had died at the age of fifty-one, Aurora's mother emerges from the clinical notes as shallow, flighty, deficient as mother (when judged by the eugenic passion of Aurora) and given to beating her daughter when she questioned her conduct (Rendueles 1989: 17). At her trial Aurora would state 'Me encontraba abandonada en el hogar, manteniendo únicamente relaciones con mi padre' [I found myself abandoned within the home, keeping up relations only with my father] (Grau, 1934a; see also Toga, 1934b). In the light of this family scenario, Aurora's project of having her own child can be seen as a bid for constancy of relation, albeit one that would be perverse in its overinvestment in control.[12] The episode in which Aurora acted as care-giver to the prodigy Pepito Arriola, only to have him removed from her care, doubtless added to the investment in her 'own' object. When that object threatened to become independent from her (in whatever manner, whether through a personal relationship, or simply through not adhering to her plans to act as redeemer for the world), then murder was the logical option, one that would preserve the object as what it had originally been intended to be. Aurora was explicit about the fact that Hildegart had replaced Pepito Arriola as an 'object' to be formed (as he had, in his turn, replaced a doll from the Philippines that Aurora received at the age of four, a gift in response to which she had said that she wanted a 'muñeca de carne') (Toga, 1934a).

A further feature of Aurora that fits with the profile of the filicide who is a perverse mother is the degree of her composure and sense of self at her trial. She attracted attention by wearing a sleeveless black velvet dress, and carrying a bunch of red carnations. In the report in the *Daily Herald* of 28 May 1934, her composure was translated into determination: 'Proclaiming passionate love for her daughter, she insisted she had good reason for shooting her, and would do so again a thousand times in the same circumstances, as she was "called to reform the world by new eugenic methods"'. This 'knowing' of what she had done, and yet detachment from its horror, is viewed as characteristic of the maternal filicide, who has a sort of 'middle knowledge' of the event 'a detached, rather abstract knowledge that does not penetrate to the affective level' (Knowles, 1997: 84).

Death of the Liga

A salient feature of the Liga in the events surrounding Hildegart's death and her mother's trial is its subsequent invisibility. It is absent from official biographies of figures such as Marañón, or from other figures of the time (such as writers and other cultural figures who were to have participated in the 1933 Eugenics Conference) who apparently had contact with it, however brief.[13] Similarly, Ellis's involvement with the WLSR is reduced to a brief treatment in Grosskurth's biography (Grosskurth, 1980: 379–80). The suggestion of Cal (1991a: 89) is that Hildegart effectively withdrew from the Liga some time before her death, although the evidence of the letters to Ellis tells a quite different story. The fact that the Eugenics Conference took place in the spring of 1933, as well as the publication of the second number of *Sexus*, is testimony that the movement was at that point in vigorous action. Notwithstanding the evidence that Hildegart continued to the end to be active in the affairs of the Liga, her connection with it was completely suppressed when her body was taken to the Círculo Federal for people to pay their last respects. Since the funeral was predominantly organized and orchestrated by Federal Republican colleagues of Hildegart, it is perhaps not surprising that Liga contacts were not in evidence, but that of the founder members only Morata should have been there is quite striking (report in *La Tierra*, 12 June 1933).[14] The Liga was thus distanced from the shocking murder, arguably put on one side by those who sought to preserve their own reputations, or perhaps more plausibly was discounted by Hildegart's political comrades as of reduced relevance.[15] If Aurora had become as much associated with the Liga as Hildegart, and formed a 'cause célèbre' in which doctors and lawyers were at odds, then it is possible that the subject of eugenics became simply embarrassing. But the funeral also shows the degree to which Hildegart's fame and public acclaim went far beyond her Liga connections.

Individuals in the public eye were notably involved in this disavowal of the Liga. The sweeping and resounding criticisms that Lafora was to make of Hildegart's ideas in her intervention in the Eugenics Conference conveniently sent to oblivion the fact that he and others had joined the Liga with which those ideas were so closely associated.[16] At the same time, as Álvarez Peláez and Huertas (1987: 186) rightly comment, what Lafora did constituted an attack as he turned on ideas that were consequently linked to madness and became totally devalued. Meanwhile, an attentive reading of the clinical assessment made by Sacristán and

Prados can be seen as a fascinating obverse of the events Hildegart had relayed to Ellis in her letters. Here Sacristán, the Liga member who had intervened to mediate between Haro and Hildegart in the conflict about the secretaryship of the movement, conveys powerfully Aurora's view of what happened, and indicates her prominence in conflict, referring to her strong reaction to seeing that she did not have her way within the Liga, whether in the appointment to offices or on matters of principle (Rendueles, 1987: 208) (see Chapter 5 pp 98–9). By contamination of association, Aurora, deemed by Sacristán and Prados to be mad, was made to undermine the credibility and respectability of the Liga her daughter had brought into being.

A more positive reading of the disappearance of the Liga from the accounts of Hildegart's death is that – posthumously – it allowed Hildegart herself to come into more prominence. An example of this is the decision taken by *El Liberal* on 10 June 1933 to print, alongside its article on the murder, an interview with Hildegart in which her political feminism was to the fore ('No es el hombre quien dirige a la mujer, sino el que es dirigido por ella' [Man is not the one who rules woman, but who is ruled by her] (*El Liberal*, 1933c)). It thus allowed Hildegart to make a final strong statement by which she might be remembered.

Let us not end on a note of sour disavowal. The killing of the 'eugenic child' occasioned grief and regret, felt by those close to Hildegart.

> Mais, pourquoi cette fin anticipée, avant d'avoir connu la vie et l'amour? Et la mère qui vit encore, qui n'a pas sucumbé à un retour terrible de sa raison perdue – cette mère qui l'enfanta dans la douleur pour la tuer plus tard, froidement, tranquillement!
>
> Cette lumière ne sera pas de sitôt remplacée par une autre ... Ce n'est pas tous les jours que naissent les fleurs rares et que s'allument dans les cieux les petites lumières qui signalent l'apparition de mondes lointains ou proches.
>
> [But why should there have been this premature end, before she had known life and love? And what of her mother, who still lives, who has not given in to the awesome return of her lost reason – this mother who bore her in pain only to kill her later in cold tranquillity!

This light will not easily be replaced by another... It is not every day that rare flowers bloom and that the glints of light that tell us of the existence of worlds near or distant can be seen in the skies.]

(Federica Montseny, July 1933)

This death has greatly shaken Havelock Ellis. He regards it as the most tragic death he ever heard of, for Hildegart seemed cut for a remarkable woman: not so much the prodigy type as the embodiment of new heroic womanhood, possessing brains, learning, health, and all that goes to make great people. Knowing as he did the mother's love for the girl, he is lost to account for the deed. (Françoise Lafitte-Cyon to Norman Haire, 13 June 1933)

NOTES

1. Cited by Rendeules (1989: 109).
2. British Library Havelock Ellis collection.
3. Partial transcriptions of the trial are provided by Pérez Sanz and Bru Ripoll, 1987: 69–107, and can be read in press accounts of the time.
4. An elaboration on this was that Hildegart had asked Aurora to murder her since she saw that 'marchaba por senderos que no le agradaban, pero que se sentía impulsada a ir por ellos' [that she was following paths she did not like but that she felt impelled to follow] (Grau, 1934a).
5. When Lafora subsequently criticized José Valenzuela Moreno, the public prosecutor for his conduct of the case, specifically in relation to the use of expert evidence, Valenzuela pointed out that Lafora's defence of Aurora was one he could have made with greater effect had he agreed to act himself as counsel for the defence (letter from Valenzuela in *Luz*, 2 July 1934, p. 3).
6. Yet more curious in the circumstances is the coincidence that the public prosecutor, Valenzuela, had been a member of the Liga. Aurora referred to this in her response to how Hildegart came to know Abel Velilla, saying that this had come about through Hildegart's work in the Liga, and adding 'Y si no estoy engañada, el fiscal que ahora me interroga también ha pertenecido a esta Liga' [And if I am not mistaken, the prosecutor questioning me has also belonged to that League] (Toga, 1934a).
7. Haire to Ellis, 16 June 1933, Sydney University Library, 3.16. It is not known whether Fajardo had access to this information, but his coyness suggests that he might have. Commenting on the oddity that four shots were fired he opts for a vagueness that is improbable, saying that the fourth shot had no fixed target (Fajardo, 1987b: 132). He repeats here the reported vagueness of Aurora, who in her account written up by Guzmán says of the final shot: 'No sé donde dio el balazo' [I do not know where the shot went] (Guzmán, 1972:

168). Aurora is reported by Cal as saying of the fourth shot that it was a *coup de grâce* in the left cheek (Cal, 1991a: 110), phrasing that simultaneously suggests intentional finality and mercy at the same time as its location (in the cheek rather than the genitals) is of pretended innocence. It is noteworthy that newspaper reporting of the murder is also vague. The front page report in *La Tierra* of 10 June 1933 (notable for its warm emotion to both mother and daughter) refers to three bullets on the right side of the face and a fourth in the upper part of the chest. The destination of the fourth bullet became vague by the time the defence sums up in the trial. As summarized by Juan de Toga (1934b), there was a bullet to the forehead, one to the temple, one to the heart, but for the fourth no destination was given, a vagueness that is potentially consistent with what the medical student told Haire.

[8] See Fajardo, 1987a: 134; Montero, 1995: 188 (names Velilla as secretary of the Partido Federal); Guzmán, introduction to Hildegart 1977: 16; Cal, 1991a: 103–4; Rendueles, 1989: 134 (suggests that Velilla had proposed marriage to Hildegart); Álvarez Peláez and Huertas, 1987: 102.

[9] Viewed in Object Relations terms, if the relationship between Hildegart and Aurora was so close as to make the independent identity of the latter problematic, then jealousy would have been impossible, since it presupposes some degree of autonomy of the 'object' provoking jealousy.

[10] This cutting from the Ellis archive in the British Library has a handwritten date of July 1933.

[11] For fuller background to Lafora's ideas on homosexuality see Cleminson and Vázquez García (2007).

[12] The details Hildegart supplies to Ellis in her letter of 2 December 1931 about her early upbringing can be read as the account of an overly controlled childhood, rather than one of natural growth.

[13] Mysteriously, when the Liga was dissolved, the 800 pesetas existing in its funds passed over to the Asociación Española de Médicos Escritores y Artistas. In an account of this association, no date is given for the transfer of funds. See www.medicosescritoresyartistas.com/abajo01_a.htm.

[14] Attendance at the funeral was predominantly by women, including Clara Campoamor (listed in *Sexus* 1 as part of the feminism and marriage section).

[15] This issue of *La Tierra* kept Hildegart's Liga activities in view in a different way. Just beneath the report of her funeral, there is an advert for one of her works, *Paternidad voluntaria* [Voluntary fatherhood] in Morata's series Cultura Sexual.

[16] Lafora had claimed (1934e) that Hildegart founded the Liga at the instigation of Aurora. Later he criticized Hildegart's paper at the Eugenics Conference as simplistic, and asserted that her work simply cherry-picked from that of others: throughout she had been inspired by Aurora (Lafora, 1934g).

Appendix I

Hildegart's Letters[1]

1. Dated 23 October 1931 [folios 1–3]

Mr. Henry Havelock Ellis.

I know that you read with special interest all letters of youths, and though this be perhaps a little longer than others we receive, I beg of you most sincerely to lend it a bit of your attention, for I am a girl, my age is sixteen years old, and I am spanish,[2] three things which I expose first as my only racommandation to you.

Though my age is not great, I have finished my lawyer proffesion on September of this year, and I am studying Philosophy and Medicine. [I] cannot notwithstanding work as a lawyer because I have not legal age, and until I am twenty one years old, law does not allow me to work in public, but I intend to profit these years in learning specially in these three proffessions which I have selected and in visiting other nations, so as to know their laws and habitudes.

Nearly a year ago. I began to read in Spain the works of our pioneers in sexual problems, Marañón, Jiménez Asúa, Vital Aza, etc. I became interested by this questions. The studies which I had received were the sufficient in Physiologie and Anatomie, to make me understand easily all the problems of humane generation. I have entered in Socialist Partie since I am fourteen years old, and thinking that the ## most necessary in these moments is to expose to workmen the problem #####################[3] of their great families which they have created in their inconscience. I beng[4] a work of divulgation writing three pamphlets, the first of them untitled: "Eugenic problem", the second: "Birth Control" and the third "Sexual Education". I intend to do inmediately the second edition of these three works that have been very diffused among workmen as was my desire. After this, I began to give some conferences over this same problem that have moved special attention of people, and which I intend to continue among us in the next month. After this, Mr. Javier Morata* which with Aguilar* – whom you will surely know for he has impressed[5] in Spain the extraordinary book: "Sex in civilisation", whose preface is yours – are the best editors which preoccupy themselves over sexual problems, begged of me a book where I exposed my points of view over love, marriage and familie. And I wrote: "The Sexual Problem studied by a Spanish woman" a big book, whose prize [6] is a dollar, which was put on sale in August, and is finishing itself.[7] Today Mr. Morata publishes another book of mine particularly endowed to new generatin, titled: "Sexual Revolt of Youth" a bit dearer than the other. I have read with special interest your works, specially the formidable ones over the Psychologie of Sex, and I find that your assurances are all true, though in Spain we think that situation here is different from that in England and other parts of world. I find that all the men of past generation, as Marañón, Jiménez de Asúa, etc – observe before this problema[8] reactionary attitude, and I think that it is own[9] to the horrible weight of twenty centuries ########[10] christianisme, that have made their consciences a grudge, and that force them to maintain the old attitudes as the natural correspondence with their marriages and families constitued following the canonical law which has mantained so many inmoral purchases. My position is thus here a revolutionary one. They find that I am very valiant, they admire themselves to find that a girl has much more courage to enterprise a mouvement in that sense than they, and I find so accomplished that the points of view of old and new generation are fully opposed.[11]

Thanks be given that they observe a comprensive attitude for our desires and don't oppose to them the critic[12] which always accompany our work, and which you have experienced in London, when you had to go to New-York to put in press your great work. Besides that, I have published two other books, all in this year one untitled: "Sex and Love" and other: "Sexual Revolution". I cannot send you one of each as would be my desire, for as they are published by editors, I Have very small number of books, and I cannot dispose of them. One of these days will appear another, that is titled: "Profilaxia Anticoncepcional. Voluntary Parenthood" in which I try, founded in the silence of actual laws over this point, and the natural liberalitie of republican gouvernment[13] to make a divulgation of most used contraconceptives. I remember the tragical cases which you expose in your book which would be exemplar for Humanekind if she had a little more sense.

You see what my work is. I am reading a great quantity of books over sexual things. Lindsey, Forel, Bloch, Van de Velde, Ellen Key, Marie Stopes, Kollontay, Renato Kohl, Sanger, and a lot of several others.[14] But the special motive of my writing to you is to beg your help for me in the work which I have enterprised. I would desire to know the laws, the propositions, the ideas and the books which are given to publicity in all countries but specially in England where you can so well know the developpement of people in this interesting object.

I that admire you so profoundly, by the great work which you have developped would desire that you would explain me the creation and accord taken by that Ligue of Sexual Reform, of which you are president in England's name, and whichosever things you would judge interesting for my work, with the only finalitie[15] that I can make my books advance with international mouvement in all the world. I hope to be so your pupil though at a great distance. Perhaps on next year I will go to England and in this case I will try to know you, as I already can by your works.

Young people are here interested by this problem. After several years pass you will be astonished to find Spanish revolt[16], and you will help a great deal to it, if you can lend me some notices and details which you would judge interesting to be know in Spain. I can write books and articles in daily Press, so that the work of divulgation is for me very easy. Hurra for you that so well understand our wishes. And hoping to receive soon your answers, I remain yours sincerely true friend and pupil.

Hildegart

I would be very grateful to you if you would send the letter that I include to Miss. Ellen Key, for you speak very much of her in all your works, but in Spain we don't know her save by several morsels of her books.

MISS HILDEGART
LAWYER
GALILEO=45=4º=derecha.
MADRID. SPAIN.

23.10.1931

2. Dated 23 October 1931 [folios 4–6][17]

Miss. ELLEN KEY.

First of all I must do[18] to the first woman which in Sweden[19] began to expose the new ideas over sexual problem, a small history. And as I know that you read with special interest all letters of youths, though this be perhaps a little longer than others you receive, I beg of you moust sincerely to lend it a bit of your attention, for I am a girl, my age is sixteen years and I am Spanish, three things which I expose first as my only racommandation to you.

Though my age is not great, I have finished my lawyer proffesion on September of this year, and I am studying Philosophy and Medicine. I cannot notwithstanding, work as a lawyer, because I have not legal age, and until I am twenty one years old, law does not allow me to work in public, but I intend to profit these years in learning specially in these three proffessions, which I have selected and in visiting other nations, so as to know their laws and habitudes.

The studies which I have received were the sufficient in Physiologie and Anatomie to make me understand easily all the problems of humane generation[20]. I have entered in Socialist Partie since I am fourteen years old, and thinking of their great families which they create in their inconscience, I began a work of divulgation, writing three pamphlets, the first of them untitled: "Eugenic Problem", the second: "Birth Control", and the third: "Sexual Education". I intend to do inmediately the second edition of these three works that have been very diffused among workmen as was my desire. After this, I began to give some conferences over this same problem that have moved special attention of people, and which I intend to continue among us in the next month. After this, Mr. Javier Morata, which with Aguilar – in one of whose books untitled: "The Sex in Humane Civilisation" appears and endowing to you and other women like you – are the best editors which preoccupy themselves over sexual problems, begged of me a book where I exposed my point of view over love, marriage and family. And i wrote: "The Sexual Problem studied by a spanish woman", a large book whose prize is a dollar, which was put on sale in August, and is finishing itself. Now, Mr. Morata publishes another book of mine, particularly endowed to new genetation, titled: "Sexual Revolt of Youth" where I speak of your interesting works, a bit dearer than the other. I have read with special interest the part of your works which I know, and I find that your assurances are all true, though in Spain we think that situation here is different from that of Europe. I find that all the men of past generation, as Marañón, Jiménez de Asúa, etc. observe before this problem a reactionary attitude, and I think that it is own to the horrible weight of twenty centuries of christianisme, and capitalist regime, that have made their consciences a grudge, and that force them to maintain the old attitudes as the natural correspondence with their marriages and families constitued following the canonical law which has mantained so many inmoral purchases.

My position is thus here a revolutionary one. They find that I am very valiant, they admire themselves to find that a girl has much more courage to enterprise a mouvement in that sense than they, and I find so accomplished that the points of view of old and new generation are fully opposed. Thanks be given that they observe a comprensive attitude for our desires, and don't oppose to them the critic[21] which always accompanies our work. Besides that I have published to[22] other books, all in this year, one untitled: "Sex and Love" and other "Sexual Revolution". I cannot send you one of each, for as they are published by an editor, I have very small number of books and I cannot dispose of them. One of these days will appear another, that is titled, "Profilaxia anticoncepcional. Voluntary Parenthood" in which I try, founded in the silence of actual laws over this point and the natural liberalitie of reublican[23] gouvernment to make a divulgation of most used contraconceptives. I remember the tragical cases which you expose, which would be exemplar for Humane Kind if she had a little more sense.

You see what my work is. I am reading a great quantity of books over sexual things. Havelock Ellis, Lind[s]ey, Forel, Bloch, Van de Velde, Marie Stopes, Kollontai, Renato Kohl and a lot of several others.[24]

But the special motive of my writing to you is to beg your help for me in the work which I have enterprised. You know well the interest that I have in knowing the law, the propositions, the ideas and the books which are given to publicity in all countries but specially in United States of America and in England where you can so well know the developpement of people in this interesting object.

I that admire you so profoundly by the great work which you have developped would desire that you would explain me the creation and accord taken by this movement in England[25], with the only finalitie that I can so make my books advance with international movement in all the world. I hope to be so your pupil though at a great distance. Perhaps on next year I will go to Europe and in this case if it is possible for me, I will try to know you.[26]

Sweden movement is here fully unknown, and your works, as they have not been translated in Spanish are not known here. ¿Could you say me if there is any transnaltion[27] in English or French in which I could read them.? Because I only know you through the great work of Havelock Ellis: "Etudies over the psychologie of sex", but I could not though[28] all my efforts acquire one of your original works.

Young people are here interested by this problem. After several years pass you will be astonished to find Spanish revolt, and you will help a great deal to it, if you can lend me some notices and details which you would judge interesting to be known in Spain. I can write books and articles in daily Press so that the work of divulgation is for me very easy. Hurra for you that so well understand our wishes. And hoping to receive soon your anwsers,[29] I remain yours sincerely true friend and pupil

Hildegart

MISS. HILDEGART.
LAWYER.
GALILEO, 45, 4º, derecha.
MADRID.
SPAIN.

3. Dated 2 December 1931 [folios 8–10v]

Mr. Havelock Ellis.

Querido maestro:

Voy a cumplir ante todo su deseo de que le diga todo lo que me sea posible sobre mí. Nací el día 9 de Diciembre de 1914, y soy una hija eugénica, esto es, no inconsciente. Mi madre se quedó huérfana de padre cuando tenía 30 años, y un año después deliberadamente vine yo al mundo. De mi educación física le puedo dar a Vd. una idea, diciéndole que hasta los siete meses estuve acostada en mi coche cuna y que a los once meses, sin que antes hubiera puesto los pies en el suelo, me puso mi madre a andar y eché a correr sin la menor dificultad y tropiezo. Me he criado sin ninguna enfermedad. Hoy mido un metro setenta centímetros y peso ochenta kilos. Soy de complexión muy fuerte y a pesar de mi peso no soy nada linfática. Tengo el pelo en tirabuzones – un poco más largos de como están en el retrato que data de hace tres meses – y tanto los tirabuzones como los ojos son negros.

En cuanto a vida intelectual se refiere, a los once meses conocía el alfabeto en un "rompecabezas" (puzzle) de varias piezas en que figuraban las letras en colores y con ellas formaba palabras de dos y tres sílabas. A los veintidós meses leía de corrido. Antes de los tres años escribía y como desde los dos años he leído mucho empecé a formarme una excelente ortografía, lo que me permitió obtener cuando tenía cuatro años el título de mecanografía en la Casa Underwood sita en Madrid en la calle de Alcalá 39. Después empecé a estudiar, pero sin ir jamás al colegio. Mi madre se ocupó de iniciarme sexualmente. Recuerdo que cuando tenía tres años, aprendiendo por entonces la historia natural, sabía que la rosa era "hermafrodita" esto es como decía macho y hembra a un tiempo. Teníamos nosotros una de las criadas que se llamaba Rosa y el mismo día en que aprendí esa lección corrí junto a ella y le dije a bocajarro: "Rosa, tú eres hermafrodita". Era ella ya de alguna edad y no comprendió, pero extrañada me preguntó qué era aquello. Le contesté ingenuamente que era macho y hembra a un tiempo. Y como Vd. puede figurarse armó un escándalo. Nadie pensaba por aquel entonces en España en ninguno de estos apasionantes problemas de iniciación sexual. Hasta los tres años viví en un hotel con un precioso jardín y rodeada de animales y flores, que siguen siendo ahora mi mayor debilidad.

Después obligada por mis estudios tengo que vivir en la capital, pero en uno de los barrios más sanos, cercanos al Parque del Oeste, y con una azotea – mi casa tiene siete pisos – cuya terraza tengo convertida en jardín por el gran numero de macetas que tengo en ella.

A los diez años entré en el Instituto de 2ª enseñanza, ya que hasta entonces no me fue posible a cursar el Bachillerato. Consta éste de siete años y Reválida. Pero cuando contaba trece años pude ingresar en la Universidad y empecé a seguir la carrera de Filosofía y Letras. Me interesó más la de abogado, y a pesar de que consta de cinco años, la he terminado ahora cuando no contaba mas que diez y seis años, estoy estudiando tercero de la de Filosofía y Letras, y Medicina.

En cuanto a mi vida literaria, empecé acudiendo a todos los certámenes y concursos literarios, donde siempre obtuve premio. Recuerdo que cuando tenía doce años planeé e hice bastante capítulos de un libro de Psicología que era la ciencia que en su aspecto experimental más me apasionaba por entonces. También hice una traducción de un libro latino del que sólo hay tres o cuatro ejemplares en las Bibliotecas de todo el mundo, un libro de Fox Morcillo, el filósofo español titulado: "De Naturae Philosophia seu de Platonis et

Aristotelis relatione".³⁰ El latín lo conozco y lo traduzco con mucha facilidad. Conozco bien el inglés y el francés y puedo traducir el portugués y el italiano, y el alemán.

He cursado también la carrera de piano, que ya tengo terminada, y me entusiasma la música. Y tengo publicadas nueve obras.

"Tres Amores Históricos. Romeo y Julieta. Abelardo y Heloísa y los Amantes de Teruel".
"El Problema Eugénico".
"La Limitación de la Prole".
"Educación Sexual".
"Sexo y Amor".
"El Problema Sexual tratado por una mujer española".
"La Rebeldía Sexual de la Juventud".
"Revolución Sexual".
"Profilaxis Anticoncepcional. Paternidad Voluntaria".³¹

Esta última obra de la que le remito un ejemplar ha tenido un éxito enorme. Hace ocho días que se ha publicado y se han vendido en Madrid dos mil ejemplares. En Barcelona se hará una edición especial. Entre nosotros representa una gran difusión por el tema tratado y por el precio bastante reducido.

Esto es cuanto tenía que decirle sobre mi vida. ¿Qué le parece?

Ahora voy a pedirle un favor. Estoy cursando el doctorado de la Facultad de Derecho y he de hacer con el Sr. Saldaña a quien Vd. conocerá seguramente por ser uno de los pocos autores que en España han tratado la materia sexual, una memoria sobre: "Criminología Sexual" (Los delitos sexuales). El Dr. Chiavacci* me ha enviado un extracto de los artículos del Código penal austríaco sobre el tema sexual. Yo deseaba saber qué disposiciones hay en Inglaterra en torno a los delitos sexuales, y si le es posible a Vd. hablar e escribir a Leunbach, cuáles son las disposiciones que hay en su país. Asimismo le agradecería me indicara qué folletos, libros, o sociedades se han encargado de tratar de este tema, ya que cuantos más datos reuna más interesante ha de ser la memoria. Me interesan todos los temas sexuales, pero en particular: "Eugénica" – "Birth Control" (he recibido las dos revistas que leeré con gran interés) y "Delitos Sexuales".

Asimismo quisiera hacerle una pregunta. ¿Cómo nació la Weltliga? ¿Quién la inició? ¿Ha publicado algún trabajo en que se resuma la labor de su Congreso o las iniciativas de la campaña por ella emprendida?

Recibí su interesante libro italiano, y le agradecería infinito que me proporcionara Vd. todos los datos que le fueran posibles en torno a las preguntas que le he hecho. Muchas gracias por el interés que se ha tomado conmigo hablando de mí a Leunbach y a Margaret Sanger. Reciba un afectuosísimo saludo de su discípula española.

Hildegart

HILDEGART.
ABOGADO.
GALILEO 45, 4º, derecha.
MADRID.
ESPANA.
=2=12=3[]

La obra sobre "Estudios de Psicología Sexual" publicada por Vd. la tengo en español: pero no consta más que de seis tomos, el último titulado " El Sexo en relación con la sociedad" ¿Ha publicado Vd. algún apéndice más sobre este mismo tema? La obra aquí en inglés es carísima, pues mientras la edición española asciende a 74 pesetas, la inglesa sube a 60 pesetas como mínimo si no asciende por las oscilaciones de la libra y la peseta.

Hilde

Mi nombre es Hildegart. No es seudónimo sino nombre laico. Es una composición alemana de "Hilde" (sabiduría) y Gart (jardín), esto es jardín de sabiduría (wisdom's garden). Hoy es un nombre bastante conocido en España tanto por mi actividad literaria como política, pues llevo tres años militando en el Partido Socialista donde he desarrollado una intensísima campaña, ya que escribo artículos en la prensa y doy "meetings" y conferencias, pues tengo gran facilidad de palabra.

Hilde

[Mr Havelock Ellis.

Dear Master:

First of all I shall do as you request and tell you everything possible about myself. I was born on 9 December 1914, and I am a eugenic child, that is, not unintentional. My mother lost her father when she was 30, and a year later I chose to come into the world. I can give you some idea of my physical development by telling you that until the age of seven months I lay in my pram, and that at eleven months, when I had never put my feet on the floor before, my mother started me walking, and I began to run without any difficulty or stumbling. I grew up free from illness. Today I am a metre seventy tall and I weigh eighty kilos. I have a strong constitution and despite my weight I'm not at all anaemic. My hair is in ringlets – a bit longer than they are in my picture which was taken three months ago – and both my ringlets and my eyes are black.

As far as intellectual life is concerned, by eleven months I knew the alphabet through a puzzle which had different parts and which had letters in colour, and I was able to form words of two or three syllables. At twenty-two months I read fluently. Before I was three I could write, and since I have read much since the age of two I began to attain an excellent level of spelling, which meant that when I was four I was able to get a typing qualification at Underwoods, situated in Madrid, Alcalá 39. Then I began my studies, but without ever attending school. My mother took it upon herself to give me my sexual education. I remember that when I was three, and at that time learning natural history, I knew that the rose was 'hermaphrodite', meaning that it was both male and female at the same time. One of our maids was called Rosa and the same day that I learned this lesson I ran up to her and said to her without more ado, 'Rosa, you're hermaphrodite'. She was of some age and did not understand, but puzzled, asked me what that was. I innocently told her that it was male and female at the same time. You can imagine what an uproar this caused. In Spain at this time no one thought about any of these fascinating problems of sex education. Until I was three I lived in a villa with a lovely garden, surrounded by animals and flowers, which are still today my greatest weakness.

Since then I've had to live in the city itself because of my studies, but in one of the healthiest neighbourhoods, near the Western Park, and with a flat roof – my house is seven storeys high – and I've turned its terrace into a garden with the large number of pots I have there.

When I was ten I went into secondary school, to an Institute, since up to that point I had not been able to follow the studies of the Bachillerato. These take seven years, with a final examination. But when I was thirteen I was able to go to University and began my studies in Arts. I was more interested in studying Law, and although this course takes five years, I have finished it now, being only sixteen. I'm now in the third year of studying Arts, and also studying Medicine.

As far as my literary life is concerned, I began to take part in all the contests and competitions, and always won a prize. I remember that when I was twelve I planned and wrote a good number of chapters of a book of Psychology, which was the scientific subject which most aroused my enthusiasm then, because of its experimental aspect. I also translated a Latin book of which there are only three of four copies in all the Libraries in the world, a book by Fox Morcillo, the Spanish philosopher, entitled: "De Naturae Philosophia seu de Platonis et Aristotelis relatione". I know Latin and translate it with great ease. I know English and French, and can translate Portuguese, and Italian and German.

I have also completed studies in piano, and love music. And I have published nine works.

Three Historic Loves. Romeo and Juliet. Abelard and Heloïse and the Lovers of Teruel.
The Eugenic Problem
Limiting Offspring
Sexual Education
Sex and Love
The Sexual Problem Discussed by a Spanish Woman
The Sexual Rebellion of Youth
Sexual Revolution
Contraceptive Prophylaxis: Voluntary Fatherhood

The last of these, of which I am sending you a copy, has been enormously successful. I am working for my doctorate in the Faculty of Law, and under Sr Saldaña who you no doubt know as he is one of the few authors in Spain to have dealt with sexual matters, I'm working on a paper on "Sexual Criminology" (on sexual crimes). Dr Chiavacci has sent me an extract of the articles of the Austrian penal code that deal with sex. I wanted to know what provisions there are in England relating to sexual crimes, and, if you were able to speak and write to Leunbach, to know what provisions there are in his country. I would also be grateful if you could tell me which pamphlets, books or societies have taken on dealing with this topic, as the more information I can put together the more interesting my paper will be. I am interested in all topics relating to sex, but in particular in "Eugenics" – "Birth Control" (I have received the two journals[32] and will read them with great interest) and "Sexual Crimes".

I would also like to ask you a question. How did the World League come into being? Who initiated it? Have you published any work that makes a resume of the work of its Congress or the initiatives of the campaign it has begun?

I have received your interesting Italian book, and I would be infinitely grateful if you could give me all the information you can in response to the questions I have posed you. Many thanks for the interest you have taken in me, talking of me to Leunbach and Margaret Sanger. Most affectionate greetings from your Spanish pupil

Hildegart

HILDEGART
LAWYER
GALILEO 45, 4º, derecha. MADRID. SPAIN

2 December 1931

I have the Spanish version of your work, *Studies in the Psychology of Sex*, but it only has six volumes, the last of them entitled, 'Sex in Relation to Society'. Have you published some further appendix on this topic? Here the English version is really expensive, because while the Spanish edition costs as much as 74 pesetas, the English one is at least 60 pesetas minimum (or more according to the movement of the pound and the peseta).

Hilde

My name is Hildegart. This isn't a pseudonym but a secular name. It is made up of the German words "Hilde" (wisdom) and Gart (garden), making garden of wisdom (Wisdom's Garden). The name is fairly well known in Spain now, both for my literary activity and work in politics, as I have been working now for three years in the Socialist Party where I have been engaged in a really intense campaign, writing articles in the press and holding "meetings" and giving lectures, as I find speaking very easy.

Hilde]

4. Dated 5 January 1932 [folios 11–16]

Mr. Havelock Ellis.
LONDON.

Dear Dr. Havelock:

You cannot imagine yourself what a great pleasure I have had when I received your letter. Today, I have had a sort of holiday for with these changes of weather, I have caught a cough, and so I am going to write to you a long, long letter.
    First of all, I will continue to tell you whatever I think interesting for you to be known of me and of Spain. You tell me that my mother is wonderful. You can well say so. When I was born she was thirty-one years old, and now she is forty eight years old, but is strong and youthful. She goes with me everywhere, and is my full and absolute companion. Her sight is not good, because of having spoiled it reading in not very good conditions, but she observes wonderfully the inner part of people, and is for me an excelent counsellor. She has advised me not to tell you anything about herself – she is so very modest – but I don't accept this forbearance, for if she had not trained me, specially in sexual problems, I could not at my age know such a great quantity of these things. You see, I am the product of a "matriarcado" following perhaps the "Mutter-recht" de [*sic*] Bachofen,[33] because nothing but her influence has been felt by me, and I am absolutely a complete work of herself.
    Secondly. What refers to my name. Munmy knew that there was in Germany (Baviera) the Santa Hildegard of which you speak to us.[34] But my name is not hers. My aunt had travelled a great deal in Germany, and spoke german very well, so my Munmy asked her to give her

several words in which there was something referent to health, wisdom, flowers, etc. for she thought that names would influde[35] in my formation, and as she tried during my gestation not to read anything refferring to war – as you know I was born in December of 1914 and during this year Great War had exploded – so as not to influde in my feelings and nervous system, she thought that name would be a great improvement for me. My aunt gave her several words and between them she selected two – "hilde", – "held" (wisdom and beauty too) and "gart" (garden). As german construction is the contrary to Spanish one, she made so "Hilde-gart" (garden of wisdom) and then she thought of no other name for me. So you will explain yourself that puzzle of my name. I am not baptised, and I have never had any religious ideas. ¿Do you explain yourself now what you asked me? ¿What do you think of it?

I am glad you like my portrait. In every one I do of myself, I appear very mature, but it is not my fault you know. But if I don't photo my face but my body also, effect is perhaps worst. Imagine yourself what I told you in past letter. I am nearly a meter and seventy centimeters hight, and I weigh seventy eight kilograms. So that I appear as a splendent woman. If it were not for my hair, my corsckrewes[36] are much longer than most in the portrait appear and we can only use this combing[37] here until we are twenty years old, people would not judgue of my age, save in my conversation and manners, and perhaps in my little experience of life. If it were not for my Munmy, I confide in everybody and that, as you know is always perilous.

You cannot imagine what a pleasure we have had when we received your photo. You look so nice in it. I had several others, in the book which you sent me. In the translation of your works what Reus has done, there is one.[38] Another in: "L'Scopo dell'Eugenica"[39] in which you have a wonderful head, for the "studio" of a painter, and another in one of the pamphlets which you sent me about you, but in this last one although so small, to see your figure so arrogant and virile and your white hairs, is a pleasure for sight. I have shown it to my particular friends and all are charmed of you. I will put it in my writing table, with a beautiful picture frame.

I have received too your pamphlet of George Ives*[40] and I am very grateful to you for it. You don't know how very grateful for several reasons. Morata that is my editor has begged of me three new books for these two past have been a great success. The first that I am doing now is untitled: "Malthusianism and neo-malthusianism". The second, I have not yet thought the title, but it will be a study of homosexuality between men. I think if will be somethink like "The prostitution between men" or a similar title. And the third which is the study which I am doing as a "doctoral thesis" over Sexual Criminologie" a very big book which will not be published until ####Autum.

I must speak to you of my second book,[41] because it will have a special interest in Spain. Reasons because I will study the cases of a great deal of our political principal figures, without telling their names, but as their cases are very well known it will be a great succes and a exemplarity too. I will tell you several of these cases. Our President, Mr.

Alcalá Zamora, and our Labour Minister,[42]. Mr Largo Caballero. (I don't know if in English Press was published a very curious fact over these two. When they were imprisoned during the first months of this year, one night there was a telephonic calling for Mr. Alcalá Zamora. An employer came to advise him## and as it was a very strange calling and at such hours – at two o'clock in the morning – two others accompanied him, and were astonished to find in the same "celda"[43] of Mr. Alcalá Zamora, to Mr. Largo Caballero.[44] They went to telephone and could not speak for communication was suddenly cut. The two explained it next day in political press saying that gouverment had intended to apply Mr. Alcalá Zamora the tragical "ley de fugas"[45] –do you know what this is?, to say that the prisoner has intented to escape although it is not true and kill him by the back, and Mr. Alcalá Zamora told that thanks to the presence of his great friend Mr. Largo Caballero whose "cell" – he told – was near, when this is not true, for it was in an opposite gallery and I have visited them several times, he would have been killed. Monarchic gouvernement was astonished, because he had not the least intentions to lill[46] Mr. Alcalá Zamora, for it would have been the inmediate sign for revolution in Spain, several investigations were made; soon it was known that the telephonic calling was fully intentioned, by several "comunist" that had their meetings in a popular "bar" and that knew by a prison's official that every night, Mr. Largo Caballero went to the cell of Mr. Alcalá Zamora and wished to give a public impression of it). Well, another pair, is our Lord Mayor, Mr. Rico[47], and the first "teniente de alcalde" that is to say, the one that follows the Major in representation Mr. Saborit.[48] People calls them the "Major" and the "Mayoress". (These four are all married). There is also our President or Lord First Minister, Mr. Azaña. This is rather a monstruous case. He has several relations with Mr Casares Quiroga (Gouvernation Ministry), Marcelino Domingo*, Agriculture and Industry Ministry) and Zulueta, the recently appointed for the International Relations Ministry. Besides that he has had a long "frinedship"[49] with Mr. Rivas Cherif*, actually artistic director of a theatre, and with whom there must have been a great familiar disease.[50] Mr Azaña is now married with a sister of that Mr. Rivas Cherif, but has no sons[51] whatever.[52] That must explain you what has happened. I am studying this case with great interest but it is one of the most monstruous one.

Besides there is another minister, the charged of Justice (I am writing to you following the denomination of our Ministers in Spain that are very different between you) – that is very strange. You will have surely heard of our Penal Director. She is a woman. She is called Victoria Kent*. Well, she lives with another woman, Julia Irureta Goyena*[53] during several years and as I can know in lesbic relations. Well. Albornow[54] that is a widow with a daughter maintains relations with the two. ¿Don't you think it strange? I have been reading your book over "Sexual Inversion" and I can't find a full explanation for It. But as I am studying the case and trying to apile materials so as to judge, when I have these cases finished I will tell you in several letters some of the small things that I judge decisive to know the character of these men and women.

But I have not finished yet. Mr. Galarza* that has been until last "crisis" Director of Policemen is known in public as "Madame. Rosita". Llopis*, the director of our Primary teaching, that is to say of our schools, is also a known homosexual of the passive kind. Jiménez Asúa, the lawyer also interested by sexual problems, and that is charged of the legislation of our new Republic is like Salazar Alonso*, the President of our Provincial Deputation, known as the "two princesses". They are both "ocassional" exactly as those poor and so ill treated "prostitutes" in our lupanars, or brothels.

Besides this, Clara Campoamor*, the other woman deputy is also a homosexual one. She lives with another woman, a german one, and I know her wince[55] I was very little and all her family.

I know many other cases in our literature world, and many others too in our political figures of second degree, of which I will speak to you in next letters. This will explain to you that our political situation is too so infirm, and that there happen so bloody facts between us. There are neither true men nor true women directing our country, so we can expect no more of them.

All these cases that I am studying will appear in my next book. So that when you ever think that there is anything interesting for me to be know over whichsoever of these three problems which I am going to study in my books, I would be very grateful to you if you send it to me.

I have not received yet your book. But that does not matter. I know that it was published in April of 1928. I went to speak with Casa Reus, that has published your first ones, and they have told me that they think there will be no inconvenient for publishing this other, and they only wish you to send me the conditions in which you would let it for Spain, for they don't remember past ones, and because perhaps you could have changed your opinion. ¿Could you then send me these conditions soon? For you know, they have to submitt them to study, and as translation always requires a bit of time, we must have all made quick. I will be very glad indeed to translate it, and I thank you very much for begging of me to do it. I will try to do it with full care and with my very best wishes.

I have received a letter from Miss Sanger*[56] and some pamphlets. I will anwser to her perhaps tomorrow. I have to make her a charge to send me several books, and among them this of which you speak to me: "My fight for brth[57] control" ant[58] others which she has collected in a small pamphlet with a very useful Bibliography. I am very grateful to her, and to you.

I send you know[59] another of my books, and one of the reffences of one of the conferences[60] which I have given. I have a great easiness of speach, and I give hear a great deal of conferences. In our socialist party, the richer of societys and the most powerful is that of masonry. Her capital is of several millions, and her number of members is great. Between all of them I have a great opinion. They call me their "red Virgin" and others the "good hit or best chance of Nature". And I give them always a great deal of conferences. I will give them in this year several "sexual conferences" of which I will speak to you in the next letter.

Now I hope that I have written a long long letter. So I must close. I thank you very much for your news about the League. Of what you tell me of Hirschfeld, I am glad. I have always had a great sympathy for jews. (You know Karl Marx was also a jew). I also like very much Leunbach letters and opinions.

So with the best wishes for the new year, receive my most affectionate greetings.

Hildegart

HILDEGART.
LAWYER.
GALILEO=45=4º=derecha
MADRID.
SPAIN.
=5=1=1932

I will send you soon several photographs and newspapers of Spain so that you can judge of the true of my opinions over our political.[61]

Hilde

Postscript dated 8 January 1932 [folio 16]

The conferences that I am giving actually in our theatre are over the following themes:

"¿DID JESUSCRIST EXIST?"
"¿HERENCE AND PHYSIOLOGIE OF JESUS"
"THE INTELLIGENCE AND THE DELIRIUM OF JESUS"
"THE AMORALITY OF JESUS".
"DIAGNOSTIC OF JESUS MADNESS".

I have received your beautiful book. It is very very nice. I am reading it at a high speed. Besides I am translating it already. Thanks very much.

Although it is against regulations, I cannot be silent. So I had to write these few words. ¿Do you pardon me? It[62] not I will cry a bit but I can't help it. It is superior to my energies.

Today. =8=1=32=[63]

5. Dated 8 February 1932 [folio 17]

Dr. Havelock Ellis,

Dear Dr. Havellock:

Only a few lines for I am working hard. On this week we will have the first meeting of W. L. S. R. in Spain.[64] There are thirty three persons and all of them physician, lawyers, teachers and writers that have a deep interest for sexual problems. We will form seven sections. One of Sexual Education. Another of Feminism and Marriage. A third one of Birth Control. A fourth of Eugenics. A fifth of Prostitution and prevention of Venereal Diseases. A sixth of Rational attitude before sexual inversion, and a seventh of legislation formed by the lawyers and preferently members of Parliament so as to make a good legislative labour. The president will be Marañón, that is as you know the best authoritie in Spain. One of the vicepresidents will be Jiménez de Asúa, that is the charged by Parliament to do all the legislative work of Republic and that will be very useful. Besides the Director of Public Heath Department that is socialist too and very charmed with these problems will help infforming the Government favourably to dispositions of public health that favours our establishment. We too have an editor, that will publish a review and severwl[65] works. I am sending you one of the works published already by this editor of one of the members of our League, Mr. Bugallo, that is as you will see very interesting for it is a full program of teaching of sexual life in schools. Besides I am trying to form a section in Valencia, and another probably in Barcelona.

You see I am working hard. I have spoken with Reus. On next week he aill[66] give me a definite anwser over your book. I will say you what happens next officially, for I think I can be the secretary of the League here, for I know several languages and I have greater time to spend on it than my other companions. I will form a section of Propagand and public diffusion, and we will make it very intensively. A great deal of thanks for all, and I remain

Yours sincerely

Hildegart

=8=2=32=
MISS HILDEGART.
LAWYER.
GALILEO=45=4º=derecha
MADRID. SPAIN.

6. Dated March 1932 [folio 18]

Dr. Havelock Ellis.

Dear Dr. Havelock:

You see I promised that I would write inmediately that we had celebrated our first meeting. So I am going to fulfil my promise. I am sending you a copy of the paper that I read in the first meeting and what happened in it. You see, Marañón was appointed President and I am already the Secretary. We are forming a catalunian section and another one in Valencia, another in Bilbao and in Asturias. I will go to Asturias on next week after this and I will remain there a week giving several lectures in the Ateneos, Universities, etc. I will send you some refferences over them.

    We are going to visit our First Minister so that he gives us a local[67] and perhaps a subvention too from the State. As there are in our League a great number of Parliament members, we hope to have a great success. Dr. Leunbach wrote to me saying that Congress in Paris was rather difficult, and that he advanced to me that if Spain would officially invite them, Congress could take place in Madrid in June of this year. We have studied with great interest this point. On June it will be impossible for me, for besides we are only constituting our League and we hope to make it each time greater, weather will be very scorching for all of you. We have acceeded[68] that Congress could take place in October. On next month, I will write to you officially with the invitation for the month of October. I would be very grateful if you could come on this month, for I have a great wishes to see you and Marañón is charmed with the idea, and we will be all sorely disappointed if you could not wait till October. Time[69] will be then wonderful in Spain and we would be all very happy to see you all.

    Besides I am sending you some of the first pamphlets that we have sent to all our members. We are already fourty, but these are only the founders. But we hope to be a hundred next month. I am sending you some slips of papaers where some news of our League have appeared. Bulletin or the Review of our League will be published perhaps on April or May. I will send you some numbers of it, for I will be his director. ¿Could you send us a work of yours for it? Don't mind if it is in English, but we would be charmed to receive it. I have received your wonderful letter and the slip of New York's newspaper with the letter of that german boy. I cannot say you how grateful I am for all your good wishes.

    Reus has told me to speak to him tomorrow. I don't know if he will acept. If that is not possible, it is nearly sure that Mr. Morata, the editor of our League, the best editor in Spain, the only one that is not topsy-turvy for all the editor houses save his are passing a very difficult moment, will perhaps do it. He is now finishing the translation of the work of Malinowsky, "Sexual life among Savages"[70] and we have spoken too of your lovely book.

A great deal of thanks and good wishes for you. And I remain

Yours sincerely

Hildegart

=[?]=3=32=
Miss Hildegart.
Lawyer.
Galileo=45=4º=
MADRID.
[The Liga foundation document was included with this letter.]

7. Dated 19 March 1932 [folios 40–2]

Dr. Havelock Ellis.

Dear Dr. Havelock:

Before beginning my letter, I must say to you that you ######[71] I am very very grateful to you for the lovely present of your book. I have read it all already and I think it is really wonderful. I am very interested in it, and in one of my next letters, I will make you some questions over some of the problems that you study in it. Besides, I received your magazine, and you cannot imagine how happy I was and my mother too when we read what you spoke of Spain and of me.[72] So that I cannot give you thanks, for I would have to be expressing my gratitude a long time.

Of what you speak of "The Eugenic Problem" my small pamphlet, you must know that it was written when I was only fourteen years old, and published when I was fifteen.[73] I had not read then many books over sexual problems, and it was my first incursion in those new fields, so that I was not very sure then. I had only read Marañón works by that time, and I was interested in the problems, though I had yet no scientific preparation for them. Besides, I had not studied Greek then, and only Latin, for I had a great interest in that dead language, and I did not know as I know now the true origin of "homosexuality" neither its true meaning, nor the idea or[74] Carpenter* "homogenic love"[75] that I think would be very interesting and suitable. But I like very much that you would say to me what you think that is wrong in my books, for it will make me progress, and I will be very grateful to you for it.

The work for me is rather difficult in Spain. You see we have a great reaction of Catholic people, and they all marvh[76] against republican government and republican work, and againsta[77] all liberal principles. You may have read in English newspapers what has happened in our University. We are in a full civil ear[78] between the students, and that is horrible for all of us. Well, this same reaction makes my work very difficult. I have to fight a great deal and with a great number of people. The work of our League will be good when this time passes. Spain is not yet as many people think, judging that we have done our revolution. That is not true. Revolution is not yet done, and we are passing a very difficult movement. Besides, there is not sufficient money in the State, and Spain is poor. You tell me that Marañón is an ideal President. I think so too. But I have to be always behind him, pushing him to go forwards. He has a great interest for all these things, but he has a great deal of things to do, and some great quantity of preoccupied sense of "the other opinions". That is very disagreable for all of us. Thanks that he is a good friend of mine, and I can push him continuously. But, objections and small quarrels with all public opinion are already usual. With one of the members of our League Dr. Sanchis Banús*, a great psychiatric, and socialist too, I had a small fight. He told to me that one of the postulates of the League was anarchic, for vov[79] spoke of delivering marriage and specially divorce from the Church and the State's tiranny. He told me that we could not speak of tyranny of the State, for we were free lovers of the State and that if I maintained that point of view, I was an anarchist. I had to anweser him, expressing what has happened in Russia, with the phrases of Karl Krautsky*[80] one of our most eminent leaders, saying that in a well organised society, neither the man nor the woman would need of a legal bond, and with some phrases of another member of the league and socialist too, Mr. Jiménez de Asúa that has always maintained this point of view saying that the State must not enter in the particular sphere of sexual life of two individuals, as he[81] doesn't enter into the sphere of friendship, for it is absolutely private whenever it has no bad or perilous consequences for the Sfate.[82] He is not convinced but at last he admitted the postulate. And so on. It is very dusagreable[83] to fight with the ignorance and the stupidness of a great deal of persons, but I don't break down. I am very healthy, and though I work a great deal, I do it with pleasure. You see, now since a week ago, I am working every day in my terrace, between my plants, and my birds, at full sun, with only a very small paper hat on my head, and with a very slight skirt on. I am of a dark complexion, but I will soon be as other summers, nearly as black as a niger. Besides, I eat well, I walk sufficiently, and I do a very healthy life.[84]

You cannot imagine yourself what a wonderful work I have displayed in Asturias. I am to return on the month of October, and to give 30 conferences, or lectures. You must know by this, how great the interest was arousen in all Asturias. I have given ten lectures, all over sexual problems. People was extremely interested. We had to speak before the radio, so that everybody could hear it from outside. In many of the cases, it was the first time that a person, not yet a woman had spoken to them over these problems, and they were astonished. I have arousen then a great deal of thoughs[85] and inquietudes,[86] and I hope that my work will be succesful. I am going to form a special section in Asturias of W. L. S. R. and I think they will go on beautifully. Today, I was to give another conference here in Madrid, organised by the F. U. E.[87] This is the most liberal association of students, that during Dictadura's time were the opposition to monarchic institutions. It was untitled: "The sexual poblem[88] before new pedagogia" and was endowed to the new teachers that are now studying their proffession in Madrid. Well, the Director of the School for training the teachers, that is Mrs Dolores Cebrián wife of one of our socialist leaders Mr. Besteiro was rather frightened before the theme and has suspended the conference. I don't mind for I will give this lecture in another place, but that is a signal to show you how difficult is fight in Spain. They don't decide to oppose freely and openly, but they put small stones in the way so as to make us fall.

Reus will not take your Eoniam book.[89] But I hope that Mr. Morata will take it. He anwsered me in the affirmatively when I spoke to him, though I did not accept inmediately for Reus had not anwsered yet. Mr. Morata is now one of the best editors of Spain. He has edited my big books, and Darwin's books in its Spanish translation and is now editing the book of Malinowsky over the savages of Trobriand's Island,[90] of which you speak os[91] often. In my next letter I will give you a definite anwser.

Now I must close, for I am wishing to sleep. I am writing to you nearly at one o'clock in the night, and I feel rather sleepy, so that I will continue to write to you over the work of our League in Spain, soon. We hope to have next meeting on next week, then I will write to you.

I have been reading the book of Margaret Sanger; "My fight for birth control".[92] She is a very darling woman, and she has proved very simpathetic for me. It is a lovely and piercing book. My fight here is not of that type, but perhaps for being smaller in degree is more difficult. We have not to fight against opposed laws, but agains envys and passions, and ruin persons, and that is generally worst.

Well, dear Dr. Havelock a great deal of thanks for your lovely present, for your remembers in the newspaper, and for everything in which you have been so wonderfully good for me. You are some sort of fairy god for all of us.[93]

I remain

Yours affectionately

Hildegart

Hernández Catá that is a very good friend of mine begs me to tell you that he knows you too and admires you very much. He has spoken a great deal to me over you. He sends you a great deal of good wishes. My mother too wishes you a happy year.

Vale

=19=3=32=
Srta. Hildegart.
Abogado.
Galileo=45=4º=derecha
MADRID.

8. Dated 30 March 1932 [folio 43]

Dr. Havelock Ellis.

Dear Dr. Havelock:

Don't you know where I am? Well. I am in Asturias in Oviedo and Mieres. I am working a great deal, for I am giving ten lectures over sexual problems in the Ateneos that are the best cultural centres in Spain. As you will see by some slips of paper, they are having a great success, and I am very happy for it. Your name is already known between all these people of Asturias for I speak a great deall of you, and they admire you all very much. I am here for a fortnight, for all are desiring to hear me, and I will return after our Congress takes place in October. Now I am writing in a very bad typewriting machine. So, please pardon me, but I have no other here. I am very, very grateful for your letters and your constant remember. Our League will march beautifully, and you will always know that it is because your[94] anwsered my first letter that I became interested and charmed with the proposition of doing some practical work in Spain.[95] Dr. Marañón is an ideal president. We are going to see the Minister of Public Instruction when I return to Madrid so as to beg of him some money from the State for our work. We will launch on beautifully.

    I cannot write you anything more today for I am very busy. These afternoon I give two lectures, one at a half past six, and another at a half past eight, so that I am doing a great effort. But I am very happy for it, and I don't mind to work. I am wishing a great deal that the month of October arrives and that you may come to Spain and that I can see you, and talk with you, and that you may see me too. We will all be very happy. You know that Spanish people are all very simpathethic, and my character is like some bells ringing, so that all the physicians and lawyers that have formed the League in Spain are charmed with me.[96]

    Until my next letter I remain

Yours truly

Hildegart

Miss Hildegart.
Lawyer.
Galileo =45=4º=derecha.
MADRID.
SPAIN.

8a Date presumed to be as above [folio 44]

Dear Dr. Havelock:

When any of your friends wants to come to Spain, will you be so dear as to give him one of the postcards I enclose. The hotel is a beautiful one, not dear, in the best place in Madrid and its owner a very good friend of mine. He is a jew too but a splendid one, and I want to help him anyway I can.

Hildegart

9. Dated 22 April 1932 [folios 47–8]

Dr. Havelock Ellis.

Dear Dr. Havellock:[97]

Next time I write to you, I will write officially and in official paper, for we have already formed our section and are hoping to get on. But I must not make you wait to say to you as a friend what I am going to say to Leunbach and Kauffman[98] as a secretary next week.

There is a bad new first. Government's help cannot come this year as a subvention for the Congress to take place in Spain. Until next year comes, nothing can be done in that sense, and we are as new, rather poor[99] to enterprise the Congress over our full and only responsibilitie. When the Congress could take place easily would be in May of next year. Then we could manage to have Government's support that we have not now by a very simple reason. In the month of October there are three congresses taking place in Spain, one of Otorrinolaringology, another of General Medicine also, and a postal[100] one, of which there will several thousand members coming to Spain. Besides as the Congresses in Spain are rather good for all, for there are a great deal of official meetings, dinners, and a good help and good wishes by the part of all the higher members of the State, a great number of people wish to have their Congresses in Spain. We have worked for long. Dr. Marañón and Jiménez de Asúa have worked with me in this, but it has been impossible, notwithstanding our great friendship with the Minister to make them help us with enough money in October. You can imagine yourself how sorry I was for it. You know how happy and interested I was to have Congress this year in Spain. You know too how I desired to know you all, and to work together. Dr. Marañón too was very interested, and you can well know that when we have to write to you to say you this, that it has been impossible, it is the mere truth and we can't help it though our wishes are great. The first members of the League (thirty five or thirty eight or forty) are only the most selected persons of Medical and Lawyers proffession. Now we will make the diffusion in whole, for everybody, and we hope to be a good number soon. How happy I would be if when you could come to Spain we would be a powerful section, with good elements, all desiring to receive and to greet you.

The commitee appointed is the following:

Presidents of Honour.	Don Santiago Ramón y Cajal. (doctor)
	Don Sebastián Recaséns. (doctor)
	Don Manuel Bartolomé Cossío. (teacher). He was appointed for the Republic's Presidence and did not accept.
President.	Dr. Marañón.
Vicepresident.	Dr. César Juarro[101]
	Mr. Ruiz Funes. (lawyer).
Secretary.	Hildegart. (Lawyer)
Treasurer.	Dr. Haro.

This last one is one of the younger but most intelligent doctors, very well known in Madrid and a great interested by sexual matters. Besides he is a pupil of Dr. Marañón and he is as I am a very good friend of him, so that we will form a good triangle for directing the League.

The other members of the Central Commitee are authomathically the presidents of the five sections constitued, and whose names are the following:

First section.	Eugenics. Dr Haro, Dr. Otaola, Dr. Sacristán.
Second Section.	Feminism and Marriage. Dr. Vital Aza, Dr. Macau, Dr. Sanchis Banús.
Third Section.	Prostitution and Venereal Diseases. Dr. Sánchez Covisa, Dr. Juarros, Dr. Sainz de Aja.
Fourth Section.	Sexual Education. Mr. Luis Huerta, Mr. Luis Blanco,[102] Mr. José Bugallo.
Fifth Section.	Legislation. Mr. Jiménez de Asúa, Mr. Saldaña, Mr. Ruiz Funes.

So that the members of the Central Commitee are Dr. Vital Aza, Dr. Sánchez Covisa, D. Luis Huerta, Mr. Jiménez de Asúa and in sustitution of Dr Haro, president of Eugenical section ans[103] that is already as treasurer in Central Commitee, Dr. Otaola. All of these are the most selected elements and we have several others that are as good or more than these and that will work with us in either of these sections.

We wre[104] forming sections in Bilbao and Santander already, and we hope to make a good work. We are hoping for the help of the State, from the Public Health Direction and from the Instruction Minister. The man that is appointed to be the future Minister of Public Health is one of the Presidents of Honour of our League, and the one that will be the true Minister, and that is the actual[105] director of Public Health, Dr. Marcelino Pascua*, is too a good member of our League. Elements are good, so I think that being always over them, as I have to be to make them move and act, we will make a good and profitable labour. If you wusg[106] to known something more about our members, I will write to you whatever you wish, and I am very, very sorry that our wishes so that Congress could take place this year have not been fulfilled. Couldn't you wait until next year, so that we would have the pleasure to know all of you and to greet you in our country? Pardon me for my requesting it again, but as it has not been our fault that it cannot take place this year and we are so sorely disappointed, we think that we must not pay for others and that we are not responsible so as to be let[107] without the great happiness that would be for all of us to see you.

I remain

Yours sincerely

Hildegart

=22=4=32=
Miss Hildegart.
Lawyer.
Galileo=45=4º=derecha.
MADRID.
SPAIN.

10. Dated 1 May 1932 [folio 49]

LIGA ESPAÑOLA PARA LA REFORMA SEXUAL SOBRE BASES CIENTIFICAS
Secretaria: Galileo, 45
Presidente: Dr. Marañón
Secretaria: Srta. Hildegart
Madrid, 1 de Mayo de 1932

Dr. Havelock Ellis.
LONDON.

Dear Dr. Havelock:

You don't know how happy I am. I told you in my past letter that next time I would write to you officially, and so it is. I am writing to you in my new sheet of paper, and it seems to me rather wonderful that the organisation of the Spanish League that I thought nearly impossible at the beginning could now have come to an end. You see I am glad and I am sorry too. And I will explain you why. I am glad because I have accomplished the first part of my work. I am sorry because this work is not already[108] mine. You see this seems a paradox, but you know generally our thoughts and our feelings are generally paradox. Before any Commitee had been named, the League was only mine. I was his only supporter and propulsor. Now, and it must be soo and I am happy for it, all the elected for the Commitee have a part in their ideas and in their love for our League and I am but one more. It seems as if I have had a child with great efforts, and seen afterwards being born, I had to give it to a nurse, for I could not give him the milk of my breast, though I know that the presence of the nurse is necessary to save the life of the child. I hope you can understand me, and you will know how I am writing this letter so happy, so happy and yet a bit sorry. Everybody is very kind for me, they love me a great deal. I find a good number of easy ways in the direction of the League, Dr. Marañón specially is a charming President, and yet I am sorry. But I hope that this will pass. I am finishing this letter and I am already happier than when I begun to write it. The League is beginning to march. We won't decay in it. I will be its supporter here, though they would tire, I would always maintain its principles. You can imagine yourself how grateful I am to you that gave me the idea with your loving letters to begin this League in Spain. I would have never thought of it if it were not for you. Besides you have helped me a great deal, you and your friends and I am very, very grateful to you. You know my last book untitled: "Voluntary Parenthood". Well, I am going to do a special luxurious edition, at a most elevated price, seven shilling, with a beautiful cliches and much more augmented so as to diffuse it among richer kind of people. Do you know how many boks[109] have been sold of that first edition? They have done three editions of ten thousand numbers each, and on the 2 of April, the last letter of my editor, tells me that there has been sold twenty thousand seven hundred and nine. We hope that on finishing this month, the thirty thousand will be sold and then we will do the enlarged and dearer edition. Besides I am going to write a big book too about nudism problem.[110] What do you think of it?

Well, I am going to close, but I will write soon. Don't forget me and write though it is a very small letter. You cannot imagine what a shouts of joy I give when the postman brings in one of your letters. A great deal of good wishes from my mother and I remain

Yours sincerely little pupil

Hildegart[111]

11. Dated 25 June 1932 [folio 50]

LIGA ESPAÑOLA PARA LA REFORMA SEXUAL SOBRE BASES CIENTÍFICAS
Secretaria: Galileo, 45[112]
Presidente: Dr. Marañón
Secretaria: Srta. Hildegart
Madrid, 25 de Junio de 1932

Mr. Havelock Ellis.
London

Mr. Havelock Ellis.
London

Dear Dr. Havelock:

Your dear and sympathetic letter arrived precisely in a very difficult moment for me. You have always the opportunitie of being in the right place and at the right moment, and your letter was at least a confort to me. I will try to say to you clearly what is happening, though I am not compelled to do so officially.

First of all; all the members of the Central Committee of our Spanish League that are most of the[113] parliamentary members and that have been the most selected here, have no special interest for the work of the League. To say this makes one's heart sad, but it is the truth. They have accepted for a compromise of friendship either with me, either with Dr. Marañón,[114] and specially because the work that they have done, the books that they have written forced them to do it, for their names were known as defenders of this cause. But now that the moment comes for working, and carrying to practise what was defended in books and lectures, they all turn backwards and don't want to advance. They have not made any diffussion whatever. On the contrary, when several young people, pupils generally have spoken to them over the opinion that they had over the League, they were rather pessimistic and told that Spain can not be occupied with these "small problems". Besides, the Republican Government helps us much less than the Dictatorial Government.[115] They have "other great problems" to discuss, and ours does not interest them. Besides, Republic is not sure. Government is the less surer yet. They have no interest but in prolonging their life the most than they can, and they have not given us a bit of official help, neither a local[116] for our Secretary nor for our Public meetings, nor any subvention for our expenses.

Second part. Dr. Marañón is a charming president. You have said me so several times, and I am convinced of it, for I am a great friend and admirer of his, and his conservative points of view are not an obstacle for our work. For example, he says repeatedly that he will never be in favour of contraceptive appliances. Well, this does not matter. We will work without him in our Section, and he will not be mixed in it if he does not like. You see then that his conservative ideas are not an obstacle to for his working in the League. Besides, though I expose those ideas in my books, I am very accustomed to my living and in good terms with everybody and in our Commitee, there are scarcely two or three persons that we may call "radical" in ideas, and I would not mind giving the League a conservative and moderate tone. What we need is that a tone whatever it may be, shall be given to it.[117] But Dr. Marañyn[118] is – and when you know him, you will find it so by personal experience – as versatile as a woman.[119] His character is – with this I don't offend him, for it is well known between his friends and pupils – rather voluble and capricious, and what he thinks most charming now, it is sure will be judged by him, not so well tomorrow, and possible bad after a week has ellapsed. The promise of the International Congress for this year had aroused him, and he was all in earnest. The not official help from the Government has made him tower.[120] The absolute carence[121] of good wishes to work of his all other companions – I have carried all the work since the beginning, and fully alone, for he has only had to sign letters, and all the propagand and all the members of our League until now are only due to me, and the only articles published are mine – has nearly put him down.

The excuse that there are other political cuestions to develop first is not to be mattered. In the times of the Dictadura, when the most urgent problem was to restore the liberties for the Spanish nation the first Eugenic Congress was held in Spain between Spanish members, and it was a success as you cannot well imagine. I was then but a small girl, but I remember quite well, that I had to go, three hours before beginning to manage to be not seated, but standing on and hear them. The sexual problem is a problem of always and for always. Thanks for that be given.

Until October we cannot begin to work. We have the intention to publish the first number of our Review on the month of October. We will have to spend over a thousand pesetas, but we will do it, and I will be charmed, if only we would have fire and he would be all ready to fight.[122] And the sorrier I am that they are all so lazy is that people is wanting it. I will tell you an example. A month ago, being one afternoon waiting to see one of our Vice presidents, Dr. Juarros that he may sign a letter instead of Dr. Marañón that was absent then, I began to think about the abolition of prostitute's reglamentation. Two of the members of our League, Dr. Sánchez Covisa and Dr. Bejarano[123] had presented a project of law abolishing it, and reglamenting the prophylaxis of venereal diseases. Besides, by a Decret[124] of Republican Government, the taxes over prostitution were fully abolished. We thought that these measures ought to be known in public – when I say we, I speak of my mother[125] – and when I passed to the room with Dr. Juarros, I told him. ¿Couldn't we possible organise a meeting to speak of this? Quite well he anwsered. We thought then that we had no money and that a theatre where we could give it, would make us spend at least three hundred pesetas. "Don't mind." I say. We can give seven meetings instead of one. We will give five small ones in the mansions of all the feminist association in Madrid, and two big ones, one in the house of the Labour Socialist Party in Madrid, the most ample local in the town, for popular people,[126] and another in the Ateneo, the best liberal centre, in Madrid and very big too. When I spoke to Juarros it was friday afternoon. We began on Monday. I was charged with all the work of organising, looking for the locals,[127] the presidents, the men and women – that were to take part in it. We began on Monday of next week. And it was a success. People crowded to hear us, and people plaudited and were interested. And then, in Parliament, we were beginning to discuss, the Catalunian Estatute,[128] and notwithstanding there was a great public interest in our meetings.

That is the saddest part of all. People would be interested. But the first workmen are not. They have not said "no", but they are moving slowly and yet more slowly, with a drowsy movement. I don't mind to work and work hard for the League if only they will help me. But i have been working the only person in it, and not for vanity but in that monotonous work of writing letters and troubling friends, and writing articles, and all to find that they are not interested in aiding you in your efforts. You see, I feel very sad. Dr. Marañón is away at present. He has gone to Bruxelles and afterward to Praga where he has to attend to a Congress of Physical Culture or something like that and he will not return till the fourteenth of next month of July. If only you could be an injection to him as you are to me, and if he could come decided to work and to help me not only with his goodness and his amiabilities – I cannot complain in that, for he is a perfect gentleman and a good friend for me – but in everything, you don't know how happy I could be. I will let you know what may happen in our League. And with the most sincere gratitude for your loving letters and your nice news of your interest in me with a great deal of good wishes from my mother I remain

Yours afectionately

Hildegart.

12. Dated 18 July 1932 [folio 51]

LIGA ESPAÑOLA PARA LA REFORMA SEXUAL SOBRE BASES CIENTÍFI-CAS
Secretaria: Galileo, 45
Presidente: Dr. Marañón
Secretaria: Srta. Hildegart
Madrid, 18 de julio de 1932

MR. HAVELOCK ELLIS.
=24= HOLMDERNE AVENUE
HERNE HILL.
LONDON.

Dear Dr. Havelock:

I am writing to you again. You are like a father to me and as you are indirectly too the father of our Spanish section of W. L. S. R. I am always wishing to let you know whatever happens in our Section, and very important discoverings have just taken place.

You know what I spoke to you in my last letter, about the discouraging acts of our dear President, Dr. Marañón. Though I knew what his character was, and how variable was it, I was astonished to find him changed whenever we were near him, and that when I spoke to him, he became enthusiastic, while when we let two or three days without visiting him, or speaking to him by telephone, we found him deppressed. But.[129] happened that made me think most of all. I think you know the name of our treasurer, Dr. Haro, that is the author of a book untitled: "Eugenics and Marriage". Well, Dr. Haro has been a pupil of Dr. Marañón, and this last one has him so as to help him to go out from the anonimous[130] in which he is actually. When I spoke with D. Gregorio about the names of the persons that were to form the Executive Committee, and I begged of him to name the treasurer, he told to me: "I think, dear Hildegart, that Dr. Haro will do quite well. Besides, the Vicepresidents will not interfere very much in our League and we need to form a "triangle" of persons that carry themselves well, so that, you, Haro and I will be quite suitable". Haro lives opposite to Dr. Marañón's house, and as he has very little proffessional work, I could telephone him whenever I wished, and if something urgent was to be said to Dr. Marañón in the morning, as D. Gregorio leaves home at seven o'clock and does not return till a #### half past one, I could telephone to Dr. Haro, at ten or eleven in the morning, and when he went to the Hospital where D. Gregorio has his daily teaching, he told him whatever I wished him to know. Everything was going on well, though I could not help being astonished at the changes of D. Gregorio, that only when I was near him became enthusiastic. But on the last days of the month of June, Dr. Haro telephoned me home. It was on thursday. On Monday, I had been speaking with Dr. Marañón, and I had to go and see him that same afternoon. He called so to me. "Please, come to see me before you go to see D. Gregorio. There are very important things that Marañón does not decide himself to say to you, and it will be best for him and for you that you know it already." I was astounded at this extrange calling, but I promised. Ordinarily, I went to see Dr. Haro after having spoken with Dr. Marañón, so as to tell him the last wishes of our President. But this day, I went to see Dr. Haro first. We were speaking about half an hour, perhaps more, but he told me the most strange things. "All the members of the League are displeased with the work of the Secretary." "Dr. Marañón is very displeased too, but it is very violent[131] for him to say to you so. . . " "Dr. Sacristán – another of the members – has told me so repeatedly, and I wish you to know. . . " "They say all these things to me, because they don't dare to say it directly to Marañón, but I have told him everything. . . " "They also wish that the Secretary is a doctor, and a proffessional one. . . " "I think, that you ought to let your place,[132] to say it so to D. Gregorio, and that the same members in the Executive Commitee could change places, so that everybody will be satisfied . . . etc. etc". You cannot imagine, dear Dr. Havelock, what a half an hour it was for me. I had to contain myself. I had been speaking very recently with most of the members of the League, for generally they were all old friends of mine, and they only had words to praise my work. They were fully enthusiastic. Dr. Marañón on Monday had been more charming than usual. My head was really topsy-turvy. ¿What had happened? Thanks that I am of a very resistent nature, and that Munmy was with me. But when I came to the outside, I could not decide myself to go to see Marañón inmediately. I must wait. I went roaming by the nearest streets, crying,[133] not to lose my place as a secretary – you see it only means work for me – but to find myself thrust so, and without any motive whatever. At last, I was calmed, though my temples ached badly, and though I was sweating, my hands and feet were deary cold. I tried to smile pleasantly, and I came up again to see Dr. Marañón. He came soon. He was rather violent[134] too. I said him simply: "I have been speaking with Haro, and I know everything." "¿Do you? he asked ###.[135] Well, if I will say you my truth, I can't think it is true. They have not said me a word. They have only said Dr. Haro all these disagreeable things. Our meeting was to be tomorrow, no?" Yes, I anwsered him. BWill[136] you please postpone it two days? I think we ought to have it on saturday..." "Very well", I said. "But I will go. It is no trouble for me, as I have no ambitions..." "Never, he anwsered me firmly. "Hasn't Haro told you what I think?" (I was going to anwser him that I knew he too was displeased of the Secretary but I didn't, and to my greatest bewilderment, I found myself hearing) "That I will only be a President having you as a Secretary. But not as a favour. The same unanimous votation that I want for me now as the indiscutible President, I want for you, as a indiscutible Secretary. Mind what you do. If you go, I will go with you, and NOTHING, remember well, NOTHING can change me in this. I feel quite decided". I was almost dumb. I spoke with him greatly about the subject. Whatever happened, he must remain. It was necessary for the work of the League, he was the only one, but he bursted: "No, my dear, it is quite impossible what you beg of me. I don't mind the League, I mind you. I love justice, and as this is an unjust thing, whatever shall be your fate, shall be mine too". He continued speaking, but you can imagine what a help it was for me to hear this. I went home relieved. And Saturday came at last. The meeting although reserved only for the members was a very important one. Only threee of the members did not come, and excussed themselves by telephone, with very amiable phrases for me and for my work. When we had studied all the points of the council, statutes, and reglaments about among them, the last one of dimissions[137] arrived. I told simply, that I did not like to be in my place when I was disliked. I knew some had said that the League was not serious with such a young girl in the first place, but the fault was not mine that I was born on the 9 of December of 1914, and was then only seventeen years old. You don't know what an uproar rose. Dr. Marañón spoke just as he had spoken to me. He insisted in abandoning his place. Everything, he said had been done because I had done it. He could not be more satisfied with my work that he was. Where we thought that we were going to find an assembly of adverse members, we found all were as I had supposed friends and good friends too. Generally all of them spoke, and had dear phrases for both of us. "You must think this well", I said. "Until next Assembly comes, we won't decide". They all insisted, but we postponed our accepting till next Assembly. When it was finished, they all came to speak to me. You cannot imagine how good they all were for me. I speak of me, for I know that Dr. Marañón was never thought to be discussed. Dr. Sacristán of whom Dr. Haro had spoken, came specially to speak with me, and had a small chat there where he had a special interest in making me know that he was quite ready to help, but that they wanted me and my activitie. Then I found Dr. Haro. I did not suspect anything them.[138] He was a bit baffled, and he said to me, "I think we will arrange this matter, having two Secretaries, you can remain as the social secretary, and we can have a scientific secretary, a proffessional doctor, and so we could be quite right". I anwsered dubitatively. I had no reason to suspect, but I did not like the idea. I did not know whwy[139] the Secretary ought to be a doctor. I thought that in a League where no special proffesssion was required, but where doctors and advocates were the most numerous, the president ought to be a doctor, and the secretary an advocate, and so, we ought not to have two Secretaries.

But something more happened. On the next day, I began to receive calls at my telephone number and several letters of generally all the members of the League. They warned me against somebody that was inside the League, and that the worst enemy was not outside, but on the utmost inside and where I did not suspect. This time, Dr. Marañón was absent, and it was then when I wrote to you. I could not speak to him of this and help me to find the man of whom all letters spoke. At last, one of the very best friends in my League, quite a charming man in fact, whose daughter is quite of my age, and that loves me dearly, for she too carries her hair in the corckscrewes like mine, and she he always think he is speaking to his daughter[140] spoke to me openly: "¿Do you know who is wanting to have the Secreatary place for himself? Dr. Haro." I was struck deaf and dumb. I could not speak. Everything began to be clear to me then. But he continued speaking "I know, for D. Gregorio has told me so, that he has been telling Marañón things about all of us, that we have never said. Every day in the Hospital where they both work, he has been trying to let him know that another member was dissatisfied with the place of the Secretary's work, that it ought to be a doctor instead. No wonder you found Marañón really troubled when you went to see him, and that only your presence could make him doubt in anybody being dissatisfied with you."

I thanked him dearly. At last I knew who was inside and working.[141] I was so angry . . . for I did not suspect. I had in him the utmost confidence, I spoke to him freely, of everything. WE have projects together. I remembered that when he was appointed treasurer, and I went to him to carry him our poor treasures, – the first time I saw him, for I had only spoken to him by telephone and by cards – I wrote to you saying I felt sorry. It seemed as if the League taht[142] had been mine until then, had been appointed to another father. I never thought that this would happen. On that day precisely, I received several letters from friends of the W. L. S. R. from Weiskoppf*[143] of Brno, and other ones. I was decided to speak to Marañón opnely[144] when he came, and to work in the League with more interest than ever. We were beginning to discuss the programs for next course that will begin in October, and I had a great wish to be avenged. But I limited myself to call him by telephone. It was late in the night. Nearly eleven o'clock. He had gone to the theatre, but he would return before twelve. Tell him, I said to the servant, to call to my home when he comes back. I don't go to bed till nearly a half past twelve, or one o'clock every day". Near twelve o'clock he called. "?Hat[145] is the matter?" he asked. "Do you know when D. Gregorio comes, I said to ask something?" "No." Well, I do. He is coming back the day after tomorrow. He wrote me a postcard this afternoon. I have very important news to say to him. I have received such a great number of letters. I feel[146] so happy that I am not going to let my place of Secretary, not before the God of the Catholics that could be before me." And I added: "So that he who is behind the Secretary place,[147] may know it already, that he won't have it." "Quite right", he said huskily, and generally he used to speak to me a great deal, but that night he wished me good night and cut the wires. You will think I am a very bad little person, but I think it was the very happier night that I have slept in this year.

When Marañón has returned, wonderfully enthusiastic, for when he was in Bruzelles and in Praga, they have spoken to him of our League and he came wishing to work, I spoke to him openly. He was astounded to find he had said me, that he was angry with his Secretary. He began to unite all the facts, and he warned me, "Never beleive what anybody will say to you about me. When I have something to say to you, I know you sufficiently to say it to you by myself."

So, now you know what the motive of the fights that I had inside our section, and of the great work I had. ¿Isn't it a pity that these persons, have so stupid ambitions, and employ so bastard means?

But now, everything is going on well. I have not visitied Dr. Haro since that day in which I called him by telephone. And I am going to play him a bad game. He is interested in his directing the Review that will appear on October. I am going to oppose him. And if he is angry, I ####[148] am going to say him several things that will get him angrier yet. I will say that our Review needs each time, one or two contributions from the membrs[149] of W. L. S. R. He cannot translate them, for he does not know languages well, and besides he cannot write to any of you, by the same reason. I think that you will have seen how he calls you in his book. He writes your name as: "Havellok Hellis". You see, he has not read neither the spanish translation of your books, where your name is rightly spelled. Don't think that many of the members of the League know it. But they are modest, they don't want to have an international relations, and they are not to be blamed. But he must know. Besides, I have other sensible reasons. All the members and future contributor have a great deal of things to do. I will have to be always over them, visiting or calling on them by telephone to have their papers in order to be edited in the Review. They won't deny their presence to a woman, by Spanish gallantry, and to a friend. But they will get sorely bored if Dr. Haro had to do this same thing. So that, the commitee of Redaction of the Review wil be formed by the Executive Commitee, but I will be too the Secretary and so indirectly the Director of the Review. I think he will get angry. But I don't mind him.

And now a special pray. I NEED a contribution of you for the first number of ####[150] our Review. You can write it in English. I will translate it for you, and I am sure you will not find yourself saying absurd things that you have never thought. I know how to translate. ¿Can we depend upon your contribution? Please say yes. It should be a real, real pleasure for me.

Well, now I have to tell you what I ought to have said at the very beginning of this letter, I am so grateful to you. Alice Withrow Field* has send me a lovely book about "Protection of Women and Children in Soviet Russia",[151] and she said you have spoken to her about my possible interest in these themes. You don't know whow[152] I loved reading it. I love to read so much, that I am absurdly grateful to you, for this, and for all your promises, and good wishes.

I think I have wrriten a enormously long letter. But I needed to. I ought to write somebody that could understand me, and this "somebody" is you.[153] I hope you will not be angry, and you will read this letter, though it is in little bits or scraps, for now at last we have the explanation of the "cross-words" which puzzled us so much at first, the alternatives of enthusiasm and despair which were my only bewilderment.

And now, with a great deal of love from my Munmy and from me, I remain

Yours sincerely

Hildegart

I have forgotten to say you in my other letters that in the darling little room where I work, and at both sides of a photograph of mine that was made in Eibar in occassion of a political propagand made there on past year, are your two photos, one I had it from your work: "L'Scopo dell Eugenica", and another from a small pamphlet you sent me. The two are lovely ones, and I like to look at them, and have them looked on.[154]

13. Dated August 1932[155] [folio 53]

Dr. HAVELOCK ELLIS.
LONDON.

Dear Dr. Havelock:

I was so charmed to receive your letter. It was for me such a great pleasure to hear from you since such a long time you hadn't written that I could not help reading it with my Munmy three or four times. I spoke with my dear friend Mr. Morata about your book. He has said me this.

He would be very keenly interested in publishing all your Volumes on Psychology of Sex. They are nearly indispensable for his Catalogue, and he would like to edit them in a presentable way, and not as Reus has done it.[156] Notwithstanding if that is not possible, he will edit the last volume next year placing it in prefferent place between all the others he has to publish. But he would desire you to make a copy of the "contrato" that you have signed with Mr. Reus about the translation of your books, and send it to us, for perhaps there is some legal term or condition that will enable us to edit here your books, without having a disagreeable incident with Mr.Martínez Reus that we could not support, however great our wishes to help you in the spanish edition of the first six or seven volumes are.

¿Will you please anwser to me about this, as rapidly as you can? I know all your other books, though I have not read them, and we will see if it is possible too a spanish edition of them, for more popular public,[157] so that your name may be known widely all over Spain.

I am so happy to know that you are sending me that piece of your book for our Review. ¿When are you going to send it? I am already wishing to read it by myself first, now that I have the privilege of reading your books before they are printed. Our dear D. Gregorio is really charmed with the English Edition of his book of Intersexuality, and is very very grateful to you. He is now in Pointillac in Royan, France, but he is going to send me a copy of this book which he has promised to me. I have already the spanish edition, but he says, he likes even best the English one. So I am wishing to see it. I am working hard now but I don't mind. I am always as happy as I used to be, and I don't get thinner nor nervous, so that I don't think I may get ill.[158] I am glad you read about me in that "Charlando con Hildegart"[159] and that you noticed too about my nice doll. I have two of my playmates of my childhood, that doll, and a very great Teddy Bear. It is so great I could not hold it in my arms when I could play with it and we both rolled in the carpet or in the grass when I was out from home, and I kissed his hairy face and he grunted – he can grunt too. Now he is enjoying a confortable jubilation.[160] He sits in my confortable bed that is very near the floor as all modern beds are and he is there in a pile of cushions attracting the attention of all my visitors that are nearly frightened at him. He has such intelligent eyes and such a cunning look. I am sure you would like him. But when I think of this, I remember you are not coming to Spain, and I feel very sorry. I don't know yet how, but I am sure I must go to England soon and see you as you do not decide yourself to cross the Channel and come to see Spain and me too. But I must not be too selfish. You have a good deal of friends all over the world, and I am sure they will all wish you to go to them, and ubicuity is not yet one of your proprieties.

I think that you received our newspapers that I have sent you. It was the best graphical infformation we had about the monarchic revolution in Spain. That is why I send it to you. Perhaps you might be interesed. When there is something that may be of interest in Spain, I will send you the newspapers there. I have all the Madrid's newspapers every day. At the end of the month it is a terribly high sum, but I don't mind, and I am always vell and goodly inffromed, so I will send you some of the graphicals that are the best published in Madrid.

Now I am going to close. I am finishing my papers for their being read in the Congress of Brno. I have sent my money already, but not yet the papers, for I have been very busy with two of my books that will appear soon. I will send you a copy of these books in the moment they appear.

A great deal of good wishes from my Munmy, and I remain

Yours most sincere Spanish pupil

Hildegart

Miss. Hildegart
Advocate
Galileo=45=4º=derecha
MADRID.
SPAIN.

14. Dated 9 August 1932 [folio 54]

Mr. HAVELOCK ELLIS.
LONDON.

Dear Dr. Havelock:

My editor, Mr. Morata is actually making the plans for the editions of his works in 1933.[161] I have spoken with him, of some interesting works that I had been charged too and specially of yours. And as I have some interesting news to say to you. I write to you again.

First of all. He thinks that you have not allowed Reus the edition of your Studies of Sexual Psychologie for always. ¿Is that true? If it is not so, or even, as the edition of your books in Spanish language is a very bad one, not in the translation but in the presentation for the public, Mr. Morata says that you could let him the edition in a new form if you wan't to add anything too, of these work in a presentable manner at least, as the Spanish edition of the book of Malinowsky that has just appeared, and that I think you will have seen, or as the edition of the book of Lipschütz*, or of the works of Van de Velde.[162] Then he could publish the eight volumes the same for hispanic than hispanoamerican lectors, and you will have a good edition and in a good fashion of them. Then you could beg of him, what we call in Spanish "un tanto alzado", that is a part which will be specially spoken before of the money that have been won, after getting aside the money spent in the edition, or only of money won.[163]

¿Would you like this? Please anwser me as soon as you can, for Mr. Morata desires to know the plan of his books for next year of 1933 in this month, and he would like to know your decision, either affirmative or not.

A great deal of love from my mother and from your Spanish little friend

Hildegart

=9=8=32

Spanish section is going on very well. I have spoken clearly to Dr. Marañón and he is working quite nicely.[164]

Miss Hildegart
Advocate
Galileo 45=
MADRIS.
SPAIN.

Thanks for all.

15. Dated 7 September 1932 [folio 55]

Dear Havelock Ellis:[165]

You can't well know how pleased I was to receive your letter and the fragment of your book for the magazine. I must question you about it. ¿Are the two fragments of the same book? In Spanish Section of W. L. S. R. we occuppy ourselves in the same section entitled: "Sex education" of sex education and "Perversions of sex". Perhaps the two fragments if they are both of the same book, could appear united though with some lines between them, and I will tell you why. I love so much the one written of Education and Sex that I am sad the spanish readers may not rejoice with it too. Besides our Review or magazine is going to be quite a big one, not like Sexus. It will have a number of pages of at least 128 or 144, and will be of the sixe[166] of your "The Eugenics Review" that I think you know. All the articles written for it, are of about 30 sheets of paper, and your will be only each, fourteen or fifteen, and both will quite suite, and make a nice long article in which we will all delight. I have got them both translated already, and I am returning you one of them which you begged back, but I wanted first to say you all about this, for perhaps you may not like, and I will only do what you tell me. Mr. Morata, my publisher is not in Madrid now. He is spending a fortnight in Alicante but he will return by the 12th or 13th of this, and I will then speak with him. I am sure he will be delighted with this new volume of Psychology of Sex that will be very useful for Spaniards that are not yet very versed in sexology. ¿Will you please say to me what size it would be? ¿Will it be like one of the other volumes of P. of Sex or of a smaller size? ¿Would you like: "The ####[167] More essays on love and virtue" that you so kindly sent me, to be translated here?[168] Perhaps it would be also a very nice book. Dr. Haire sent me the other day a book of Evans that he has published in that Bibliothek of Sexology which he leads in England.[169] It is a very nice book too. I think you have read it already. I think that all can be arranged nicely for you both.

I was very pleased to receive that note from the Times you sent me. I sent you too some of the most interesting papers from here.

I will be indeed very pleased to see Mme. Cyan*[170] and although I don't know her yet, Munmy and I send her our best regards, for to be your friend and to be able to help you in everything is for us the highest commendation and for her too, for not many women can claim the privilege of being your true friends, and even between them, she has that of being near you and helping you more directly than any of us.

Now I must close. I am very busy these days, so, please pardon me for not writing a nice long letter, but I have to arrange my Magazine, so that it may appear on the last days of October and be put on sale on November. Dr. Marañón comes back on the twelfth and I have to have work ready for him. He too is writing in this first number, but his, we desire it is a long article, as the magazine deserves.

With the best wishes from my Munmy, I remain

Yours very sincerely

Hildegart

=7=9=32=
Miss Hildegart
Advocate
Galileo# 45=
MADRID.
SPAIN.

16. Dated 6 October 1932 [folio 56]

Dr. HAVELOCK ELLIS.
LONDON.

Dear Dr. Havelock:

Just a few lines of gratitude for all your kindness. Spanish section of W. L. S. R. is passing a very bad time, and I have to use all my power of diplomacy so as to sustain itself. I use a very useful method, that of constant contradiction. For those that inside our League are ennemies, the League is dead. For those friends, it revives; for those other that besides friends are "brothers" in a spiritual communion, they don't know what happen, for I have begged of them by the privilege of "sister" to help and be silent. If you saw me here, such a young and inexperienced woman, going over all the fences and obstacles set by, always smiling though many times, despairing, you would be wondered.[171] Dr. Marañón is now rather ill. He is in the "menopausic" period, he has a horrible "impetigo" all over his body; the doctors order him to be away from all active work, he is loosing memory and faculties; in fact he is not the same Dr. Marañón he was, though his great will will maintain him up perhaps some more years. Besides, unfortunately for him; he is like a good woman, very jealous of me and of the name I have already in Spain. You see, his works are all copies of german books and not original of his own; they are not sold now in Spain, and his name is not respected as it was, and as he is the pail of the wheel that goes down, and I go up for I have all the future before me, he is monstrously jealous of me, and has done and is doing all that is in his power to undo our Section and break it down. Now he has dimitted the Presidence with the idea of making me despair and set away the League, and he returning to it, with some of his friends after two or three months, and without me this time.[172] But he is not now sufficiently strong to be a perilous ennemy – those enemies that are even worst than those known, because we continue our very friendly relations – and I am sure Spanish Section will spring up. Our Review is going to start in its first number on the first ten days of November, I think perhaps before, but he has no time to write for it; in fact this is true, for he is as I told you very ill, though he is very angry if any of us may tell him so, and I never mention this subject beside him. I have not told a bit of this to all the other members of W. L. S. R.; I only tell them the truth, that Marañón is ill and the doctors have ordered him to withdraw from all work. But as you are for me like a father I tell you all the truth. The moment is difficult. Thanks that we have at least a small help from the State, we have some money, good elements, some ambitious men that wish to work and get known and with all these elements, we can succeed in our enterprise.

¿What conditions would you like for your book? Morata accepted it at once, but I am not sure if he is going to publish it yet. Nevertheless, for his part he is very decided. He told me that if you were sending us the proofs when they appear in English, and we would return them to you inmediately, so as to have the chapter translasted[173] each at once, perhaps the Spanish edition would appear at the same time or nearly so than the English one. ¿Could that be possible? Nevertheless tell me how much do you want for your book, if it is going to be a volume like the others of "Sex studies", or one like "More Essays". I will be very glad to receive one of the last vopies[174] of "Man and Woman". I have the old one in the Spanish translation, but I think that yours as everything that you have done, will be very interesting.

I think that you will be astonished on reading this letter. What a lot of personal ambitions around this great problem of sex... Nevertheless, I don't despair, though I have very hard moments, and I think that two or three months after this, work will be definitely begun, and without no fear of being destroyed. But I have to be silent, patient and cunning, and I am so a great deal. Munmy besides helps me a lot with her useful counsels.[175] I most sincerely beg yours. ¿What must I do?

My best remembers and those of my mother for Madame Cyon and her children of whose success I will always be very pleased, and you know I am devotedly your

Hildegart

=6=October=1932=
Miss Hildegart
Advocate
Galileo=45=

If I doubt of Mr. Morata publishing your book, it is because he nearly never pays the author of his books, for what they are worth, and I am going to speak to the publisher of a very interesting work of "Biology and Pathology of Woman", in fifteen volumes that is a very serious editor. I only wish what will be best for you, and I don't want for you what I don't like for me. The Review of our League is not done too by Morata by the same reasons: he never pays the prints.[176]

17. Dated 22 October 1932 [folio 57]

Dr. HAVELOCK ELLIS.
LONDON.

Dear Dr. Havelock:

Just received your nice letter and your lovely book. I could not anwser you inmediately, for I have been tremendously busy with my review, and it will apear on the 4th or 5th of November at last, but I have been correcting proofs, choosing models, papers, prints, etc. so that it has been a monstrous work. Thanks be given that it is nearly over for it is a great strain for me, united to the many things that I always have to do as you well know.

I am going to anwser now your letter, but you will please excuse it is not a long one, for work is not yer[177] over. I corrected yester evening the proofs of your own essay for our Spanish Review. I think you will like how the translation is done. I have some important news to give to you. I am nearly sure that in the next Commitee we will have on the first week of November when the Review is already in the streets, we will have to exclude of[178] our work both President and Treasurer; Dr. Marañón and Dr. Haro. Perhaps you will be astonished by this but you can't imagine what a hard work it has been for me to manage and move the League until now, and what a coarse fighting has taken place some time ago. ¿Can you suppose that, having first promised to arrange the International Congress this year, to make our Section enter directly into the W. L. S. R., to make Dr. Hirschfeld come to Spain, I would have been so much to blame as not to fulfill all my promises? I think you cannot imagine what a great soreness of spirit I had not to be able to fulfil my promise and have my word out, for I so dearly wished that all these things could happen and although you thought me the greatest to blame in all this, I could not tell you but that I was unable to achieve all these things, and I couldn't say how the President with the greatest smiles and the "truest" friendship for me was interposing his work so as to make me tumble in all my purposes. Our future President, the actual first Vice-President, Dr. Juarros, is a great fighter for the abolition of prostitution, has had a special interest for the pathology of sex and has written lovely books specially about this, like: "Sex in chains" that is a fine one, he has a very important place in Le [sic] Société des Nations, and is the doctor and the best friend of the President of Republic so that we don't lose in social respect, and win a faithful man to our cause. At last,[179] Dr. Juarros has never taken other men's works and signed them as his own, as Marañon has done. I hope you know that the work of Dr. Marañon just translated into English, Intersexual States,[180] is but a copy of another one published in german, I think in Vienna. I will send you soon a number of one of the best Medical Reviews in Spain, untitled : Crónica Médica, published in Barcelona in October of the past year of 1931[181] where a very long essay is endowed to show to public all the paragraphs Dr. Marañon fully copied without any notice whatever of the paragraphs of that german work. The name of Dr. Marañon is not now respected in Spain as it was. You know that the is not fault of his alone for it is difficult to maintain a popular name, but I mean to show to you that we are not losing much with his departure. You know he wrote his letter dimitting[182] his place, but speaking to his friends that are both his and mine, and that love me dearly, he told them that he did not wish to have anything to do with the W. L. S. R. and that he would like to dissolve our League here so as to make a new one, fully dessintegrated from International League and without my work too.[183] We will then accept his dimission, but the League will not be dissolved by this. everything will continue as before. I Think that only three or four member#s will perhaps go with him, but he won't get his wish to form a Society without me nor without the international help.

I am perhaps boring you with all these things, but you are for me like a spiritual father and I always tell you everything: so that it is a great halp[184] for me. You know I never go to church to confess myself, so I have to confess myself with you. Pardon me for this letter, I will see Mr. Morata on the 30 of this month, for he has gone to Barcelona, and Valencia, but I am not sure that he will pay you, that is why we will have to make a contract here, so that he shall pay you the money – he nearly never does, as he has done to Prof. Malinowsky whom he has paid in two times. I will continue to say you what happens in our Section, that I hope will be something good, for the two bad elements will be out of it. And with Munmy's best wishes and mine for Mme. Cyon, I remain

Yours sincerely

Hildegart

=22=10=32=

I was very glad to receive your book, but as I love as much the book as your writing I was very sorry that you had written nothing in it. I won't pardon you for that forgetfulness. Thanks for all.

Hilde

Miss Hildegart
Advocate
Galileo=45=
MADRID.
SPAIN.

17. Dated 6 November 1932 [folios 58–9]

Dr. Havelock Ellis.
=24=HOLMDENE AVENUE.
HERNE HILL.
LONDON.

Dear Dr. Havelock:

I suppose the postman knows already your letters, for when one of them arrives, the penny I give him for every one he brings, and they are quite a lot I assure you, is even more graciously offered. Your last one was a delicious long letter, and I spent a lot of time in commenting it with Munmy, so you see it was a rest in my work. But I must now speak as a business like little woman, and I must be serious.

    The new publisher with whom I have spoken wants to publish inmediately: "More essays on love and virtue" and wants to know the conditions of it, but is not so interested in the new volume just appearing. So if you can manage the English publisher to find a Spanish one I will not object to it, and I can give the proof you sent me to the Spanish publisher that he may find, for I am a friend of all the publishers in Madrid. You see Mr. Morata did not object to publishing the book, I don't like him because he never pays neither the authors nor the print, but if your publisher writes to him directly and officially, I think it may be best. I will speak about: "Man and woman" to this other editor. I am sure he will be very interested in it, for he wants a scientific book, as he ##############[185] publishes medical books and for medical students, so that I will speak with him as soon as possible.

I find that you are somewhat mistaken in thinking that Dr. Marañón has a great reputation. He is in the descending point of his life: none of his books are now sold in Spain, the publishers Mr. Morata too know it but too much; people don't respect him as they did, they generally mock at him, he is generally called "Gorgonio", and even the journalists laugh between themselves – I know this last thing for I am now a journalist like them, and I work too in their professional meetings – of Gorgonio's ridicule own doings. Between the medical class he had – that is the truth – a great many envies. Now, no. They all pity him, for his loss has been a rapid one. I too am sorry for him. I did not think that some months could be enough to make such a change. What I think is that this was already existent before-hand, but has just sprung now and seems more overwhelming and appaling.

The people that before filled his waiting rooms has disappeared. That I know quite well, and not by refference as I visit him very often. He has had – as all the others – great proffesional error, but people has profited of it to make things worse. Besides, now the medical class has learnt german and can read german books quite easily, and two medical publishers have published many german books here about Psychology, Pathology, Biology of Women and Sexual Matters in a great many volumes, that have made all the works of Marañón appear as simple copies from them. Besides, he did not translate well, and he mistook some things; for example speaking of the picnic[186] type, that is the ideal type of woman, he said everything different; besides in the book you have reviewed he speaks of "homosexuality" as a congenital state, and in the prologue that he wrote to Maliowsky's[187] book he says it is exclusively due to the atmosphere or "medium". All these contradictions have been observed, and between the medical class he has lost all his reputation. That is why I told you that you were perhaps mistaken when you told me that. You can't imagine what are the comments that are being done in Madrid with the "doctor honoris causa" in La Sorbonne. He hated "La Sorbonne" for this University never acknowledged him before, ###[188] and even when I begun the League he hated France and the French and was very interested in Germany; but he has a great friendship with Mr. Herbette,[189] the ambassador of France in Madrid, and perhaps with someone else, and he adores France and French, and hatez Germany. You see his character is like that of a bright little girl of six, and that is a pity in him.[190] I am enclosing you the first page of the picture paper I usually send to you uentitled: "Ahora", where you will find a very curious photograph that was commented in Madrid, and laughed at in public. The attitude of Marañón is as you can see a very funny one. All his femenine self appears in the photo, in that attitude of his body, hands and face towards Herriot.[191] Unfortunately for him, he was already ## away from Madrid, and the order from his familliars to buy all the edition and not let any number be sold did not arrive till the afternoon of that same day, and the newspaper was sold inmensely and commented in the stretts, in the Atheneum, in our Círculo de Bellas Artes, Academia de Medicina, and so many places as the newspaper arrived. You cannot well imagine what a blow it has been that for the reputation of our poor friend. I am never glad of the bad fate of another, and I can't be happy with this; I regret this, and it is for me a good lesson so as to maintain me aside from all the many factors that have led him to this state of disgrace. His reception as "doctor honoris causa" has been badly acknowledged between doctors, and even the newspapers speak very lightly of it. Politically, he formed a Association, a few months before Republic: – he never was a republican he is not yet one, but a monarquic with the red cap on – it was a horrible failure: he voted in the most unproceeding manner, and always against public opinion with the greatest fault of discretion,[192] and at last, decides him to abstain from politics and limit himself to diplomatic functions as in the visit of M. Herriot. But even then, the photographs[193] are always ready, hiding in asome[194] bushes near to make a photo zo unpleasant and ridicule for him as that I am just sending you.

I hope I will write to you how all the difficulties pass away. I am quite ready to fight and will fight. On the fifteenth I think the Review will appear. I will inmediately send it to you.

Good bye now. A great many remembers from my mother for you and Mme. Cyon and her children, and I remain

Yours sincere little friend

Hildegart

=6=11=32=
Srta. Hildegart
Advocate
Galile[o] =45=
MADRID.

The political situation in Spain is not what is reviewed in the public press. It is quite different, because all the newspapers are bought by the Government that have formed with four of them a trust and has bought the actions of the other three by some of the Ministers privately. So that the press does never tell the truth. Perhaps I will speak to you some day about it.

Vale

18. Dated 18 February 1933 [folio 60]

Dra. Hildegart
Abogado
Galileo, 51
Teléf: 34033[195]

Dear Dr. Havelock:

You can't well know how busy I have been lately. I couldn't neither write to you, though I wished it greatly. I have some more books in preparation, and besides several articles for Spanish and foreigner Reviews. I suppose you have received a number of "La Gaceta Médica". It is the best medical Review we have in Spain, and the directors are great admirers of my work. They have begged of me insistently to write something for them, but I couldn't until the month of January of this year, in which I sent it, and I gave them your adress that they may send you a copy. They are some of the richer men here in Madrid, specially between the Medical class, and fully "anti-marañonists". You can't well know what a group of persons of great political and social meaning is already with us, opposite to Marañón. I think that I will give you soon some interesting news, and when time passes, you will see how I was in the truth when I told you his name was already declining. But you must not forget that only those persons that have economical independence can afford too their spiritual independence. I have no need to depend on them, and on Marañón less than all, and as I have assured my economical freedom, I can tell the truth, though it may trouble them, to all the persons that surround me. That as you may see is very important. All the independent persons here, specially between the medical class, among whom are my best friends here are already against him, and now the "consigna"[196] as we say in Spanish is to tell "Against Marañón" or "Marañón is not with us" to decide them to join our group. If you lived here in Spain, you would see how easily this goes on, and you will see once more how there is not a small ennemy. I suppose that Marañón never could think me in this point as a very important factor. But however small is an enny, you must be aware of him![197] and unfortunately for him, I am not too small an ennemy. I mean an ennemy in best sense of the world, proffessionally speaking, as there is nothing that may be called "personal" between us, and we continue in the best terms of apparent friendship.[198]

I am speaking to Mr. Aguilar, the editor of "Sex in civilisation" about your book.[199] He is going to publish two of mine in the present year. I think he will be very interested in "More essays on love and virtue" at first, and inmediately afterwards we will try to find either by himself, either[200] by some of his friends a publisher for the other two: "Man and Woman" and "Eonism", though I think that the new volume of "Studies of Sexual Psychology", of which I have at home half of the first prints, will be the most apt for our public. I hope to have an anwser next week. I will forward it inmediately to you.

¿Do you know Dra. Paulina Luisi?* She is actually in Madrid, but she is a funny sort of woman, very irritable, and a bit mad. She is sorely cerebrally wounded with a "psicosis urémica", and her conversation is always a tremendous shock for all. She is very indignated for the medical proffession here has not accepted her, and does not help her either, and she is giving some small lectures in a feminist association over here. She can't undersantstand[201] at her sixty years, how a girl of eighteen – I have just entered in my eighteenth year – can be so dearly loved and respected in Spain, and have so many friends and hearers everywhere. She is a funny sort of woman, and I thought inmediately to ask you if you knew her. She seems to have known Forel in a Congress of Sexual Education and Prophylaxis of Venereal Diseases. But I don't know anything more of her.

I am sending you two of my photos just taken here. One of them is with what we call here the "toga" and "birrete" that are the symbols of my proffession.[202] The other is with a street dress, taken the same day. I think you will like them. But I must beg something too. I want a photo of yours. I have only a very, very small one, but not a nice one where you appear just as you are. I think I deserve one, and would be very grateful if you sent it, and I will put it in the desk where I work, that you may be always besides me.

My best regards for Mme. Cyan, and with the sincerest wishes from Munmy I remain Yours very sincere little friend

Hildegart

19. Dated 10 April 1933 [folio 61]

Dra. Hildegart
Abogado
Galileo, 57
Teléf: 34033

Dr. HAVELOCK ELLIS.
ENGLAND.

Dear Dr. Havelock:

You can't well know how grateful I am to your lovely photographs, and how pleased too of receiving your dear little letter. I have been enormously busy these days, in political meetings, and going to bed at five o'clock a.m. every morning and getting up at nine, after taking my cold bath and breakfast to begin again. Besides the Spanish section of the W. L. S. R. is taking now an exceptional activity. All the branches in each of the provinces, 51 are being #####[203] begun actually. We are arranging a great Congress of Eugenical problems that will last since the twentieth of April until the 12th of May,[204] with lectures during the morning, afternoon and nights, in our Medical Faculty and Atheneum, with the best lecturers, Marañón too among them, and our Chief minister Mr. Azaña,[205] and many other members of Government, and a great many of the most distinguished between medical class, for we have twentyfour "cursos" of six lessons each over each branch of medical and juridical knowledge in relation with Eugenics, that are all given by specialists. I have six lectures about birth control, and hope to make them very interesting with lantern slides, etc. Besides the second number of SEXUS is just going to appear, for the ##############[206] first day of May, and as nothing was done, I am quite busy arranging it. As our number of members have increased greatly in Madrid, we are, in these fifteen[207] days more than a hundred and fifty, and more will soon come, I have to work greatly. I hope to have soon a special "taquimecanograph"[208] to help me, as a special secretary.

I would be very grateful if you could send me as soon as possible a brief opinion over the first number of SEXUS to get it published in the second just going to appear. My best regards for François,[209] and from my Munmy for both of you and love from

Hildegart

20. Dated 16 May 1933 [folio 62]

Dra. Hildegart
Abogado
Galileo 57
Telef: 34033

Dr. Havelock Ellis.
LONDON.

Dear Dr. Havelock:

I ought to have anwsered you long ago, but I have been so busy lately that it has been really impossible for me. I am going to depart from Madrid possibly next Saturday to Portugal. I am going to give several lectures in my own proffession of criminal laws and studies in the Universitys of Porto, Coimbra and Lisboa. But I will return soon. Probably on the second day of June I will be back in Madrid and quite ready to start afresh with new work.

You must not be worried for my health.[210] I am quite healthy. I think Dr. Haire has spoken to you about me. He will tell you I am ###### very tall[211] for what women are generally in Spain (I am actually growing now) and very healthy. I measure one and seventy one centimetres and I weigh seventy seven kilograms. Munmy besides cares greatly of me, but you see I can't be healthy nor happy if I haven't work, much more than I can at first sight achieve. Now I begin to work in my own proffession as a lawyer, and I am trying to have a special permission so as to be able to ACT in public as a lawyer as I am but eighteen now, and I can't exercise until I am twenty-three. I think my permission will be ready for October and all this while I work united to some other lawyers here that sign my works and act instead of me. I suppose you received and[212] interview I publish with Dr. Haire in the best periodical newspaper of here. Daily Liberty.[213] It is one of the biggest and the best judged between us.

Now I want to beg of you a great favour.

Our Eugenical Conference has finished with enormous success. We are actually arranging the great book in two or three volumes that will contain the seventy five lectures that have been pronounced here. But there is a theme which no-one between us can developpe. It is entitled: "Psychopathology of love". The organiser Committee of our Eugenical Conference wants me to beg of you if possible to send us your contribution to this theme, with what you have written, or what you actually would say about it, for although the Eugenics Conference is a Spaniard one, your name and specially in this theme is absolutely indispensable for us. Then we could profit of this so as to make that part of the book a public hommage of simpathy and respect for your own marvellous book, and make your work known all through the Spanish countries for the book will be sold and spread widely not only in Spain but in all America. We would like a soon anwser to this question. If you accept, I would be extremely pleased, and I could then translate your work into Spanish. I think you may have observed by the first number of SEXUS, I translated your own contributions quite clearly and distinctly. We want as soon as anwser as possible and hope that this anwser will be in the affirmative as it will be the greatest pleasure for us.

Spanish section is going on quite ahead, at last.

Hope you have received my book, and some other articles from me here.

I am sending you now two other ones.

The best regards from my Munmy and hoping that François Cyan has returned quite well from her holiday, I remain

Yours very sincerely

Hildegart

=16=5=33=

NOTES

[1] In this transcription of the letters held in the Havelock Ellis papers in the British Library the following conventions have been observed. Misspellings are retained, as is her erratic capitalization, and where necessary, the word intended is given in the notes. Accents have been provided for proper names,

and for Hildegart's letter in Spanish. Where the problem has simply been one of the typewriter jumping, this has been corrected. The punctuation is as it is in the original, but spurious full stops have been deleted before question marks, and some missing bits of punctuation have been supplied (e.g. completion of quotation marks). The letters have a number of crossings out. Minor or insignificant ones are not recorded, but where it is possible to read what has been deleted, or it is otherwise of interest, this has been noted. Letter headings (of headed paper) are given in italics. Hildegart's signature and occasional longhand notes are indicated by a different font. The details of the address and date at the foot of the letters are retained as they allow us to track changes in Hildegart's residence, professional status and sense of professional self.

2 Hildegart is inconsistent in her use of capitals for nationalities and days of the week. The original form has been preserved.
3 The typing crossed out here is evidence that Hildegart had a longhand draft first and then typed a fair copy. Under the crossing out are the words 'of divulgation writing three pamphlets, the first' and which appear lower down.
4 i.e. 'began'.
5 i.e. 'printed'.
6 i.e. 'price'.
7 i.e. 'is now running out'.
8 probably should read 'problem a'.
9 i.e. 'owing'.
10 'to maint' crossed out here, an indication that Hildegart is making a fair copy, and has slipped a line.
11 See Coca (1931) (one of the cuttings sent to Ellis), where Hildegart makes the same point in an interview.
12 i.e. 'the criticism'.
13 Hildegart is writing under the newly elected Republican government.
14 Hildegart's references here show her wide and eclectic reading. The figure referred to as Renato Kohl is in fact Renato Kehl, the Brazilian eugenicist (1889-1974).
The texts alluded to are probably: Ben Barr Lindsey, *Companionate Marriage* (written with Wainwright Evans, introduction by Mrs Bertrand Russell), 1928; Auguste Forel, *Sexual Ethics*, English translation 1908; Iwan Block, *The Sexual Life of our Time in its Relations to Modern Civilization*, 1907; Theodore H. Van de Velde, *Ideal Marriage: its Physiology and Technique*, 1926; Marie Stopes, *Married Love*, 1918, *Contraception: its Theory, History and Practice*, 1923; *Early Days of Birth Control*, 1922; Aleksandra Kollontai, *Sexual Relations and the Class Struggle*, 1921, *Red Love*, 1923, *Prostitution and Ways of Fighting It*, 1923; Renato Kehl, *Eugenia e medicina social; problemas da vida* [Eugenics and Social Medicine; Problems of Life] second edition, 1923.
15 i.e. 'objective'.
16 i.e. 'that those in Spain rebel'.
17 This letter closely resembles the first letter to Ellis, apart from specific comments relating to Key.
18 i.e. 'give'.
19 'Sweden' inserted in Hildegart's longhand.
20 i.e. 'reproduction'.
21 i.e. 'the criticism'.
22 i.e. 'two'.
23 i.e. 'republican'.
24 See note to first letter to Ellis on this.

Appendix I   211

25 Hildegart presumably intends 'Sweden' here but is copying from the letter to Ellis.
26 i.e. 'to get to know you'.
27 i.e.'translation'.
28 i.e. 'despite'.
29 Hildegart's regular misspelling of 'answer'.
30 *De naturae philosophia, seu, De Platonis, & Aristotelis consensione*, Lugduni Batavorum: Iacobi Marci, 1622. Note the ingenuous assertion that there are only three or four copies of this in the world.
31 See bibliography for publication details.
32 This may mean 'the two copies of the journal'.
33 Johann Jakob Bachofen (1815–87), *Das Mutterecht* (1861), whose proposition was that a state of mother-right came before that of father-right.
34 An example of how Hildegart includes her mother as a recipient of the letters of Ellis, something repeatedly implied.
35 i.e. 'have an influence on'.
36 'corkscrews' i.e. 'ringlets'.
37 i.e. 'hairstyle'.
38 Her reference here is to the 1913 publication by Reus of *Estudios de Psicología Sexual, Hombre y mujer (Introducción): La evolución del pudor, Fenómenos de periodicidad sexual, El autoerotismo* (Vol. I); *Inversión sexual* (Vol. II); *El impulso sexual, Amor y dolor* (Vol. III); *La selección sexual en el hombre* (Vol. IV); *El simbolismo erótico; El mecanismo de la detumescencia ; El estado psíquico durante la preñez* (Vol. V).
39 This is the Italian 1922 edition of *The Task of Social Hygiene* (1912).
40 It is not clear which pamphlet Ellis has sent, but from what follows it would appear to relate to homosexuality and the law.
41 What Hildegart has in mind here is *¿Quo vadis burguesía?*, her novelette of September 1932, published in the series La novela proletaria (see Chapter Four). In the cutting sent to Ellis from *El Socialista*, 5 December 1931, with her interview with Coca, Hildegart declares that her current enthusiasm is for a book she is engaged on, *Casos patológicos de perversión sexual* [Pathological Cases of Sexual Perversion] in which she proposes to look at major figures of Spanish public life.
42 i.e. Minister of Labour.
43 i.e. 'cell'.
44 i.e. 'to find Mr. Largo Caballero in the same "celda" as Mr. Alcalá Zamora'.
45 The law under which it was licit to kill a prisoner trying to escape, notoriously misused. The law originated with Zugasti, Governor of Córdoba 1870–4 (Brenan, 1962: 156 n. 1).
46 i.e. 'kill'.
47 Pedro Rico, who became Mayor of Madrid in April 1931.
48 Andrés Saborit, socialist, elected a deputy to the Cortes in 1931.
49 i.e. 'friendship'.
50 The allusion is to some hereditary disease.
51 i.e. 'no children'.
52 It is unclear what basis Hildegart had for her suspicions that those she lists were homosexual. A curious coincidence is with freemasonry. Ferrer Benimeli lists Azaña, Casares Quiroga and Zulueta as believed to be masons (1987, vol. II: 218–22). Rumours about the homosexuality of Azaña are expanded on by Carlavilla in his rather sensationalist account: his chapter on Azaña, originally drafted in 1933–4, describes him as 'euconoide', and asexual, rather than homosexual, although he alleges that at some point he would have been a

passive homosexual (Carlavilla, 1956: 137–9). Given Aurora's apparent support for masonry, and antagonism towards homosexuality, Hildegart's position here encapsulates some of the internal inconsistencies of her mother's attitude. At best she reacts against her mother's espousal of masonry with accusations of homosexuality to undermine it. Alternatively she reacts against the politics of a Republic that is already not radical enough for her.

53   i.e. Julia Iruretagoyena.
54   The reference is probably to Concha Albornoz, daughter of the mason Álvaro de Albornoz.
55   i.e. 'since'.
56   Presumably this letter from Margaret Sanger came at the prompting of Ellis.
57   i.e. 'birth'.
58   i.e. 'and'.
59   i.e. 'now'.
60   i.e. 'lectures'.
61   i.e. 'politicians' or 'politics'.
62   i.e. 'if'.
63   This is a postscript, with reference presumably to some suggestion from Ellis that she should write less.
64   In this letter Hildegart seems to anticipate the foundation meeting of the Liga of 3 March 1932.
65   i.e. 'several'.
66   i.e. 'will'.
67   i.e. 'place to meet'.
68   Presumably 'agreed'.
69   i.e. 'the weather'.
70   Published in 1932, with prologue by Marañón, translated from English by Ricardo Baeza as *La vida sexual de los salvajes del noroeste de la Melanesia*, Madrid: [n.p.] Ellis wrote a preface for the 1929 London edition of this work. See note 91.
71   'you are' crossed out.
72   There is no record of this article in Grosskurth (1980) or other works on Hildegart.
73   Hildegart's reference is to *El problema eugénico: punto de vista de una mujer moderna* [Madrid: Gráfica Socialista]. The 1930 edition make no mention of an earlier one, which according to this letter, would have been 1928.
74   i.e. 'of'.
75   The work referred to is *Homogenic Love and Its Place in a Free Society* (1894).
76   i.e. 'march'.
77   i.e. 'against'.
78   i.e. 'war'.
79   Characters crossed out here. The reference is probably to Prince Yorgi Yevgenyevich Lvov, Prime Minister of Provisional Government 1917, under whom marriage was a question of registration, and divorce was granted on request.
80   i.e. Karl Kautsky.
81   i.e. 'the State'.
82   i.e. 'State'.
83   i.e. 'disagreeable'. The number of mistypings in this letter may suggest stress, particularly given the end of this sentence.
84   Hildegart seems to be reassuring Ellis of her well-being perhaps in the light of some expression of concern on his part.
85   i.e. 'thoughts'.
86   i.e. 'anxieties'.

Appendix I 213

87 i.e. Federación Universitaria Española.
88 i.e. 'problem'.
89 Her reference is to *Eonism and Other Supplementary Studies (Studies in the Psychology of Sex*, Vol. VII), Philadelphia: F. A. Davis. There is no record of a Spanish edition of this volume (which discusses cross-dressing) in the Biblioteca Nacional catalogue, but there is a French edition, *L'Eonisme ou L'Inversion esthéthico-sexuelle*, Paris, Merovre de France 1933.
90 See note 70. The full title of the Malinowski work referred to earlier is *The Sexual Life of Savages in North-Western Melanesia: an Ethnographic Account of Courtship, Marriage, and Family Life Among the Natives of the Trobriand Islands, British New Guinea.*
91 i.e. 'so'.
92 Margaret Sanger, *My Fight for Birth Control* (London: Faber & Faber, 1932). An example of how up to the minute Hildegart was in her reading, perhaps here prompted by Ellis.
93 See Chapter Seven.
94 i.e. 'you'.
95 This is one of the strongest and clearest acknowledgements Hildegart makes of Ellis's support and significance.
96 The exhuberance of Hildegart is quite notable here, almost to the degree of being manic. It will contrast with the distress and paranoia shown in later letters when things in the League turn difficult.
97 Hildegart corrects her spelling here from 'Havellock' to 'Havelock': an interesting detail.
98 The publishers Wilhelm Kauffmann in Berlin published *Sexus: Internationale Vierteljahresschrift für die gesamte Sexualwissenschaft und Sexualreform* 1 for the Institute for Sexual Science in Berlin in 1933 (Dose 2003: 2).
99 i.e. 'since we are new, we are rather poor'.
100 i.e. 'of postal services'.
101 i.e. Juarros.
102 As listed in the account of the Liga sections given in *Sexus I*
103 i.e. 'and'.
104 i.e. 'are'.
105 i.e. 'current'.
106 i.e. 'wish'.
107 i.e. 'left'.
108 Hildegart's meaning here is 'ya no', i.e. 'no longer'.
109 i.e. 'books'.
110 It is striking that Hildegart perceives this as a problem (unlike anarchist naturists).
111 There is a stamp at the foot of the page with LIGA ESPAÑOLA PARA LA REFORMA SEXUAL MADRID.
112 The official address for the Liga is Hildegart's home address.
113 Unnecessary comma in text here.
114 i.e. 'with either me or with Dr. Marañón.'
115 This is an interesting commentary on the affairs of the Liga under Primo and under the Republic, the latter perceived as unstable, and hence unable to provide support.
116 i.e. 'place to work'.
117 Two things are of interest here: first that Hildegart, despite her left-wing associations in politics, and her revolutionary approach to sexual reform, is happy for the Liga to be moderate in tone, and second that she (rightly)

perceives the need for the Liga to have a 'tone', seeing perhaps its disparity of approach deriving from the heterogeneous nature of its members as a major problem.
118 i.e. 'Marañón' (an unusual mistyping).
119 Longhand insertion after this sentence: 'but not as a normal woman, but as a hysterical one'.
120 i.e. 'the lack of official help. . . .has made him falter' (?).
121 i.e. 'absence'.
122 'fire' is unclear, and corrected in Hildegart's longhand, as is 'he' and 'to'.
123 Méndez Bejarano is not listed as a founding member in the document Hildegart sends Ellis about the setting up of the Liga.
124 i.e. 'decree'.
125 Significant indication of Aurora's intervention in the Liga's business.
126 i.e. 'people of the *pueblo*'.
127 i.e. the places for the meetings.
128 The 1931 statute of the Second Republic establishing a high degree of Catalan autonomy.
129 Eccentric punctuation as in original. This letter, where the content is stressful, has a number of minor errors and corrections.
130 i.e. 'to leave the anonymity'.
131 i.e. 'difficult' or 'disturbing'.
132 i.e. 'to give up your place'.
133 It is not clear whether her mother is there as she does this.
134 i.e. 'disturbed'.
135 'him' crossed out.
136 i.e. 'Will'.
137 i.e. 'resignations'.
138 i.e. 'then'.
139 i.e. 'why'.
140 'she' is redundant: Hildegart's meaning is 'he always thinks he is speaking to his daughter when he speaks to me'.
141 Hildegart has identified Haro as the 'enemy'.
142 i.e. 'that'.
143 i.e. Dr Joseph Weisskopf.
144 i.e. 'openly'.
145 i.e. 'What'.
146 Corrected from 'felt' in Hildegart's longhand.
147 i.e. 'so that he who is after the secretary's place'.
148 'have' crossed out.
149 i.e. 'members'.
150 'your' crossed out.
151 This work is a first edition (New York: Dutton, *c.* 1932), and an indicator of Hildegart's foreign contacts of her own generation.
152 i.e. 'how'.
153 This encapsulates the whole of the relationship between Hildegart and Ellis, particularly in conjunction with the postscript of the letter.
154 Notwithstanding the apparently positive resolution of Hildegart's situation in the Liga, this is the last letter to Ellis written on official Liga paper.
155 The date is given in the hand of neither Hildegart nor Ellis, so may be that of an archivist.
156 See above, note 38.
157 Note Hildegart's desire to disseminate ideas to a broad public including the working class.
158 An indication perhaps that Ellis has expressed concerns about her health.

159 Her reference is to a cutting sent to Ellis of an interview with Alfonso Cernada, probably dated between March and August of 1932.
160 i.e. 'retirement'.
161 i.e. that Morata is looking at what he is planning to publish in 1933.
162 There is no record of any of Van der Velde (see note 11) having published with Morata in this period, although *El matrimonio perfecto* appeared in 1931 (Madrid: Prensa Moderna), and *Fertilidad y esterilidad en el matrimonio* in 1932 (Madrid: Juan Pueyo).
163 Hildegart seems to be suggesting that Ellis ask for a fixed fee for his book. The definition of 'el alzado' given in the Diccionario de la Real Academia is 'el ajuste o precio que se fija en determinada cantidad, a diferencia de los que son resultado de evaluación o cuenta circunstanciada', while María Moliner, *Diccionario del uso del español* defines 'un tanto alzado' as 'Precio en que se ajusta una cosa, particularmente una obra, que es el total de él, sin detallar los distintos conceptos'. The idea of 'un tanto alzado' is that instead of getting royalties the writer receives a fixed sum (perhaps even an 'advance'?). Hildegart's suggestion is that if Ellis asks for a fixed fee then he would not have to wait until the costs of the edition were covered before receiving royalties, nor would what he got depend on the number of copies sold. In this context 'won' needs to be read as 'earned'. My thanks to Ángeles Carreres and Francisco Vázquez García for clarification here.
164 These two sentences added in Hildegart's longhand.
165 No indication of the reason for this changed salutation.
166 i.e. 'size'.
167 'little' crossed out here.
168 i.e. *Little Essays of Love and Virtue* (London: Black, 1922).
169 Charles Benjamin Shaffer Evans (b. 1901), *Man and Woman in Marriage*, with a preface by Norman Haire and an introduction by Rudolph Weiser Holmes (London : J. Lane, 1932), part of the series of The International Library of Psychology and Sexology, edited by Norman Haire.
170 The reference here is to Françoise Lafitte, whose married name was Cyon, and who was Ellis's companion in the period Hildegart was writing to him. See Grosskurth (1980).
171 In this commentary Hildegart presents herself as both central and isolated, a perception that may be hers alone, or already indicating the increasing influence of her mother.
172 Hildegart's level of suspicion, and the sequence of her reasoning, is suggestive of the influence of Aurora.
173 i.e. 'translated'.
174 i.e. 'copies'.
175 A further indication of the presence of Aurora, notable now that Hildegart is reporting her perception of difficulties in getting the Liga to progress.
176 This postscript typed partially on the vertical at the left, to fit it onto the page.
177 i.e. 'yet'.
178 i.e. 'exclude from'.
179 i.e. 'at least'.
180 i.e. 1932 edition of *La evolución de la sexualidad y los estados intersexuales*, translated as *The Evolution of Sex and Intersexual Conditions*, produced by Allen and Unwin.
181 This seems to refer to an article by Oliver Brachfeld in the *Revista Médica de Barcelona* which appeared in December 1931, with the title 'Crítica de las teorías sexuales del Dr Marañón' (548–61).
182 i.e. 'resigning'.
183 If Hildgart is correct in this, Marañón's manoeuvre seems an extraordinary

216   Sex and Society in Twentieth-Century Spain

one, designed to make the Spanish Liga independent and freed from having to adopt the more revolutionary aspects of sexual reform. In the event it appears that he formed no such separate organization.

184 i.e. 'help'.
185 'edits specialll' crossed out.
186 A reference to Kretschmer, *Körperbau und Charakter* (1921), the pyknic type being rotund and with a tendency to fat. Kretschmer wrote on his work in the *Revista de Occidente* in 1923, with particular emphasis on the pyknic form.
187 i.e. 'Malinowski's.
188 'but' crossed out.
189 Jean Herbette (1878–1960).
190 Ironically Hildegart's image here is like that used by Mrs Gillett-Gatty to describe her own behaviour (see Chapter Seven, p. 128).
191 Édouard Herriot (1872–1957), French Prime Minister in 1932.
192 i.e. 'lack of discretion'.
193 i.e. 'photographers'.
194 i.e. 'some'.
195 Note the change of address, the new titled paper, and the styling of Hildegart as Dra. Hildegart.
196 i.e. 'watchword'.
197 i.e. 'him'.
198 See the letter of 6 October 1932 where Hildegart initiates discussion of the 'enemy'. While she may simply be recording political infighting in the Liga, Aurora's paranoia in relation to enemies is possibly also being expressed, albeit in apparently rational tone.
199 The Aguilar catalogue at the back of Max Nordau, *La esencia de la civilización* (Madrid: Aguilar) lists a series called Biblioteca de Ideas y Estudios Contemporáneos. This includes two works by Georges Lakhovski, one of which is *El sexo en la civilización*, which had an introduction by Havelock Ellis.
200 i.e. 'or'.
201 [*sic*] i.e. 'understand'.
202 These signs of Hildegart's professional status fit with the new titled paper.
203 Second 'being' crossed out.
204 Hildegart's reference here is to the Eugenics Conference (Noguera and Huerta, 1934).
205 Azaña provided the closing words for the 'Social Course' that opened the conference, but this was not published in the proceedings.
206 '15 of May' is crossed out.
207 i.e. 'fifteen'.
208 i.e. 'shorthand typist'.
209 i.e. Françoise Cyon, Ellis's companion.
210 The impression given here is that Ellis has expressed concern for Hildegart's health, either by letter or through Norman Haire.
211 'rather' is crossed out: Hildegart's correction here shows an interesting decision on emphasis. A note in Ellis's handwriting converts this height into 5'7".
212 i.e. 'an'.
213 The interview was published as 'Una figura de las Jornadas Eugénicas: El doctor Haire, presidente de la Liga Mundial para la Reforma Sexual' [A figure of the Eugenics Conference: Dr Haire, President of the World League for Sexual Reform], *La Libertad*, 11 May 1933, pp. 3–4. In the interview Hildegart makes much of Haire's having come from a large family, being the youngest of eleven children born between 1875 and 1892, and of the subsequent reluctance of several of them to have children.

Appendix II

Brief Bio-Bibliographical Guide to Figures Mentioned in the Text

Aguilar, Manuel, set up his publishing company in 1923, and was a major contact in Spain for H. G. Wells and G. B. Shaw. His *Biblioteca de Ideas y Estudios Contemporáneos,* set up in 1926, contained a section of 'Biology and Sexology' (Aguilar 1963: 178, 187–90, 196).

Alcalá Zamora, Niceto (1877–1949), President of the Second Republic 1931–6.

Alcalá Santaella, Rafael (1896–1963), doctor who wrote mainly in the field of anatomy and urology.

Aza Díaz, Vital (1890–1961), pupil of Recaséns, a gynaecologist who founded the Sanatorio de Santa Alicia, which specialized in gynaecology and obstetrics. He founded the Sociedad Española para el Estudio de la Esterilidad [Spanish Society for the Study of Sterility]. Author of hundreds of articles on gynaecology and abdominal surgery. In 1917 he published a work on the uterus with Macau. His most significant work in relation to the WLSR by the time of its founding was *Feminismo y sexo* [Feminism and Sex] (1928); his prescriptive attitude to woman was confirmed by two works of 1934, *Porqué la mujer no tiene hijos* [Why Women do not have Children] and *Derechos y deberes de la mujer* [Duties and Rights of Woman].

Azaña, Manuel (1880–1940), Prime Minister and President of the Second Republic until his resignation in September 1933. Carlavilla (1956) writes about his 'euconoide' state (that of passive homosexual).

Baeza, Ricardo (1890–1956), journalist and theatre critic, regular correspondent for *El Sol* in the 1920s, and based in London and Dublin 1920–1, translated Malinowski, *La vida sexual de los salvajes del noroeste de la Melanesia* [Sexual Life of the Savages in the North-east of Melanesia],

Madrid: [n.p.]. Ellis wrote a preface for the 1929 London edition of this work, and Marañón for the 1932 Spanish edition.

Barcia Goyanes, Juan José (1901–2003), doctor, neurologist and rector of Valencia university, wrote *Los fundamentos científicos de la Anatomía: La vida, el sexo y la herencia*, [The Scientific Foundations of Anatomy: Life, Sex and Heredity] (1928).

Barrio de Medina, J. (1895–1954), dermatologist, worked in the asylum of San Juan de Dios, where he specialized in sexual disorders, publishing in 1930 the *Tratado español de venereología y sifiliografía* [Spanish Treaty on Venereal Disease and Syphilis]. His publications were predominantly technical and professional, not populist.

Bejarano: see Méndez Bejarano.

Besteiro, Julián (1870–1940), became central in Spanish socialism after the death of Pablo Iglesias. His correspondence with his wife, Dolores Cebrián, until he died in prison, was published in 2004, *Cartas desde la prisión: 110 cartas a su esposa Dolores Cebrián* (Madrid: Biblioteca Nueva).

Bloch, Iwan, (1873–1923) dermatologist from Berlin, known as the 'father of sexology'.

Brachfeld, Ferenc Oliver (1908–67), Hungarian psychiatrist who worked in Spain, and later moved to Venezuela. His article 'Crítica de las teorías sexuales del Dr Marañón' [Critique of the Sexual Theories of Dr Marañón], *Revista Médica de Barcelona* (548–61) (December 1931), was followed by *Polémica contra Marañón* [Polemic against Marañón] (Barcelona, 1933). Brachfeld studied psychoanalysis with Adler in Vienna, researched the remnants of Hungarian folk culture in Catalan folk art, and translated Hungarian works into Spanish and Catalan from Hungarian and other European languages.

Bravo Sanfelíu, Julio (1894–1987), a doctor with a career of distinct international quality, mainly in the activity of hygiene and publicity. As a doctor, he was involved in work against venereal disease in England and Belgium in 1925, and received a Rockefeller grant to study in the United States, 1926–7. He was head of the Oficina Técnica de Propaganda Antivenérea [Technical Office for Anti-VD Propaganda] from 1929, and lectured in the Escuela Nacional de Sanidad [National School of Health] from 1931. He headed the Sección de Propaganda Sanitaria de la Dirección General de Sanidad [Section of Sanitary Propaganda in the General Institute of Health] from 1933 and would be known for the work on health posters through to 1950. He was also a dramatist and novelist.

Bugallo Sánchez, José, a lawyer whose publications reveal a strong social concern, including various reports and pamphlets such as: *Los reformatorios de España* [Reformatories in Spain], dealing with delinquent children and adolescents (1916). Various of his works were published with Morata, including *La delincuencia infantil: ¿Cómo debe prevenirse? ¿Cómo debe castigarse?* [Child Delinquency: How Should it be Prevented? How Should it be Punished? (1926), and *La higiene sexual en las escuelas* [Sexual Hygiene in Schools] (1930). He showed a different approach to knowledge in *El espiritualismo y la ciencia* [Spiritualism and Science] (1933).

Campoamor, Clara (1888–1972), was one of the three Spanish women deputies elected to the 1931 Cortes. Champion of votes for women and listed by Ferrer Benimeli as believed to be a mason (1987, vol. II: 218–22).

Campoy Ibáñez, Antonio , doctor and author of *El amor y la patología* [Love and Pathology] 1931.

Cansinos-Assens, Rafael (1883–1964), a critic, novelist, journalist and translator with prodigious output, mainly remembered for his associations with the avant-garde. He worked however, as a journalist on other publications: *La correspondencia de España* (Madrid) until 1921; as literary critic for *La Tribuna* until 1923, and for *Los Lunes del Imparcial* until 1924. From 1925 he collaborated in *La Libertad*. In 1919–21 he spearheaded *ultraísmo*, with its reviews *Grecia, Ultra, Perseo*, and 1918–22 he directed the Spanish section of Hispanoamerican journal *Cervantes*. His links with other members of the WLSR would appear to have some basis in his work as a translator, but also in his works on the erotic. He translated from Nordau, *Matrimonios morganáticos* [Morganatic Marriages] (1904), Gina Lombroso, *El alma de la mujer* [The Soul of Woman] (1926), Alfred Bruce Douglas, *Oscar Wilde y yo* [Oscar Wilde and I] (1925), and Benjamin Barr Lindsey, *El matrimonio de compañía* [Companionate Marriage] (1930). His own writings on the erotic include *Estética y erotismo de la pena de muerte* [Aesthetics and Erotics of the Death Penalty] (1916), *Ética y estética de los sexos* [Ethics and Aesthetics of the Sexes] (1920), *Los valores eróticos en las religiones: de Eros a Cristo* [Erotic Values in Religión: From Eros to Christ] (1925). He was also translator of *El sexo en la civilización* [Sex in Civilization] (1930), a collection edited by V. F. Calverton and S. D. Schmalhausen, which had an introduction by Havelock Ellis. He published *Maternidad última: novela inédita* [Final Motherhood: Unpublished Novel] (1924), in La Novela Corta series. It is possible his interest in the WLSR related also to his own reputed homosexuality (see Eisenberg 1999: 25).

Carpenter, Edward (1844–1929), writer and champion of rights of women and homosexuals, friend of Ellis.

Carrasco i Formiguera, Manuel (1890–1938), Catalan politician and lawyer (later to be executed by the Nationalists), brother of the physiologist Luis Carrasco Formiguera, his writings include *Diari de presó (1923–1924)* [Prison Diaries 1923–1924] (1999), and *El pacte de San Sebastián* [The Pact of San Sebastian] (1931).

Casares Quiroga, Santiago (1884–1950), Minister for the Navy in the Second Republic, then Minister of Goverment (till 1933).

Chiavacci, L., editor of the Berlin 1933 publication of *Sexus: Internationale Vierteljahresschrift für die gesamte Sexualwissenschaft und Sexualreform* 1. See Dose (2003: 2).

Cifuentes Díaz, Pedro (1880–1960), a urologist with an international profile, he founded the Servicio de Urología [Urology service] in the Hospital de la Princesa. He had membership of international societies of surgery, including those of Portugal, Germany, Rumania and France. In the meeting to set up the Liga, Hildegart refers the plank on prevention of prostitution and venereal disease to him as a doctor. He was also director of the Asilo Hospital de San Rafael (for weak and disabled children). His publications were restricted to his area of professional expertise.

Civera Martínez, Marín (1900–75), editor of the Cuadernos de Cultura (Valencia 1930–3) in which works by various Liga members appeared, including Hildegart. Valencia is referred to in *Sexus* 1 (2), 102 as the oldest section of the Liga. He was one of the masons in the Liga (approximately one sixth of the founding members were reputed to be masons). His publications include *España contra el fascismo* [Spain Against Fascism (1938?)], *La formación de la economía política* [Development of Political Economics] (1930), *El marxismo: origen, desarrollo y transformación* [Marxism: Origins, Development, Transformation] (1930), *El sindicalismo: historia, filosofía, economía* [Sindicalism: History, Philosophy, Economics] (1931).

Cossío, Manuel Bartolomé (1858–1936), educationalist, art critic, lecturer in the School of Criminology, and a mainstay of the Junta para Ampliación de Estudios and the Residencia de Estudiantes.

Cyon: see Laffitte.

Dantín Cereceda, Juan (1881–1943), a regular contributor to *Revista de Occidente* in the 1920s, writing reviews on geography and anthropology. His publications include: *Agricultura* [Agriculture] (1925), *Cómo se enseña la geografía* [How to Teach Geography] (1923), *La vida de la tierra* [Life of the Earth] (1922).

Domingo, Marcelino (1884–1939), first Minister for Public Instruction in the Second Republic.

Field, Alice Withrow (1909–60), socialist, sex reformer and criminologist, whose work in the 1950s would focus on sex offenders in the US.

Forel, Auguste (1848–1931), Swiss psychiatrist, director of the Burghölzli Clinic, and professor at the University of Zurich, he was the pioneer of sexology in Switzerland.

Galarza, Ángel, Head of Police, who would become Minister of the Interior in 1936.

Giner de los Ríos, Francisco (1839–1915), founder of the Institución Libre de Enseñanza (1876).

González Blanco, Edmundo (1878–1938), a novelist and prolific translator and writer of prologues. Like Cansinos-Assens, he published in La Novela Corta, with *Dos mujeres fáciles* [Two Women of Easy Virtue] (1925). Other publications include *El feminismo en las sociedades modernas* [Feminism in Modern Society] (1904), *Crónica científico-filosófica: El anarquismo como creencia* [Scientific-Philosophical Chronicle: Anarchism as a Belief, (1904–16), in 6 parts, *El profesor Saldaña y sus ideas sociológicas* [Profesor Saldaña and his Sociological Ideas] (1921), *La familia en el pasado, en el presente y en el porvenir* [The Family in the Past, Present and Future] (1930) as part of the Marín Civera series Cuadernos de Cultura, in the section of Sociología General, which also contained two works by Hildegart, *Sexo y amor* (1931), and *La Revolución sexual* (1931). His prologues included those for Kropotkin, *El anarquismo* [Anarchism] (1931) and Lenin, *El comunismo* [Communism] (1934).

Haire, Norman (1892–1952), Australian gynaecologist and proponent of birth control who had an extensive correspondence with Ellis. See Crozier (2003).

Haro García, Francisco, gynaecologist, referred to at length in Hildegart's letters as the member of the WLSR who tries to oust her from the position of secretary. Among his publications is *Eugenesia y matrimonio: El certificado médico prenupcial* [Eugenics and Marriage: The Pre-Nuptial Wedding Certificate] (1928, reprinted with foreword by Marañón in 1932). He joined with others of the group (such as Vital Aza and Marañón) in offering advice to women. His *Fases biológicas de la mujer (Cartas a Paloma)* [Biological Phases of Woman: (Letters to Paloma)] (1934) is a case in point. See Richards (2004: 833).

Hernández Alfonso, Luis (1901–79), a journalist, political and literary writer who had studied both medicine and law, and was involved in republican ideas from 1919. Author of *¿Miedo al porvenir?: Democracia y comunismo* [Fear of the Future?: Democracy and Communism] (1931), and *Eugenesia y derecho a vivir* [Eugenics and the Right to Live] (1933), both published with Morata. Also *Verdad y mentira de la República española* [Truth and Lies of the Spanish Republic] (1933). Published '¡Prostitutas!' [Prostitutes!] in *Estudios* 14: 149 (1936).

Hernández Catá, Alfonso (1885–1940), a novelist born in Spain, but who went to Cuba where he was a journalist. In 1909 he embarked on a diplomatic career, with postings in Europe, including Madrid. Known for having made some of the first representations of homosexuality in Cuban literature, as in *El ángel de Sodoma* [The Angel of Sodom] (1928). His other literary works include *El pecado original* [Original Sin] (1908), *El placer de sufrir: novela* [The Pleasure of Suffering: Novel] (1921, with four further editions). He also published in the series of La Novela Corta, with *El aborto* [Abortion] (1922), *Una mala mujer* [A Bad Woman] (1922), *Los siete pecados* [The Seven Deadly Sins] (1930), *El manicomio (Novela misteriosa)* [The Asylum (Novel of Mystery)] (1933).

Hirschfeld, Magnus (1868–1935), sexologist who founded the World League for Sexual Reform in 1928, and focused in particular on promoting knowledge about and acceptance of homosexuality.

Hoyos Sainz, Luis de (1868–1951), physical anthropologist who was elected to the Chair of Physiology and Hygiene in Madrid in 1909.

Huerta, Luis, listed as 'doctor' in the *Gaceta Médica española*, interested in pedagogy as well as paediatrics. Concerned with infant mortality, he saw the solution as birth control and sex education. He published, as did Hildegart and González Blanco, in the *Cuadernos de Cultura* of Marín Civera Martínez, with *La vida (biología)* [Life (biology)] (Valencia, 1930). In January 1933 he wrote in the *Gaceta Médica Española* on prostitution, including a summary of the work of the WLSR, and the Liga (under Hildegart) in Spain. In June 1933 in *Gaceta Médica Española*, his review of Hildegart's 'trilogy' (*El problema sexual tratado por una mujer española; La rebeldía sexual de la juventud; Malthusismo y neomalthusismo*), an article in press at the time of her death, was a further occasion for him to stress her importance and value. With Enrique Noguera he edited the proceedings of the 1933 Eugenics Conference (1934).

ILE: Institución Libre de Enseñanza, founded in 1876 by Francisco Giner de los Ríos.

Ives, George Cecil (1867–1950), writer and criminologist, dedicated to homosexual law reform, in touch with Hirschfeld, Ellis, Wilde and Carpenter, and one of the founders in 1914 of the British Society for the Study of Sex Psychology.

JAE: Junta para Amplicación de Estudios, set up in 1907 to enable Spaniards to study outside Spain.

Jiménez de Asúa, Luis (1889–1970), lawyer and writer, who spent 1925–6 in the US, including some time in Argentina. His publications focus on criminal law, and show a high level of international awareness. His approach to eugenics, and matters such as venereal disease, and euthanasia, was from the legal aspect. His publications include: *La lucha contra el delito de contagio venéreo* [The Struggle against the Crime of Contagion of Venereal Disease] (1925), *Libertad de amar y derecho a morir* [The Freedom to Love and the Right to Die] (1928), *Al servicio de la nueva generación* [In the Service of the New Generation] (1930) (an 'ethical' work, published with Morata), *Valor de la psicología profunda: (psicoanalisis y psicología individual en ciencias penales* [The Value of Depth Psychology: Psychoanalysis and Individual Psychology in Criminal Science] (1935). He provided a prologue to J. Mª de Barbáchano, *Hacia el divorcio en España* [Towards Divorce in Spain] (1931). He was elected deputy to the Cortes in 1931. Ferrer Benimeli (1987: 218–22) lists him as a mason.

Juarros Ortega, César (1879–1942), a neuropathologist who had worked in the army and was director of the Central School for the Subnormal. An energetic popularizer of knowledge, he wrote books, lectures and articles in his campaign for physical education and efforts to have norms of sexual hygiene accepted. He also wrote popular novels, many with a didactic purpose. He was elected deputy to the Cortes in 1931. His publications include *De la falta de personalidad clínica de las psicosis histéricas* [On the Lack of Clinical Personality in Hysterical Psychosis] (1908), *El breviario sentimental de la madre* [Sentimental Handbook of the Mother] (1921), *El amor en España: características masculinas* [Love in Spain: Masculine Features] (1927), *Los senderos de la locura (Divulgaciones psiquiátricas)* [Paths of Madness (Psychiatric Musing] (1927), *Los horizontes del psicoanalisis* [Horizons of Psychoanalysis] (1928), with the more florid and popular *Los engaños de la morfina* [The Deceits of Morphine] (1929), where a healthy sexual life is billed as being incompatible with the consumption of morphine.

Kautsky, Karl (1854–1938), author of *Terrorism and Communism* (1920), widely available in Spain through the Biblioteca Nueva series Nuevas Doctrinas Sociales.

Kehl, Renato (1889–?), Brazilian eugenicist, active in eugenics between 1917 and 1937, author of *Eugenia e medicina social; problemas da vida* [Eugenics and Social Medicine: Problems of Life] (second edition, 1923). Hildegart had planned to write two works in collaboration with him, *Cómo escoger un buen marido* [How to Choose a Good Husband] and *Cómo escoger una buena esposa* [How to Choose a Good Wife].

Kent, Victoria (1898–1987), one of the three women deputies elected in 1931 (by an all-male electorate), and the first Republican Director General of Prisons. Kent opposed giving the vote to women, believing that it would place the Republic in danger. She successfully defended Álvaro de Albornoz when he was tried for his involvement in the revolutionary coup of December 1930.

Key, Ellen (1849–1926), Swedish reformer, feminist and strong advocate for motherhood to be accorded a greater respect.

Kollontai, Aleksandra (1873–1952), Russian revolutionary and novelist.

Iruretagoyena, Julia, daughter of the republican mayor of Irún, and wife of the socialist Tomás Meabe.

Lafitte, Françoise, whose married name was Cyon, was Ellis's companion in the period Hildegart was writing to him. See Grosskurth (1980).

Lafora: see Rodríguez Lafora.

Largo Caballero, Francisco (1869–1946), General Secretary of the UGT, Minister of Labour in the Second Republic. Listed as believed to be a mason by Ferrer Benimeli (1987, II: 218–22).

Lessa, Almerindo (1909–97), Portuguese eugenicist just starting out on his career when he published in the second number of *Sexus*, when he was president of the Professional Association of Students of Medicine in Oporto.

Leunbach, J. H., Danish physician who edited, with H. Reise, the proceedings of the Sexual Reform Congress held in Copenhagen 1928, and the proceedings of the Second Congress of the WLSR, Copenhagen and Leipzig, 1929.

Lindsey, Benjamin Barr (1869–1943), US jurist and reformer.

Lipschütz, Alexander (1883–1980), born in Latvia, studied in Germany and Austria, and was in Chile 1927–36, specializing in endocrinology and oncology. Two of his works came out with Morata, *Las secreciones internas de las glándulas sexuales* [Internal Secretions of the Sexual Glands] (Madrid: Morata, 1928) and *Trabajos recientes sobre secreciones internas* [Recent Studies on Internal Secretions] (Madrid: Morata, 1932).

Llopis, Rodolfo (1895–1983), socialist, and Director General of primary education in the Second Republic in 1931. Listed as a mason by Ferrer Benimeli (1987, vol. II: 218–22).

Lombroso, Cesare (1835–1909), founder of the Italian School of Criminology, who believed that the tendency towards crime was hereditary, and could be detected in the physiognomy.

López Ureña, Francisco, a biologist, author of *El misterio de la vida: Ensayo de Biología universal* [The Mystery of Life: Essay of Universal Biology] (1929).

Luisi, Paulina (1875–1950), Uruguayan doctor, feminist and social reformer.

Nordau, Max (1849–1923), initially a doctor, but better known for his promotion of theories of degeneration, summarized in *Degeneration* (1895), a work widely translated throughout Europe.

Macau Moncaunt, José (1890–1952), doctor, named clinical director of the Casa de Maternidad de Santa Cristina, becoming its subdirector in 1930. In 1917 he published with Vital Aza on cancer of the uterus. Also published in *Sexualidad* on 8 March 1925, 'La embarazada y su protección' [The Pregnant Woman and How to Protect Her].

Madrazo, Enrique Diego de (1850–1942), a 'socialist' who wrote on eugenics, sometimes described as father of Spanish eugenics. His publications include *Cultivo de la especie humana* [Cultivation of the Human Race] (1904), *Un siglo de civilización bajo la influencia eugenésica* [A Century of Civilization Under the Influence of Eugenics] (1930), and *Pedagogía y eugenesia* [Education and Eugenics] (1932). He was one of the speakers at the 1933 Eugenics Conference.

Marañón, Gregorio (1887–1960), pupil of both Ramón y Cajal and Recaséns, with a strong national and international reputation. President of WLSR in Spain, promoter of eugenics, publicist, connected with the Residencia de Estudiantes, he wrote on sexual reform, but also on literature, culture and gender, with a mixture of conservative and liberal attitudes. His notable breadth of interest and expertise is shown by his membership of the five Royal Academies of Language, Medicine, Exact, Physical and Natural Sciences, History and Fine Arts. He published on sex (*Tres ensayos sobre la vida sexual*), eugenics, and wrote a number of psychobiographies. He also engaged in popular dissemination of medicine and published *El problema social de la infección* [The Social Problem of Contagion] (1929) in the series El Libro del Pueblo. There is no sign of his association with the WLSR in biographical accounts, although Álvarez-Sierra (1963) lists some of his relevant publications

Méndez Bejarano, Mario (1857–1931), an early mentor of Hildegart who had published widely in the arts and humanities. See Chapter Three.

Morata, Javier, publisher, arguably one of the key figures of the Liga. In the series Temas de Nuestro Tiempo [Themes of Our Time] of twenty-six volumes, twelve titles referred to sex, marriage or eugenics. In a 1933 list, Otros Libros de Interés [Other Books of Interest], of seventy books, forty-four are on sex and marriage, and six carry 'eugenesia' in the title (Álvarez Peláez and Huertas, 1987: 194). He published works by twelve founding members of the Liga, and by a further four from the list of provincial contacts. He figures prominently as a publisher in Hildegart's letters to Ellis.

Nelken, Margarita (1897–1968), socialist and champion of women's rights, and educational reform.

Navarro Fernández, Antonio (1870–1931), specialist in dermatology and venereology. In 1925 he organized the meetings of a campaign for social hygiene at which Hildegart spoke in her early teens, and on which his attitude to prostitution was that of an abolitionist. The meetings were reported in the journal *Sexualidad* of which he was director (see Cleminson, 2000: 79). He was also involved in the *Archivos de Higiene y Sanidad Pública* [Archives of Hygiene and Public Health] of which Mario Sánchez Taboada was manager and which served as a network and meeting point for various WLSR members, including Marañón, Juarros, and Pittaluga. His publications include: *La prostitución en la villa de Madrid* [Prostitution in the City of Madrid] (1909), *Conciencia y voluntad sociales* [Social Will and Conscience] (1909), *Dactiloscopia en España* [Finger-printing in Spain] (1912), *El porvenir de la raza blanca* [Future of the White Race] (1912), *Presérvate del amor impuro: (enfermedades venéreas)* [Keep Yourself Safe from Impure Love; (Venereal Disease)] (1931).

Noguera, Enrique, hygienist who studied under Marañón, and left medicine for journalism. Director and chief editor of the *Gaceta Médica Española*, founder and director of the Servicio y Escuela de Perfeccionamiento Sanitario [School and Service of Sanitary Improvement], Member of Academia Médico-Quirúrgica, and Sociedad Española de Higiene and of the Junta Directiva de la Asociación de Escritores Médicos. By the time of *Sexus* 1(2) (May/June 1933) he had become President of the Spanish Liga. With Luis Huerta he edited the proceedings of the 1933 Eugenics Conference (1934).

Nóvoa Santos, Roberto (1885–1933), doctor (pathologist) and publicist of conservative views on gender, who had periods of study in France, Austria and Germany. His publications included: *La indigencia espiritual del sexo femenino* [The Spiritual Poverty of Woman] (1909?), *La mujer, nuestro sexto sentido y otros esbozos* [Woman, Our Sixth Sense and Other Sketches] (1929), *Cuerpo y espíritu: Fragmentos para una doctrina genética y energética del espíritu* [Body and Mind: Fragments for a Genetic and Energetic Theory of Mind] (1930), *Patografía de Santa Teresa de Jesús y el instinto de la muerte* [Pathography of St Teresa of Jesus and the Death Instinct] (1932).

Oriol Anguera, Antonio, who wrote *Física de la psique: Monogamía, Poligamia* [Physics of the Psyche: Monogamy, Polygamy] (1930), in the Morata collection of Temas de Nuestro Tiempo.

Ortiz de Pinedo, José (1881–1956), a prolific writer of novels published in series such as La novela corta, and Los contemporáneos. These include: *El afán de vivir* [The Desire to Live] (1917), *El derecho de vivir contento* [The Right to Live Happily] (1920), *Eva curiosa: novela* [Curious Eve] (1920), *El árbol del bien y el mal* [The Tree of Good and Evil] (1921), *Casa de amor* [House of Love] (1931), *El superhombre* [Superman] (1932).

Otaola y Richter, José María de, gynaecologist, author of *Aborto, su tratamiento* [Abortion and its Treatment] 1927, and of an article on conception and contraception in Noguera y Huerta (1934), he was a frequent contributor to the *Gaceta Médica Española*.

Pascua, Marcelino (1897–1977) was prominent in health reform in the first two years of the Republic.

Pestaña, Ángel (1886–1937) labour leader prominent in the Confederación Nacional de Trabajo (CNT).

Pi y Suñer, Augusto (1879–1965), doctor and physiologist. His writings include lectures such as *El problema del metabolismo* [The Problem of the Metabolism] (1917), *El hambre en los pueblos* [Hunger in the Villages], lecture (1922).

Pittaluga Fattorini, Gustavo (1876–1955), doctor working in public health, but also well known in the Residencia de Estudiantes for his musical activities. He devoted particular attention to malaria. Of Italian origin, he went in 1903 to Spain for a Congreso Internacional de Medicina, eventually taking Spanish nationality, and with Huertas spoke on the epidemiology of malaria ('Etiología y epidemiología del paludismo' [Aetiology and Epidemiology of Malaria]) which led to work with Dr Felipe Jiménez Asúa. He was Consejero de Sanidad and Vice-President of Sociedad Española de Higiene [Spanish Hygiene Society]. His publications include: *El problema político de la sanidad pública* [The Political Problem of Public Health] (1921), *El vicio, la voluntad, la ironía* [Vice, Willpower, Irony] (1927/8), *Ensayo de una teoría biológica del vicio* [Essay on a Biological Theory of Vice] (1925).

Prados Such, Miguel (1894–1969) psychiatrist, pupil of Kraepelian, former clinical director of asylum of San José, Malaga, co-author with Sacristán of clinical report for the defense on Aurora. His publications include *La psicología de la multitudes: conferencia* [The Psychology of Crowds: lecture] Madrid, Cosano, 1928.

Ramón y Cajal, Santiago (1852–1934), clearly the most eminent and internationally recognized scientist of the group, eighty at the time it was set up. A histologist, he won the Nobel Prize for medicine in 1906, and was first president of the Junta para Ampliación de Estudios. He was honorary member of many foreign medical academies, including those of New York, Vienna, Berlin, Paris, London, Göttingen, Oxford, Basel, Rome, Cambridge, Lisbon, Brussels, Stockholm and Leipzig.

Recaséns, Sebastián (1893–1956) was dean of Faculty of Medicine of University of Madrid, and held the chair of Gynaecology. Through the 1920s he had links with Germany, France, Italy, Lisbon and Buenos Aires. Organizer of the 1928 Eugenics Conference, he spoke on 'Eugenesia y Procreación' [Eugenics and Procreation], and president of the Real Academia de Medicina in 1928. His publications, apart from the Eugenics Conference paper, are all within his professional field of obstetrics and gynaecology.

Remartínez, Roberto (1895–1977), a naturist doctor who published *Universo* [Universe] in the Cuadernos de Cultura of Valencia. Most of his works now exist in modern editions, including *Comer para vivir, no vivir para comer* [Eating to Live, not Living to Eat] (1958), *Lo que debe conocer toda madre: preguntas y respuestas de Eugenesia y Puericultura* [What Every Mother Should Know: Questions and Answers on Eugenics and Puericulture] (1948), *Vitalidad y alimentación racional* [Vitality and Rational Nutrition] (1981).

Rivas Cherif, **Cipriano** (1891–1967), early twentieth-century dramatist and theatre director.

Rocamora: this may be either R. S. Rocamora (b. 1880) or Jaime Peyri Rocamora. R. S. Rocamora was a writer and lawyer, also interested in Sociology and Esperanto. The interest in Esperanto forms a possible link to the Liga in that various social reformers of the period also embraced the idea of a universal language. A report in the *Archivos de la Higiene y Sanidad Pública* in August 1925, for example, is on the Centro Esperantista de Madrid (see also Chapter Three, note 5). R. S. Rocamora's publications include *Los conflictos jurídico-sociales que plantean las dolencias venéreas y sifilíticas* [Legal and Social Conflicts Posed by Venereal and Syphilitic Illnesses] (1916), a reference to which is made in *Sexualidad* 1 (17), 24 May 1925, 12, in 'Bibliografía'. Jaime Peyri Rocamora was a dermatologist, whose publications included the *Manual de enfermedades intersexuales* [Manual of Intersexual Illnesses] (1928). He was the translator of Edmund Lesser, *Tratado de las enfermedades de la piel y venéreas* [Treaty on Venereal Disease and Skin Complaints] (1914).

Rodríguez Lafora, Gonzalo (1887–1971), an energetic and internationally known doctor who was a pupil of the psychiatrist Simarro in Spain, of Alzheimer in Munich, and worked with Ramón y Cajal in Histology. 1910–12 he was a histopathologist at the Government Hospital for the Insane in Washington. He was active in journalism, contributing regularly to the debate on medical education in the daily paper *El Sol* in the early 1920s and reviewed Freud's *Interpretation of Dreams* for the *Revista de Occidente* in 1924. His numerous professional publications include *Los niños mentalmente anormales* [Mentally Subnormal Children] (1917), *Diagnóstico y tratamientos modernos de la neurosífilis* [Modern Diagnosis and Treatments of Neuro-Syphilis] (1920), *Impotencia sexual masculina de forma psíquica* [Psychic Variety of Masculine Sexual Impotence] (1925), while more widely ranging and accessible works include the *Estudio psicológico del cubismo y expresionismo* [Psychological Study of Cubism and Expressionism] (1921) and *Don Juan, los milagros y otros ensayos* [Don Juan, Miracles, and Other Essays] (1927). In 1925 Lafora was co-founder of the journal *Archivos de neurobiología, psicología, fisiología, histología, neurología y psiquiatría*, now titled *Archivos de neurobiología*.

Ruiz Funes, Mariano (1889–1953), an academic lawyer who was elected deputy of Cortes 1931, and was head of Acción Republicana. He spoke on 'La nueva política y la maternidad consciente' [New Politics and Conscious Motherhood] in the 1933 Eugenics Conference. His publications include: *Endocrinología y Criminalidad* [Endocrinology and Criminality] (1929), *Delito y libertad* [Crime and Freedom] (1930, and later published by Morata in 1931). He translated and wrote an introductory study of Emile Durkheim, *El suicidio: estudio de sociología* [Suicide: a Sociological Study] (1928).

Sacristán, José María (1887–1957), pupil of Ramón y Cajal, specialized in neuropathology; being assistant to Simarro, he studied further in this area in Germany. Member of the Junta para Ampliación de Estudios when Ramón y Cajal was at its head, he became director of the Manicomio de Ciempozuelos para mujeres (the asylum where Aurora was sent eventually), and testified for the defence at her trial. His publications include a review of Freud, *The Ego and the Id* in *Revista de Occidente* (1923), work on Kretschmer (1926) and a translation of Kretschmer's *Hysteria* (1928).

Sainz de Aja, Enrique Álvarez (1884–1965), a doctor who specialized in dermatology and the treatment of syphilis. Hildegart refers the plank of the Liga on prevention of prostitution and venereal disease to him. His publications concentrated on venereal disease, including *Terapéutica de enfermedades sexuales* [Treatment of Sexual Diseases] (1914), *Sífilis, blenorragia y matrimonio* [Syphilis, Blenorrhagia and Marriage] (1920), later becoming a pamphlet, *Lo que todo el mundo debe saber sobre la sífilis* [What Every One Should Know About Syphilis] (1946).

Salazar Alonso, Rafael, who would become Ministro de Gobernación in Samper's 1934 government. Listed as a mason (*www.fuenterrebollo.com/masoneria.html*).

Saldaña, Quintiliano (1878–1938), lawyer and writer, with clear international profile. He supervised Hildegart's law dissertation, and was possibly her first initial contact with the work of Ellis. His wide-ranging publications cover culture, psychology, sexology, law and literature (directed, as are those of Juarros, to dissemination of ideas about society and sexuality), including: *La locura de Don Quijote* [The Madness of Don Quixote] (1916), *El atentado social* [Social Attack] (1927), *Capacidad criminal de las personas sociales* [The Criminal Capacity of People in Society] (1927), *Siete ensayos sobre sociología sexual* [Seven Essays on Sexual Psychology] (1928), *La sexología* [Sexology] (1930). His novels include *Las corridas* [Worldly Women] (1914). Pérez Sanz and Bru Ripoll (1987: 50) comment on how the majority of those writing 'erotic novels' were professionals from medicine, law, journalism, that is, the professions of those most involved in eugenics.

Sánchez Covisa, José (1881–1950), doctor specializing in treatment of syphilis, to whom Hildegart refers in the discussion of the plank on prevention of prostitution and venereal disease. His publications focus on syphilis and other contagious diseases such as leprosy, including *Problema social de la lepra en España* [Social Problem of Leprosy in Spain] (1928).

Sánchez de Rivera y Moset, Daniel, a doctor whose interests included areas of hygiene and culture. His publications include: *El cólera y los medios de evitarlo* [Cholera and How to Avoid It] (1908), *Degeneración por sífilis adquirida* [Degeneration Acquired Through Inherited Syphilis] (1911), *Lo sexual: (peligros y consecuencias de los vicios y enfermedades sexuales)* [The Sexual: (Dangers and Consequences of Sexual Vices and Diseases)] (1924), and *La ruta del matrimonio* [The Path to Marriage] (1929).

Sánchez Taboada, Mario S., manager of the *Archivos de Higiene y Sanidad* and listed as medical correspondent in this journal and for *El Liberal* (1925). The *Archivos* were a central networking point, publishing work by Marañón, Juarros and Pittaluga.

Sanchis Banús, José (1893–1932), considered one of the best psychiatrists in Spain, one of those who introduced psychoanalysis to Spain. He spoke at the 1928 Eugenics Conference and was one of the organizers of the Liga de Higiene Mental, and president of Colegio de Médicos de Madrid. A socialist, he was elected deputy to the Cortes in 1931. His publications include work on the delinquent, on menopausal epilepsy, and *La Psiquiatría en la novela española contemporánea* [Psychiatry in the Modern Spanish Novel], a paper read at the Ateneo de Madrid in 1922.

Sanger, Margaret (1879–1966), Irish-American pioneer of birth control who contacted Ellis by letter December 1914 and with whom a close relationship developed (Grosskurth, 242–53).

Santullano, Luis, involved in cultural exchange, became secretary of the Patronato de Misiones Pedagógicas (1933).

Stopes, Marie (1880–1958) British feminist and birth control campaigner.

Tomás y Samper, Rodolfo, educationalist, translated and wrote the prologue and notes for the *Sistema de educación de Pestalozzi* [Educational Scheme of Pestalozzi] (1932).

Torrubiano y Ripoll, Jaime (b. 1879), writer and publisher of philosophy and theology. A Catholic commentator, he spoke at the 1933 Eugenics Conference on 'El Cristianismo es el mejor auxiliar de la Ciencia Eugénica' [Christianity is the Best Support of Eugenic Science]. His publications include: *¿Son ellos adúlteros? para mujeres casadas y casaderas y para gente de sotana* [Do They Commit Adultery? For Married Women and Those About To Marry, and For Men of the Cloth] (1921), *Teología y eugenesia* [Theology and Eugenics] (1929), *Política religiosa de la democracia española* [Religious Politics of the Spanish Democracy] (1931). He contributed regularly in *Sexualidad* through 1925 in a section called 'Teología sexual' [Sexual Theology], and the review carried an advert for his matrimonial advice section, describing him as Catedrático de Derecho Matrimonial [Professor of Matrimonial Law].

Varela Radio, Manuel (1875–1962), a gynaecologist who travelled in England and Germany to further his professional expertise. He was appointed to a chair of Obstetrics and Gynaecology in Santiago de Compostela in 1905, transferred to Madrid in 1918 and was named director of the Maternidad de Santa Cristina, where he stayed till 1936. He was consulted about the provisions in setting up the Junta para Ampliación de Estudios, specifically about possible advisers on applications for studying medicine (Castillejo, 1997: 345–6), and went on the 1922 visit to Las Hurdes with Alfonso XIII.

Van de Velde, Theodore H. (1873–1937), Dutch physician and gynaecologist, author of *Ideal Marriage: its Physiology and Technique* (1926). In Spain this appeared in 1931 (Madrid: Prensa Moderna), and *Fertilidad y esterilidad en el matrimonio* [Fertility and Sterility in Marriage] in 1932 (Madrid: Juan Pueyo).

Weisskopf, Joseph , local organizer of the congress of the World League for Sexual Reform in Brno, Czechoslovakia in 1932.

Wells, H. G. (1866–1946), author of novels and science fiction, journalist, well known in Spain through the press and publicity attached to his visits in the 1920s and 1930s.

Zozaya, Antonio (1859–1943), translator and publisher who founded the Biblioteca Económica Filosófica in 1880, with emphasis on translations of philosophy. He also wrote popular novels in series such as La Novela Mundial and La Novela Semanal. His non-fiction publications include: *La guerra de las ideas: la filosofía, el derecho, la moral, la historia, la estética, la* *sociología* [The War of Ideas: Philosophy, Law, Morality, History, Aesthetics, Sociology] (1915), *Libertad, propiedad y alma colectiva* [Liberty, Property and Collective Soul] (1935), *Libertad e individualismo* [Liberty and Individualism] (1935). His translations of philosophy include: J. S. Mill, *El utilitarismo* [Utilitarianism] (1891), Plato, *Diálogos polémicos* [Polemic Dialogues] (1896), Descartes, *Meditaciones metafísicas* [Metaphysical Meditations] (1904), *Aforismos y pronósticos de Hipócrates* [Aphorisms and Predictions of Hippocrates] (1904), Kant, *Crítica de la razón práctica* [Critique of Practical Reason] (1907), Spencer, *Clasificación de las ciencias* [Classification of the Sciences] (1928).

Zulueta, Luis de (1878–1964), pupil of the *Institución Libre de Enseñanza*, regular contributor to the *Revista de Occidente* 1925–9.

Bibliography

Adams, Mark B. (1990) 'Toward a Comparative History of Eugenics', in Mark B. Adams (ed.), *The Wellborn Science*, Oxford, Oxford University Press, pp. 217–31.
Aguilar, Manuel (1963) *Una experiencia editorial*, Madrid, Aguilar.
Álvarez Junco, José (1989) 'Racionalismo, romanticismo y moralismo en la cultura política republicana de comienzos de siglo', in Jean-Louis Guereña and Alejandro Tiana (eds), *Clases populares, cultura, educación. Siglos XIX-XX. Coloquio Hispano-Francés Junio 1987*, Madrid, Casa de Velázquez/UNED, pp. 355–75.
Álvarez Peláez, Raquel (1988) 'Origen y desarrollo de la eugenesia en España', in José Manuel Sánchez Ron (ed.), *Ciencia y sociedad en España. De la Ilustración a la guerra civil*, Madrid, CSIC, pp. 179–204.
Álvarez Peláez, Raquel and Rafael Huertas García-Alejo (1987) *¿Criminales o locos? Dos peritajes psiquiátricos del Dr Gonzalo R Lafora*, Madrid, CSIC.
Álvarez-Sierra, José (1963) *Diccionario de autoridades médicas*, Madrid, Héroes.
Amador, Nicolás (1914) 'La eugénica y sus relaciones con la sociología y economía política. El factor biológico', *Estudios*, 7, 1–9, 167–99.
Anderson, Benedict (1983) *Imagined Communities: Reflections on the Origin and Spread of Nationalism*, London, Verso.
Aza, Vital (1932) 'Algunos comentarios clínicos y sexuales sobre la fecundación artificial', *Sexus*, 1, 1, 34–43.
Baroja, Pío (1900) 'Patología del golfo', in *Vidas sombrías (Cuentos)*, Madrid, Caro Raggio.
Baroja, Pío (1904) 'Mala hierba', in *El Tablado de Arlequín*, Madrid, Caro Raggio.
Baroja, Pío (1911). *El árbol de la ciencia*, Madrid, Caro Raggio/Castalia.
Barriobero y Herrán, E. (1930). *Los delitos sexuales en las viejas leyes españolas*, Madrid, Mundo Latino.
Bécarud, Jean and Evelyne López Campillo (1978) *Los intelectuales españoles durante la II República*, Madrid, Siglo XXI de España.
Bernaldo de Quirós, Constancio and José Llanas Aguilaniedo (1901) *La mala vida en Madrid*, Madrid, Rodríguez Serra.
Brandhorst, Henny (2003) 'From neo-Malthusianism to Sexual Reform: The Dutch Section of the World League for Sexual Reform', *Journal of the History of Sexuality*, 12, 1, 38–67.

Brenan, Gerald (1962) *The Spanish Labyrinth*, Cambridge, Cambridge University Press.

Burgos, Carmen de (1927) *La mujer moderna y sus derechos*, Valencia, Sempere.

Caamaño Alegre, Beatriz (2004) *Mujeres nuevas, viejas ideas: Contradicciones y fisuras en la construcción de la feminidad en la II república española y la dictadura franquista*, PhD dissertation, New Brunswick, Rutgers, State University of New Jersey.

Cacho Viu, Vicente (1962) *La Institución Libre de Enseñanza I. Orígenes y etapa universitaria (1860–1881)*, Madrid, Rialp.

Cal, Rosa (1991a) *A mí no me doblega nadie. Aurora Rodríguez: su vida y su obra*, La Coruña, Ediciones do Castro.

Cal, Rosa (1991b) 'Tras el padre de Hildegart', *Cambio 16*, 1045, 125–6.

Carlavilla del Barrio, Mauricio (1956) *Sodomitas*, Madrid, Nos.

Carr, Raymond (1966) *Spain 1808–1939*, Oxford, Oxford University Press.

Castillejo, David (1997) *El epistolario de José Castillejo. I. Un puente hacia Europa 1896–1909. Cartas reunidas por David Castillejo*, Madrid, Castalia.

Cernada, Alfonso [1932?] 'Charlando con Hildegart: Sobre la Liga española para la reforma sexual'. Source unknown [March 1932?], British Library Havelock Ellis archive.

Certeau, Michel de (1984) *The Practice of Everyday Life*, Berkeley, University of California Press.

Chesterton, G.K. (1922) *Eugenics and other Evils*, London, Cassell.

Cleminson, Richard (1994) 'Eugenics by Name or by Nature? The Spanish Anarchist Sex Reform of the 1930s', *History of European Ideas*, 28, 5, 729–40.

Cleminson, Richard (2000) *Anarchism, Science and Sex: Eugenics in Eastern Spain, 1900–1937*, Oxford, Peter Lang.

Cleminson, Richard (2003) '"Science and Sympathy" or "Sexual Subversion on a Human Basis"? Anarchists in Spain and the World League for Sexual Reform', *Journal of the History of Sexuality*, 12, 1, 110–21.

Cleminson, Richard (2006) 'A Hundred Years of Eugenics: Dr. Enrique Diego Madrazo, socialism and scientific progress', *Dinamis 26* (2006) forthcoming.

Cleminson, Richard and Efigenio Amezúa (1999)221–51 'Spain: the Political and Social Context of Sex Reform in the Late Nineteenth and Early Twentieth Centuries', in Lesley Hall, Gert Hekma and Franz Eder (eds), *Sexual Cultures in Europe: National Histories*, Manchester, Manchester University Press, pp. 173–96.

Cleminson, Richard and Francisco Vázquez García (2000) '"Los invisibles": Hacia una historia de la homosexualidad masculina en España, 1840–2000', *International Journal of Iberian Studies*, 13, 3, 167–83.

Cleminson, Richard and Francisco Vázquez García (2007) *'Los invisibles': A History of Male Homosexuality in Spain, 1850–1939*, Cardiff, University of Wales Press.

Coca (1931) 'Con la camarada Hildegart, propagandista de la rebeldía sexual de la juventud', *El Socialista*, 5 December 1931, 1.

Criado y Romero [1932?] 'Los orientadores del feminismo', *El Heraldo de Madrid* [1932?], in British Library Havelock Ellis archive.

Crozier, Ivan (2003) '"All the World's a Stage": Dora Russell, Norman Haire, and the 1929 London World League for Sexual Reform Congress', *Journal of the History of Sexuality*, 12, 1, 16–37.

Dasí, Pilar (1997) 'Los estragos de la interpretación materna: Hildegart o El jardín de la sabiduría', *Finisterre Freudiano (Revista de la Sección de Galicia de la Escuela Europea de Psicoanálisis)*, 7, 99–102.

Davies, Rhiân (2000) *'La España Moderna' and 'Regeneración': a Cultural Review in Restoration Spain, 1889–1914*, Manchester, Manchester University Press.

Delisle, Françoise Roussel (1946) *Friendship's Odyssey: [an autobiography]*, London, Heinemann.

Dose, Ralf (2003) 'The World League for Sexual Reform: Some Possible Approaches', *Journal of the History of Sexuality*, 12, 1, 1–15.

Dubois, Antonio (1934a) 'La trágica muerte de Hildegart: ¿Es la procesada una simuladora o no?', *La Libertad*, 25 May 1934, 4.

Dubois, Antonio (1934b) 'La trágica muerte de Hildegart: ¿Es doña Aurora paranoica, paranoide o semiloca?', *La Libertad*, 26 May 1934, 4.

Dubois, Antonio (1934c) 'La trágica muerte de Hildegart: La madre, parricida responsable', *La Libertad*, 27 May 1934, 4.

Eder, Franz X., Lesley A. Hall and Gert Hekma (eds) (1999). *Sexual Cultures in Europe: National Histories*, Manchester, Manchester University Press.

Eisenberg, Daniel (1999) 'Introduction', in *Spanish Writers on Gay and Lesbian Themes. A Bio-Critical Sourcebook by David William Foster*, Westport CT, Greenwood, pp. 1–21.

Ellis, Havelock (1906) 'Eugenics and St Valentine', *Nineteenth Century*, 59, 780–1.

Ellis, Havelock (1912) *The Task of Social Hygiene*, London, Constable.

Ellis, Havelock (1915) 'War and the Birth-Rate', *Nation*, 25 September 1915.

Ellis, Havelock (1916) 'Thinking for the Future', *Nation*, 23 December 1916.

Ellis, Havelock (1917) 'Birth-control and Eugenics', *Eugenic Review*, 9, 34–41.

Ellis, Havelock (1920–8) *Studies in The Psychology of Sex*, Philadelphia, Davis.

Ellis, Havelock (1922) *Lo scopo dell'eugenica* [Italian translation of the Task of Social Hygiene], Rome, Leonardo da Vinci.

Ellis, Havelock (1932) 'El infierno de la patología sexual', *Sexus*, 1, 1, 44–57.

Ellis, Havelock (1933) 'El infierno de la patología sexual', *Orto*, 16, 33–4.

Ellis, Henry Havelock (1894) *Man and Woman*, London, Heinemann.

Ellis, Henry Havelock (1899) *Man and Woman. A Study of Human Secondary Sexual Characters*, London, Walter Scott.

Ellis, Henry Havelock (1908) *The Soul of Spain*, London, Constable.
Ellis, Henry Havelock (1933) 'The Red Virgin', *The Adelphi*, June 1933, 174–9.
Espectador (1928) 'Pro Cultura Sanitaria', *Sexualidad*, 5, 140, 3–5.
Fajardo, José Manuel (1987a) 'Aurora Rodríguez, la tragedia de la Eva futura', *Cambio 16*, 806, 130–6.
Fajardo, José Manuel (1987b) 'Un delirio redentor', *Cambio 16*, 806, 132–3.
Farrall, Lyndsay (1970) *The Origins and Growth of the English Eugenics Movement 1896–1925*, Indiana, Indiana University.
Feinstein, H. M. (1964) 'Group Therapy for Mothers with Infanticidal Impulses', *American Journal of Psychiatry*, 120, 880.
Ferrer Benimeli, José Antonio (co-ordinator) (1989). Masonería, política y sociedad. 2 vols. Zaragoza, Centro de Estudios de la Masonería Española.
Forrester, John (1990) *The Seductions of Psychoanalysis: Freud, Lacan and Derrida*, Cambridge, Cambridge University Press.
Freeden, Michael (1979) 'Eugenics and Progressive Thought: a Study in Ideological Affinity', *The Historical Journal*, 22, 3, 645–71.
Freud, Sigmund (1905) 'The Sexual Aberrations', in Angela Richards (ed.), *On Sexuality: Three Essays on the Theory of Sexuality and Other Works*, Pelican Freud Library, Harmondsworth, Penguin Books, vol. 7, pp. 45–87.
Freud, Sigmund (1909) 'Family Romances', in Angela Richards (ed.), *On Sexuality: Three Essays on the Theory of Sexuality and Other Works*, Pelican Freud Library, Harmondsworth, Penguin Books, vol. 7, pp. 217–25.
Freud, Sigmund (1910) 'A Special Type of Choice of Object Made by Men', in Angela Richards (ed.), *On Sexuality: Three Essays on the Theory of Sexuality and Other Works*, Pelican Freud Library, Harmondsworth, Penguin Books, vol. 7, 227–42.
Freud, Sigmund (1927) 'Fetishism', in Angela Richards (ed.), *On Sexuality: Three Essays on the Theory of Sexuality and Other Works*, Pelican Freud Library, Harmondsworth, Penguin Books, vol. 7, 345–57.
Glick, Thomas (1981) 'Psicoanálisis, reforma sexual y política en la España de entre-guerras', *Estudios de Historia Social*, 16–17, 7–25.
Glick, Thomas (1982) 'The Naked Science: Psychoanalysis in Spain, 1914–1948', *Comparative Studies in Society and History*, 24, 533–71.
Glick, Thomas (2003) 'Sexual Reform, Psychoanalysis, and the Politics of Divorce in Spain in the 1920s and 1930s', *Journal of the History of Sexuality*, 12, 1, 68–97.
González-Blanco, Edmundo (1921). *El profesor Saldaña y sus ideas sociológicas*, Madrid, Reus.
Grau, Carlos (1934a) 'La madre que mató a su hija', *Luz*, 25 May 1934, 8–9.
Grau, Carlos (1934b) 'La madre que mató a su hija', *Luz*, 26 May 1934, 11.
Grau, Carlos (1934c) 'La madre que mató a su hija', *Luz*, 24 May 1934, 4.
Grosskurth, Phyllis (1980) *Havelock Ellis: a Biography*, London, Allen Lane.

Gureña, Jean-Louis (2003) *La prostitución en la España contemporánea*, Madrid, Marcial Pons.
Guzmán, Eduardo (1977) Prologue to Hildegart, *La rebeldía sexual de la juventud*, Barcelona, Anagrama, pp. 7–26.
Guzmán, Eduardo and Ezekiel Endériz (1972) *Aurora de Sangre*, Madrid, G. del Toro.
Hackl, Erich (1990) *Aurora's Motives*, Vintage Books.
Haire, Norman (1933) '¿En qué consiste la reforma sexual?', *Sexus*, 1, 2, 37–47.
Harder, T. (1967) 'The psychopathology of infanticide', *Acta Psychiatrica Scandinavica*, 43, 196–245.
Haro, Francisco (1934) 'Concepción y anticoncepción', in Enrique Noguera and Luis Huerta (eds), *Libro de las primeras jornadas eugénicas españolas: Genética, eugenesia y pedagogía sexual I*, Madrid, Morata, pp. 310–366.
Herbert, S. (1931) 'Norman Haire, Sexual Reform Congress: Proceedings of the Third Congress of the World-League for Sexual Reform, London 1930', *Eugenics Review*, 23, 2, 166–8.
Hildegart (1930a) *La limitación de la prole: un deber del proletariado consciente*, Madrid, [Gráfica Socialista].
Hildegart (1930b) *El problema eugénico: punto de vista de una mujer moderna*, Madrid, [Gráfica Socialista].
Hildegart (1930c) *Tres amores históricos: estudio comparativo de los amores de Romeo y Julieta, Abelardo y Eloísa y los Amantes de Teruel*, Teruel, *La Voz de Teruel*.
Hildegart (1931a) *Educación sexual*, Madrid, [Gráfica Socialista].
Hildegart (1931b) *El problema sexual tratado por una mujer española*, Madrid, Morata [Gráfica Literaria].
Hildegart (1931c) *Profilaxis anticoncepcional. Paternidad voluntaria*, Valencia, [Pascual Quiles].
Hildegart (1931d) *La rebeldía sexual de la juventud*, Madrid, Morata [sucesores de Peña Cruz].
Hildegart (1931e) *La revolución sexual*, Valencia, Cuadernos de Cultura.
Hildegart (1931f) *Sexo y amor*, Valencia, Rip. P. Quiles.
Hildegart (1932a) 'Endocrinología, delincuencia y eugenesia', *Sexus*, 1, 1, 77–91.
Hildegart (1932b) 'Historia del movimiento internacional y español de Reforma Sexual', *Sexus*, 1, 1, 104–15.
Hildegart (1932c) *Malthusismo y Neomalthusismo. El control de la natalidad*, Madrid, Granada Urania.
Hildegart (1932d) *¿Quo vadis, burguesía?*, Madrid, Ediciones Libertad.
Hildegart (1932e) *¿Se equivocó Marx . . . ?*, Madrid, Ediciones Boro.
Hildegart (1933a) 'Ensayos en torno a la criminología sexual', *Sexus*, 1, 2, 48–60.
Hildegart (1933b) 'Sugestiones en torno al problema de la bisexualidad', *Gaceta Médica Española*, 7, 77, 140–4.
Hildegart (1933c) 'Una figura de las Jornadas Eugénicas: El doctor Norman Haire, presidente de la Liga Mundial para la Reforma Sexual', *La Libertad*, 11 May 1933, 3–4.

Hildegart ([1933d]) *Venus ante el derecho*, Madrid, Castro.
Hildegart (1934) 'Maternidad consciente', in Joaquín Noguera and Luis Huerta (eds.), *Libro de las primeras jornadas eugénicas Genética, eugenesia y pedagogía sexual*. I, Madrid, Morata, pp 203–44.
Hildegart (1977a) *El problema sexual tratado por una mujer española*, Madrid, Morata.
Hildegart (1977b) *La rebeldía sexual de la juventud*, Barcelona, Anagrama.
Hildegart (1978) *Medios para evitar el embarazo. Paternidad voluntaria*, Zaragoza, Guara.
Hildegart ([1985]) *Paternidad voluntaria*, Barcelona, Hacer.
[Hildegart?] (1932) 'Instituciones de tipo científico sexual: un internado en regimen de coeducación. Beacon Hill School', *Sexus*, 1, 1, 96–103.
Huerta, Luis (1933a) 'El problema de la prostitución, ¿es insoluble?' *Sexus*, 1, 2, 22–36.
Huerta, Luis (1933b) 'En torno al problema de la prostitución: I. Situación actual de los problemas del sexo', *Gaceta Médica Española*, 7, 76, 193–205.
Huerta, Luis (1933c) 'En torno al problema de la prostitución: II. La prostitución como plaga social', *Gaceta Médica Española*, 7, 77, 270–7.
Jagoe, Catherine (1998) 'Sexo y género en la medicina del siglo XIX', in Catherine Jagoe, Alda Blanco and Cristina Enríquez de Salamanca, *La mujer en los discursos de género*, Barcelona, Icaria, pp. 305–67.
Juarros, César (1932) 'Normas básicas de la educación sexual', *Sexus*, 1, 1, 7–19.
Kehl, Renato (1933) 'Por qué soy eugenista', *Sexus*, 1, 2, 12–21.
Keller, Gary (1977) *The Significance and Impact of Gregorio Marañón: Literary Criticism, Biographies and Historiography*, New York, Bilingual Press.
Keown, Dominic (1999) 'Feminism, Politics and Psychosis in Fernán Gómez's *Mi hija Hildegart* (1977)', in Peter William Evans (ed.), *Spanish Cinema: the Auteurist Tradition*, Oxford, Oxford University Press, pp. 147–63.
Kevles, Daniel (1985) *In the Name of Eugenics: Genetics and the Uses of Human Heredity*, Harmondsworth, Penguin.
Knowles, Jane (1997) 'Women who Murder Their Children', in Estela V. Welldon and Cleo Van Velson (eds), *A Practical Guide to Forensic Psychotherapy*, London and Bristol, Pennsylvania, Jessica Kingsley, pp. 84–7.
Labanyi, Jo (1999) 'Gramsci and Spanish Cultural Studies', *Paragraph*, 22, 1, 95–113.
Liberal, El (1933a) 'Una conferencia del Sr Ruiz Funes sobre la nueva política y la maternidad consciente', *El Liberal*, 5 May 1933, 8.
Liberal, El (1933b) 'Un doloroso drama de familia: La notable abogada y periodista Hildegart Rodríguez es muerta por su madre de cuatro tiros de revolver', *El Liberal*, 10 June 1933, 11.
Liberal, El (1933c) 'No es el hombre quien dirige a la mujer, sino el que es dirigido por ella, dice la señorita Hildegart', *El Liberal*, 10 June 1933, 11.

Louis, Anja (2005) *Women and the law: Carmen de Burgos, an early feminist*, Woodbridge, Tamesis.
Mancebo, Julián (1904) 'Las Hurdes en la historia (III)', *Las Hurdes*, 1, 9, 194–8.
Marañón, Gregorio (1925) *La edad crítica: estudio biológico y clínico*, Madrid, n.p.
Marañón, Gregorio (1930) *La evolución de la sexualidad y los estados intersexuales*, Madrid, Morata.
Marañón, Gregorio (1967) 'Los estados intersexuales en la especie humana', in *Obras completas*, Madrid, Espasa-Calpe.
Maristany, Luis (1973) *El gabinete del doctor Lombroso: Delincuencia y fin de siglo en España*, Barcelona, Anagrama.
Martín Gaite, Carmen (1982) *La búsqueda del interlocutor y otras búsquedas*, Barcelona, Destino.
Massa, Pedro (1934) 'Epílogo de un crimen sensacional', *Crónica*, 31–2.
Mattingly, Cheryl (1998) *Healing Dramas and Clinical Plots: the Narrative Structure of Experience*, Cambridge, Cambridge University Press.
Mazumdar, Pauline M.H. (1992) *Eugenics, Human Genetics and Human Failings: The Eugenics Society, its Sources and its Critics in Britain*, London and New York, Routledge.
McFadden, Margaret (2004) 'In/Outsider: Hella Wuolijoki's *Identities* and Virginia Woolf's *Three Guineas*', in Johanna Gehmacher, Elizabeth Harvey and Sophia Kemlein (eds), *Zwischen Kriegen: Nationen, Nationalismen und Geschlechterverhältnisse in Mittel- un Osteuropa, 1918–1939*, Osnabrück, Fibre, pp. 261–74.
Monlau, Pedro Felipe (1847) *Elementos de higiene pública*, Barcelona, Imp. de Pablo Riera.
Monlau, Pedro Felipe (1853) *Higiene del matrimonion o el libro de los casados*, 3rd enlarged edition, Madrid, Rivadeneyra, 1865.
Montero, Rosa (1995) 'Madre Muerte', in *Historias de mujeres*, Madrid, Alfaguara.
Montseny, Federica (1933) 'Une lumière qui s'éteint: Hildegart', British Library Havelock Ellis Archive, July 1933.
Nash, Mary (1992) 'Social Eugenics and Nationalist Race Hygiene in Early Twentieth-Century Spain', *History of European Ideas*, 15, 4–6, 741–8.
Noguera, Enrique (1934) 'Cómo se yuguló la generosa ideal del Primer Curso Eugénico Español', in Enrique Noguera and Luis Huerta (eds), *Libro de las primeras jornadas eugénicas españolas: Genética, eugenesia y pedagogía sexual. II.* Madrid, Morata, pp. 399–412.
Noguera, Enrique and Luis Huerta (eds) (1934) *Libro de las primeras jornadas eugénicas españolas Genética, eugenesia y pedagogía sexual*, 2 vols, Madrid, Morata.
Noguera, Joaquín (1930) *Moral, eugenesia y derecho*, Madrid, Morata.
Nordau, Max (1913) *Degeneration*, London, Heinemann.
Nordau, Max (1901) *Psicofisiología del genio y del talento*, Madrid, Sáenz de Jubera.
Nordau, Max (1902) *Degeneración*, Madrid [A. Marzo].
Nordau, Max (1911) *El sentido de la historia*, Madrid, Rivadeneyra.

Nordau, Max ([1902]) *Las mentiras convencionales de nuestra civilización*, Valencia, Sempere.

Noroeste, El (1932) 'La conferencia de Hildegart Rodríguez sobre "homosexualismo"', *El Noroeste*, Gijón, 27 March 1932.

Nóvoa Santos, Roberto (1929) *La mujer, nuestro sexto sentido y otros esbozos*, Madrid, Biblioteca Nueva.

Nóvoa Santos, Roberto (1932) *Patografía de Santa Teresa de Jesús y el instinto de la muerte*, Madrid, Prensa Moderna.

Oliver Brachfeld, R. (1931) 'Crítica de las teorías sexuales del Dr. Marañón', *Revista Médica de Barcelona*, 16, 96, 548–61.

Otaola, José María (1932) 'De re eugénica y euthénica', *Sexus*, 1, 1, 20–33.

Pérez Sanz, Pilar and Carmen Bru Ripoll (1987) 'La sexología en la España de los años 30: I. Las jornadas eugenésicas de 1928 y 1933 II. Hildegart o la historia de Aurora Rodríguez Carballeira, su madre', *Revista de Sexología*, 32, 1–119.

Poldervaart, Saskia (1995) 'Theories about Sex and Sexuality in Utopia Socialism', *Journal of Homosexuality* 29 (2–3), 41–67.

Polo, José (1904) 'Para Don Ramón Escalada', *Las Hurdes*, 1, 6, 124–7.

Pulido Fernández, Ángel (1876) *Bosquejos médico-sociales para la mujer*, Madrid, Imp. de Víctor Saiz.

Redondo Álvaro, Francisco L. (n.d.) Untitled article on Asociación Española de Médicos Escritores y Artistas at *www.medicosescritoresyartistas.com/abajo01_a.htm*.

Rendueles Olmedo, Guillermo (1989) *El manuscrito encontrado en Ciempozuelos: análisis de la historia clínica de Aurora Rodríguez*, Madrid, Ediciones de la Piqueta.

Richards, Michael (2004) 'Spanish Psychiatry c.1900–1945: Constitutional Theory, Eugenics, and the Nation', in Alison Sinclair and Richard Cleminson (eds), *Alternative Discourses in Early Twentieth-century Spain: Intellectuals, Dissent and Sub-cultures of Mind and Body*, special issue of *Bulletin of Spanish Studies* 81, 6, 823–48.

Robinson, Paul (1976) *The Modernization of Sex: Havelock Ellis, Alfred Kinsey, William Masters and Virginia Johnson*, London, Paul Elek.

Rodríguez Lafora, Gonzalo (1933) 'La reforma de la moral sexual', *Revista de Occidente*, 11, 116, 150–73.

Rodríguez Lafora, Gonzalo (1934a) 'La paranoia ante los tribunales de justicia: Primera parte', *Luz*, 20 June 1934, 3.

Rodríguez Lafora, Gonzalo (1934b) 'La paranoia ante los tribunales de justicia: Parte Segunda', *Luz*, 21 June 1934, 4.

Rodríguez Lafora, Gonzalo (1934c) 'La paranoia ante los tribunales de justicia: Tercera parte', *Luz*, 22 June 1934, 3.

Rodríguez Lafora, Gonzalo (1934d) 'La paranoia ante los tribunales de justicia: Parte Cuarta', *Luz*, 25 June 1934, 3.

Rodríguez Lafora, Gonzalo (1934e) 'La paranoia ante los tribunales de justicia: Parte Quinta', *Luz*, 27 June 1934, 3.

Rodríguez Lafora, Gonzalo (1934f) 'La paranoia ante los tribunales de justicia: Parte VI', *Luz*, 6 July 1934, 11.

Rodríguez Lafora, Gonzalo (1934g) 'La paranoia ante los tribunales de justicia: Parte VII', *Luz*, 9 July 1934, 3.
Rodríguez Lafora, Gonzalo (1934h) 'La paranoia ante los tribunales de justicia: Octava Parte', *Luz*, 12 July 1934, 3.
Rodríguez Lafora, Gonzalo (1934i) 'La paranoia ante los tribunales de justicia: Parte Novena', *Luz*, 18 July 1934, 4.
Rodríguez Lafora, Gonzalo (1934j) 'La paranoia ante los tribunales de justicia: Parte Décima', *Luz*, 21 July 1934, 3.
Rodríguez Lafora, Gonzalo (1934k) 'La paranoia ante los tribunales de justicia: Parte XIII [*sic*]', *Luz*, 24 July 1934, 2.
Rodríguez Lafora, Gonzalo (1934l) 'La paranoia ante los tribunales de justicia: Parte XII y última', *Luz*, 27 July 1934, 2.
Rodríguez Lafora, Gonzalo (1935) 'La plasmación de los delirios grandiosos', *Revista de Criminología, Psiquiatría y Medicina Legal*, 130, 495–506.
Ruiz Pérez, Jesús (2003) *Masonería y posibilismo libertario: La actividad masónica de Marín Civera*, X Simposio Internacional de Historia de la Masonería Española, Leganés (Madrid).
Ruiz Salvador, Antonio (1976) *Ateneo, Dictadura, República*, Valencia, Fernando Torres.
Sacristán, José M. and Miguel Prados y Such (1933) *Informe sobre el estado psíquico de la procesada Aurora Rodríguez*, report for the defence at trial of Aurora Rodríguez Carballeira, Madrid, 1933.
Sainz de Aja, Enrique (1946) *Lo que todo el mundo debe saber sobre la sífilis*, Madrid, Dirección General de Sanidad.
Saldaña, Quintiliano (1929) *Siete ensayos sobre sociología sexual*, Madrid, Mundo Latino.
Saldaña, Quintiliano (1930) *La sexología (Ensayos)*, Madrid, Mundo Latino.
Saldaña, Quintiliano (1932) 'El matrimonio ante la sexología y el derecho', *Sexus*, 1, 1, 58–76.
Sánchez Ron, José M. (1988) *1907–1987, La Junta para Ampliación de Estudios e investigaciones científicas 80 años después*, Madrid, CSIC.
Sanger, Margaret (1932). *My Fight for Birth Control*, London, Faber and Faber.
Scanlon, Geraldine (1986) *La polémica feminista en la España contemporánea (1868–1974)*, Madrid, Akal.
Schneider, William H. (1990) 'The Eugenics Movement in France 1890–1940', in Mark Adams (ed.), *The Wellborn Science*, Oxford, Oxford University Press, pp. 69–109.
Sinclair, Alison (1998) *Dislocations of Desire: Gender, Identity and Strategy in 'La Regenta'*, Chapel Hill, University of North Carolina.
Sinclair, Alison (2001) *Uncovering the Mind: Unamuno, the Unknown and the Vicissitudes of Self*, Manchester, Manchester University Press.
Sinclair, Alison (2003) 'The World League for Sexual Reform in Spain: Founding, Infighting and the Role of Hildegart Rodríguez', *Journal of the History of Sexuality*, 12, 1, 98–109.
Sinclair, Alison (2004a) 'Interior and Internal Spain: Visions of the Primitive at the Cultural Interface', *Romance Studies*, 22, 3, 209–21.

Sinclair, Alison (2004b) 'Spain's Love Affair with Russia: The Attraction of Exotic (Br)Others', *European Review of History*, 11, 2, 207–24.

Sinclair, Alison (2004c) '"Telling it like it was?" The "Residencia de Estudiantes" and its image', in Alison Sinclair and Richard Cleminson (eds), *Alternative Discourses in Early Twentieth-century Spain: Intellectuals, Dissent and Sub-cultures of Mind and Body*, special issue of *Bulletin of Spanish Studies* 81, 6, 739–63.

Sinclair, Alison (2005) '"Though I Speak with the Tongues of Men and of Angels . . .": Rhetorical Practices in Medical and Religious Discourse in Nineteenth-century Spain', *Nineteenth-Century Prose*, 32, 1, 97–127.

Sinclair, Alison (forthcoming) 'Love, Again: Crisis and the Search for Consolation: The *Revista de Occidente* and the Creation of a Culture, 1923–1936', in Luisa Passerini and Liliana Ellena (eds), *New Dangerous Liaisons*, Oxford and New York, Berghahn.

Sinclair, Alison and Richard Cleminson (2004a) *Alternative Discourses in Early Twentieth-century Spain: Intellectuals, Dissent and Sub-cultures of Mind and Body*, special issue of *Bulletin of Spanish Studies* 81 (6) (September 2004).

Socialista, El (1932) 'Una interesante conferencia de la compañera Hildegart Rodríguez', *El Socialista*, 16 January 1932, 4.

Stanton, Josephine and Alexander Simpson (2002) 'Filicide: a Review', *International Journal of Law and Psychiatry*, 25, 1, 1–14.

Stepan, Nancy Leys (1991) *The 'Hour of Eugenics': Race, Gender, and Nation in Latin America*, Ithaca and London, Cornell University Press.

Summers, Anne (1991) 'The Correspondents of Havelock Ellis', *History Workshop Journal*, 32, Autumn 1991, 167–83.

Taboada, Doctor (1933) 'Eugénica y Reforma sexual: una entrevista con el doctor Juan Noguera', *El Liberal*, 2 May 1933, 14.

Toga, Juan de (1934a) 'El parricidio de que fue víctima la señorita Hildegart Rodríguez', *El Liberal*, 25 May 1934, 5–6.

Toga, Juan de (1934b) 'El parricidio de que fue víctima la señorita Hildegart Rodríguez: Los peritos médicos discrepan acerca del estado mental de la procesada', *El Liberal*, 26 May 1934, 5–6.

Toga, Juan de (1934c) 'El parricidio de que fue víctima la señorita Hildegart Rodríguez: El jurado dicta veredicto de culpabilidad', *El Liberal*, 27 May 1934, 5–6.

Torrubiano Ripoll, Jaime (1925) 'Títulos de nuestra audacia: fuentes de nuestros estudios', *Sexualidad*, 1, 31, 2–3.

Torrubiano y Ripoll, Jaime (1929) *Teología y eugenesia*, Madrid, Morata.

Trend, J.B. (1921) *A Picture of Modern Spain: Men and Music*, London, Constable.

Trend, J.B. (1934) *The Origins of Modern Spain*, Cambridge, Cambridge University Press.

V., A.V. de la (1932) 'Lo que significa La Liga para la Reforma Sexual', *Heraldo de Madrid*, 31 March 1932, 15.

Vázquez García, Francisco and Andrés Moreno Mengíbar (1997) *Sexo y razón: una genealogía de la moral sexual en España (Siglos XVI–XX)*, Madrid, Akal.

Weldon, Estela V. (1988) *Mother, Madonna, Whore: the Idealization and Denigration of Motherhood*, London, Free Association Books.
Weldon, Estela V. and Cleo Van Velsen (1997) *A Practical Guide to Forensic Psychotherapy*, London, Jessica Kingsley.
WLSR (1928) *Sexual Reform Congress, Copenhagen 1–5 July*, Copenhagen, Levin and Munksgaard; Leipzig, Georg Thieme Verlag.
WLSR (1929) *Sexual Reform Congress*, Sexual Reform Congress, London 8–14 September 1929, London, Kegan Paul.

Index

Abolition
  Abolitionist Society 54
    establishment 54
    draft law on venereal disease 66
    gender inequality, and 53
    Hildegart on 70, 99
    regulation of prostitution, of 33
    Semana Abolicionista 53
    sexual morality, by WLSR, of 19
    'technical courses' 118
Abortion
  1928 Penal Code 53
  prison sentences for
    abortions under 53
  spread of information about 19
Aguilar, Manuel 217
Alcalá Santaella, Rafael 217
Alcalá Zamora, Niceto 77, 78, 217
Alcoholism
  images of Spain, and 5
Anarchism
  companion, ideal of 47
  eugenics activities of anarchists 104
  Saldana's views, and 47
  Salud y Fuerza 36
  Spanish involvement with 5
Archivos de Higiene y Salud Pública 44
  bibliography and reviews in 44
  international character 44
  Navarro Fernández, Antonio, contributions to 44
Aurora SEE Rodríguez, Aurora
Aza, Vital 87, 95, 107, 130, 217
  'Algunos comentarios clínicos y sexuales sobre la fecundación artificial', as 108
  artificial insemination, on 109
  'proper' sexuality, on 74
Azaña, Manuel 217
  public figures Hildegart suspects of homosexuality 78, 118
Baeza, Ricardo 217–218
  private library 15–16
Barcia Goyanes, Juan José 91, 218
Barrio de Medina, J. 111, 112, 218
Besteiro, Julián 99, 218
Birth control
  economics, and 68
  Hildegart, and
    aims of WLSR, and 86
    drive to disseminate knowledge on 65
    lectures at Eugenics conference 115
    letters to Ellis, and 68
    publication of writings on 69
  international conference on, 1933 98
  Liga sections 87, 95

My Fight for Birth Control 130
  prohibition of advice on 54
  Saldana's views on 46
Bloch, Iwan 46, 218
Brachfeld, Ferenc Oliver 218
Bravo Sanfeliú, Julio 44, 76, 218
Brothels
  assumption all Spanish males will attend 115
  attempted suppression of 34
  Haire on 115
  premises associated with 'pathological' behaviour 35
Bugallo Sánchez, José 56, 67, 95, 218–219
Campaña Sanitaria SEE Hygiene Campaign
Campoamor, Clara 78, 219
Campoy Ibáñez 56, 67, 91, 219
Cansinos-Assens, Rafael 57, 76, 91, 219
Carpenter, Edward 219
Carrasco i Formiguera, Manuel 91, 219
Casares Quiroga, Santiago 31, 78, 219
Casti connubii 108
Chiavacci, L. 220
Cifuentes Díaz, Pedro 220
Civera Martínez, Marín 9, 69, 220
  editor of *Cuadernos de Cultura* 9
  Hildegart's pamphlets 69
  mason, as 220
  membership of Liga 91
Communism
  Comunismo y matrimonio 113
  César Falcón 119
  Morata's books 67
  recognition of secular unions 92
  Spanish involvement with 5

Congresses
  Brno Congress, September 1932 16
  Congress of Berlin, September 1921 16
    Sexualidad reports of 45–46
  Copenhagen Congress, July 1928 16
    executive board of 18
    planks listed in proceedings of 16, 91–92
    emancipation of homosexuals, and 19
  First International Eugenics Congress, London, 1912 14
    language at 18
  London Congress, September 1929 16
    Ellis' absence from 18
    Hirschfield's presidential address to 18
    Sexus I reports of 110
  Vienna Congress, September 1930 16
    Spaniards' attendance at 87–88
Contraception SEE Birth control
Cossío, Manuel Bartolomé 220
Criminality
  criminal sexual acts 17
  deliberate contagion of venereal disease 53
  inheritance of 12
  pimping, of 34
  'reform' of homosexuals 35
  Ruiz Funes' *Endocrinology and Criminality* 56
  sexual abnormality, of 153
  sexual acts, of 73
  sexual variation, of 73
Criminals
  prostitutes as 32
  provincial authorities' lists of 33

restriction of birth of 14
Criminology
  Bernaldo de Quirós 45
  Hildegart, and
    Essays on Sexual Criminology 80
  images of Spain, and 5
  Juarros 107
  Rafael Salillas 45
  School of Criminology 45
Cuadernos de Cultura	9
  Civera Martínez, Marín (editor) SEE Civera Martínez, Marín
  Hildegart's pamphlets 69
  Valero, Fernando 118
Dantín Cereceda, Juan 91, 220
Decalogue SEE ALSO 'Planks'
  Biblical associations with term 91
  dissidence, and 91–95
  'planks', and 91
Degeneration
  como anormales, como degenerados 150
  concerns of reformers 24
  Degeneración por sífilis adquirida 57
  degenerate bourgeois 77
  'degenerate constitution' 118
  homosexuality as characteristic of 75, 79
  Kehl's statistics on 113
  Las Hurdes as epitome of 30
  Marañón, and 140
  murder of Hildegart to protect her from 151
  Nordau, ideas contained in 8, 224
  physical signs of 75
Dictatorship
  Primo de Rivera, Miguel, of 7
    censorship under 64
    coming of 38
    ending of 64
    growing up under 41–62
    opportunities offered by end of 67
    Spanish public life post-dictatorship 64–67
  Soviet Russian 92
Disease
  awareness of 38
  birth restrictions on disease-stricken 14
  concern of reformers 24
  containing excesses of 65
  Las Hurdes, in 30
  spreading information about 36
  venereal SEE Venereal disease
Divorce
  divorce law, 1932 20
  'equal' treatment for men and women 20
  images of Spain, and 5
  reform under Second Republic 6–7
  Saldaña's position on 47
  venereal infection as grounds for 66
  WLSR planks of belief, and 16, 73, 92
Doctors
  Aurora, treatment of 26, 27
  'authorization' of procreation by 109
  Colegio de Médicos 45
  editorial board of *Sexus I* 106
  enhanced authority of taxonomist, and 80
  eugenics, and 9, 152
  Hildegart, and 80
    promotion of standing of 80
  imposition of hospitalization by 34–35
    treatment of venereal disease, for 34–35
  lawyers, and 64, 158
    competitiveness between 64

participation in structures of
power 64
politics, and 9, 64
prominence in public life 97
social activists, as 9
Domingo, Marcelino 78, 220
Education
access to whole culture through
6
Aurora's account of her own
35, 70, 126
educational approach to
eugenics 12
feeling in man, of 114
focus of reformers 23
future Spanish mothers, of 45
Nelken, Margarita on 45
good eugenic practice, into 37
Herencia y educación. Ideal de vida
30
Hildegart's 1, 7, 42, 135, 150
Liga de Educación Social 58
placing of mentally deficient
children in special schools
11
prevention of homosexuality
through 93
'preventive' eugenics through
14
prime resource for curing ills,
as 24
processes of modernization,
and 6
sex education SEE Sex
education
Spanish style of eugenics, and
10, 17
WLSR planks of belief, and 17
Ellis, Havelock
eonism, and 18
'fairy god', as 129–131
Hildegart's father figure, as
133, 140
Lees, Edith, and 13

marriage certificate, and 12
reception of works in Spain 12,
14, 15–16
sterilization of the unfit, and
12, 24
Task of Social Hygiene 24
'The Red Virgin' in *The Adelphi*,
and 125, 127, 131–132
WLSR, and
explanation of association
with 15
Grosskurth's biography, and
158
honorary president, as 13
Endocrinology
Endocrinología y Criminalidad 56
Eugenics conference 1928 on
118
explanation of homosexuality
through 80
Hildegart's article on 80, 110
close study of 155
Marañón, and 80
Eonism
Ellis' theory of 18
Eonism and Other
Supplementary Studies 15
Estudios
Centro de Estudios Históricos
118
Dactiloscopia en España: Estudio
médico forense de la identidad
43
Estudio de la prostitución; ¿Qué es
el abolicismo de la
prostitución? 70
Estudio medicosocial del Niño Golfo
57
Estudio psicológico del cubismo y
expresionismo 59
Estudios de Psicología Sexual 46
Junta para Ampliación de
Estudios 6

Tres amores históricos: estudio comparativo de los amores de Romeo y Julieta, Abelardo y Eloísa y los Amantes de Teruel 68
Eugenics
  aims 17
  Aurora's approach to 152
  awareness of fates awaiting children 38
  contribution of publishers 66
  definition 10
  driving model of 64–65
  education in 37
  educational approach to 12
  England, in 10–11
    Eugenics Education Society 11
    Mendelian ideas of heredity, and 19
  eugenic children
    Chesterton, GK, on 24–25
    Eugenette Bolce 24
    Hildegard as 1, 24–25, 67–71, 134
  Eugenics and Other Evils 11, 23
  Eugenics conference 1928 8, 54–55, 89
  Eugenics conference 1933 20, 45, 111–113, 158
    planning and execution of 116–120
  Eugenics Education Society 11
  gender equality, and 73
  hard-line 108
  Hildegart, and
    desire for better race 110
    eugenics child, as 1, 24
    lectures on birth control 115
    Liga activities, and 86
    pamphlet setting out case for 68
    writings on topics linking to 49
  hygiene, and 104
  Marañón, and 140
  meetings at the Real Academia de Medicina concerned with 59
  'naturalness' of body in 108
  negative 35
  obligations suggested to society by 12
  Peláez, Álvarez on 8
  physical process of procreation, and 29
  precision of term 10
  problems in development of in Republic 65
  prostitution, and 32
  'pure' form 10
  reform in 104
  regenerationist ideas as impetus to growth of 7
  role of general vigilance
  Spain, in 73
  sex education, and
    new discourse 36
    providing positive face of 35
  sex reform, and 104, 105, 113, 125, 153
  Spain, in 23
    'Latin' tradition of 28, 29, 35
    satire on 25
    structures and varieties of 14–15
  unitary form of, whether 10
  variable local forms 10
  WLSR agenda, and 16
    improving race through eugenics 93
    plank two, and 92
    ten planks, and 73
Euthanasia 55
Fatherhood 69, 172
Feminism 56, 87, 92, 95, 129, 159
Field, Alice Withrow 220
Forel, Auguste 37, 220

executive board of Copenhagen
    Congress 18
Freemason(ry)
    Aurora, and
        desire for daughter to follow
            ideals of 26
        father as mason 26
        persecution of grandfather
            because of 26
    Campoamor, Clara, as 219
    Civera Martínez, Marín, as 220
    Hildegart, and
        source of references 51
    Jiménez de Asúa, Luis, as 222
    Largo Caballero, Francisco, as
        223
    Llopis, Rodolfo, as 224
    Philippine masonic lodges 26
    Salazar Alonso, Rafael, as 229
Freud, Sigmund 81, 116
    concept of transference 132
    'family romance' 136
    Hildegart's correspondence
        with Ellis, and 129, 133
    reception of works in Spain
        8–9, 15
    sexual theory of paranoia 155
    WLSR Vienna Congress 88
Gaceta Médica Española 58–59
    aims 58
    Eugenics conference 1934, and
        117
    founding of 58
    Hildegart's article in 79, 80
    Noguera, Dr Juan 112
Galarza, Ángel 220
Galton, Francis 12
    definition of eugenics 10
Gillett-Gatty, Katherine 128
Giner de los Ríos, Francisco 220
    Institución Libre de Enseñanza,
        founding of 6
González Blanco, Edmundo 76,
    91, 221

Haire, Norman 221
    dissolution of WLSR 19
    Ellis, correspondence with 79,
        125, 127–128, 154
    Hildegart, correspondence with
        89, 125
    Hildergart's murder, on 154
    London Congress welcome
        address 18–19
    Sexus, and 112, 114–115
    WLSR planks of belief, and
        16–17
Haro García, Francisco 221
    editorial board of *Sexus I* 106
    editorial board of *Sexus II* 111
Heredity 19, 33, 56
    negative burdens 38
    race, and 30, 65
Hermaphrodites
    Hildegart, and 35–36
Hernández Alfonso, Luis 67, 221
Hernández Catá, Alfonso 56, 76,
    221
Heterosexuality 75
Hildegart
    birth control, and
        aims of WLSR, and 86
        drive to disseminate
            knowledge on 65
        lectures at Eugenics
            conference 115
        letters to Ellis, and 68
        publication of writings on 69
    'Cain y Abel' article 137
    education 1
        sexual 36
    Ellis, Havelock, correspondence
        with 2–3, 11, 24, 68, 80,
        123–145
        apprenticeship, as 110
        Asturias lecture tour 95
        attitude to homosexuality
            74–75
        Aurora, and 99

descriptions of herself
134–135
doubts about authorship of
126–129
Ellis as confidant 131
Haro, and 97
Hildegart's sex education 35
ideal interlocutor, Ellis as
132–133
interpretation of Hildegart's
approach 133–134
language 131–132
Liga, and 87, 88, 97, 98,
138–145
membership of Socialist
Party, and 72
pathology of Aurora, and 138
photographs sent 130
political rivalries and
homosexuality 78–79
presence of Aurora in 136
¿Quo vadis, burguesía? 75–76,
77
reasons for 129
reservations about WLSR
planks of belief 17
eugenic child, as 1, 24–25, 134
Aurora's choice, and 25–26
father of 25–27
'ideal' father, whether 27
mason, as 26
Gillett-Gatty, Katherine, on 128
Haro, conflict with 97, 112,
142–144
bad object, as 142, 143
homosexuality, and
accusations of homosexuality
by 63
affinity with artistic
tendencies, and 75
Aurora's influence 80
degeneration, and 75
homosexuality as pathology
17

more flexible view of 79
private views of 74
problematic engagement
with 64
public figures suspected of
being homosexual 78, 141
recommendation to shut
away homosexuals 17
support for WLSR planks,
and 74
treatment for homosexuals
81
women, in 78
Hygiene Campaign, and SEE
ALSO Hygiene Campaign
articles 48
attendance at meetings 48
final appearance at 52
interpretation of move out of
71
lectures by 71, 74–75
Asturias lecture tour 95
birth control, on 115
Liga, and SEE ALSO Liga
activity in foundation
meeting 86
advice from Ellis on
establishing 2
conflict with Haro 47, 96–97,
138
effect of murder 2
H. G. Wells on 96
history of 25, 55
mother as cause of problems
in 98–99
relationship with 85
secretary of Liga, as 95–96,
112
time involved in 85
mother SEE Rodríguez, Aurora
murder of 2, 26, 72, 98–99,
127–129, 148–151
publications 68–69
contagion, and 36

dissemination of knowledge on sexual matters, and 65
Second Republic, under 69
sex reform, and
   Hildegart's education 43
   tensions in Liga, and 86
socialism, and
   'falling out' with socialism 71
   involvement in socialist activity 71
   late nineteenth-century socialist utopians 126
   membership of Socialist party 72
   mother's father's library, and 1
   resignation from activities associated with 72
Velilla, Abel, and 72, 154
Wells, H.G., and 96, 125, 126
Hirschfeld, Magnus 222
   death of 19
   Ellis, and 18
   emancipation of homosexuals, and 19
   Hildegart, correspondence with 89
   interview with Hildegart 110
   Liga executive board 18
   sexology, on 18
   Sexus articles 107
   WLSR, founding of 16
Homosexuality
   Aurora, and
      descriptions of her sister 32
      reasons for murdering Hildegart 155
      views of 80
   condition to be treated, as 116
   degenerate condition, as 75
   Ellis, and 13, 109
      result of hereditary factors, as 109
   emancipation of homosexuals 19
      methods of bringing about 19
   endocrinology explaining 80
   eugenics, and 73
   Hildegart, and
      accusations of homosexuality by 63
      affinity with artistic tendencies, and 75
      Aurora's influence 80
      degeneration, and 75
      homosexuality as pathology 17
      more flexible view of 79
      private views of 74
      problematic engagement with 64
      public figures suspected of being homosexual 78, 141
      recommendation to shut away homosexuals 17
      support for WLSR planks, and 74
      treatment for homosexuals 81
      women, in 78
   Hirschfield's work on 18
   'homosexual crimes' 115
   Homosexualität 18
   legislation on 54
   Marañón, on 93
   'reform' or 'cure' of homosexuals 35
   Saldaña on 47, 93
   significance of prostitution to 32
   pathology, as 17
   WLSR planks, and 17, 93
      Liga members support for 73
Hoyos Sainz, Luis de 222
   1928 Eugenics Conference, and 54

Huerta, Luis 37, 222
   article on prostitution 113
   Aurora's trial, and 149, 152
   children, on 38
   Institute of Social Medicine 58
   Liga sections 95
   Russia, and 113–114
   Sexus I editorial board 106
   Sexus II, role 111
   WLSR founding members 38
Hygiene
   Archivos De Higiene y Sanidad Pública 44
   chairs of 28
   Comité de Higiene de las Naciones 44
   Hildegart, and
      reading of books on 26
   Higiene de la pubertad 37
   Higiene del matrimonio 28, 33
   Higiene Sexual del soltero 37
   hygienists
      control of veneral disease, and 32
      Fernández, Navarro, as 44
      Pittaluga as 57
      work on marriage and 30
      work of early 28
   La higiene sexual en las escuelas 56
   'Latin' eugenics, and 28
   Liga Española de Higiene Mental 65
   marriage, and 29–30
   medical officers responsible for 34
   obrero, and 48
   prostitution, and 32–33
      regulations of 34
      'special hygiene' 33
      reform in 7
   Reglamentación higiénica de la prostitución 32
   Sexualidad, and 104
   significant concept in Spanish medicine, as 28
   The Task of Social Hygiene 12, 24
Hygiene Campaign
   activities of 44
   publication of in *Sexualidad* 44
   Hildegart, and 1, 36, 43
      articles by 48
      attendance at meetings 48
      final appearance at 52
      interpretation of move out of 71
   Liga members 55
   meetings of 48
   Navarro Fernández, Antonio 43, 104
   parochial nature of 44
   Institución Libre de Enseñanza (ILE) 6, 9, 222
   Institute of Social Medicine SEE Instituto de Medicina Social
Instituto de Medicina Social 37, 58
Interlocutor
   Ellis, Havelock, as 126, 131–133, 142–144
   Freud's concept of transference, and 132
   implied 133
   inferred 133
   Martín Gaite's model 132
   narrative and 132–133
Intersexuality
   Hildegart, and
      'Algunos comentarios en torno al problema de la intersexualidad' 79
      acceptance of idea of intersex state 80
   'intersex' state 73
   Marañón, on 73, 79

Inversion 13, 47, 78, 87, 175, 178
Inversión 47, 63
Iruretagoyena, Julia 78, 223
Ives, George Cecil 222
Jiménez de Asúa, Luis 54, 55, 119, 222
   'crime of venereal infection' 66
   Hildegart on 87, 130
   Sexus I editorial board 106
Jornadas Eugénicas SEE Eugenics
Juarros Ortega, César 222–223
Junta para Ampliación des Estudios (JAE) 6, 9, 222
Kautsky, Karl 223
Kehl, Renato 71, 112, 113, 223
Kent, Victoria 78, 223
Key, Ellen 13, 223
   free love, article on 44–45
Klein, Melanie 47
Kollontai, Aleksandra 223
Lafitte, Françoise 223
Lafora SEE Rodríguez Lafora
Largo Caballero, Francisco 77, 78, 223
Las Hurdes 30–31
Lawyers
   authority of taxonomist, and 80
   Hildegart, and
      qualification as 65
      speaking as 115
   Liga members 2
   Liga section consisting of 87
   politics, and 64
   Second Republic, in 2, 64
Lesbianism
   Aurora, and
      sense of suppressed lesbianism 80
Lees, Edith (wife of Havelock Ellis) 13
Lessa, Almerindo 112, 223
Leunbach, J. H. 69, 224
   dissolution of WLSR 19
   general secretary of Copenhagen Congress 18
   Hildegart, correspondence with 89
Liga Mundial Para la Reforma Sexual (Liga)
   coming of Second Republic, and 1–2
   creation of the Instituto de Medicina Social, and 37
   death of 157–160
      Hildegart's murder, and 158–160
   declared aims 94
   Ellis, Havelock
      'father' of Liga, as 96
      mentor in establishment of 2
   establishment of 87–89
      foundation meeting 88, 130
      Hildegart's correspondence with Ellis 87
      Hildegart as prime instrument in 87
      report of foundation meeting 88–89
   Eugenics Conference, and 117
   formalization as 55
   foundation of 1–2
   Hildegart, and
      activity in foundation meeting 86
      advice from Ellis on establishing 2
      conflict with Haro 47, 96–97, 138
      effect of murder 2
      H. G. Wells on 96
      history of 25, 55
      mother as cause of problems in 98–99
      relationship with 85
      secretary of Liga, as 95–96, 112
      time involved in 85

internal dissent in 138–145
    Aurora, and 139, 142–143
    Haro, and 141, 143–144
    Marañón, and 139–141, 144
Juarros, César, founding
    member, as 34
legislative change, involvement
    in 116
membership of 1–2
    committee for drafting law
        on venereal disease, and
        66
    founding members 38, 86,
        89–91
    Institute of Social Medicine,
        and 58
    medical affiliation, and 45
    members in public eye 38
    novels written by members
        76
    participation in *Sexualidad*,
        and 44
    publications by founding
        members 56
    squabbling between
        members 96, 138
Morata, and 66–67
professional self-awareness
    within 107
'public face' of SEE *Sexus*
sections 87
Sexus SEE *Sexus*
WLSR's ten planks, and 91–95
    appeal of to members 17,
        73–74
    Decalogue 91–95
    discussion of 91–92
    'Octologue' 93–94
Lindsey, Benjamin Barr 224
Lipschütz, Alexander 224
Llopis, Rodolfo 113, 224
Lombroso, Cesare 224
    Ellis, and 12
    ideas of degeneration 8

López Ureña, Francisco 56, 224
Luisi, Paulina 224
Lupanar SEE Brothels
Macau Moncaunt, José 224
Madrazo, Enrique Diego de 30,
    86, 224
    optimistic concept of life, on
        119
    power of education, on 30
Malthusianism SEE ALSO
        neo-Malthusianism
    Malthusismo y neomalthusismo 56,
        69
Marañón, Gregorio 224–225
    articles by 38
    election to 1931 Cortes 64
    Hildegart's criticisms of 79, 139
    Hildegart's frustrations with
        96–97
    homosexuality, on 80
    Institutio de Medicina Social
        37–38, 58
    intersex state 73
    Las Hurdes, and 30
    Liga President, as 1
    'menopausic', as 140
    Sexualidad, and 44
    Tres ensayos sobre la vida sexual
        59
Marriage
    certification 24
    Comunismo y matrimonio 113
    divorce law 1932, and 20
    Ellis, Havelock, on 13
    Eugenics Conference 1928, and
        55
    freeing up of institution of 73
    Higiene del matrimonio 28, 33
    Hildegart and 86
    hygiene, and 30
    issuing health certificate before
        12, 29
    Key, Ellen, on 13
    Liga sections 87, 95

new concepts of 113
Otros libros de interés 67
religion and law and 110
rethinking of 5
Saldaña on 47
sexual activity outside norms of 28
Sífilis, blenorragia y matrimonio 36
'Temas de nuestro tiempo' series 67
WLSR planks of belief 16, 92
Masonry SEE Freemason(ry)
Masturbation SEE ALSO Onanism
  activity to be avoided, as 32–33
  far reaching consequences of 32–33
  Monlau on 34
  prostitution, and 32
Maternology 118
Méndez Bejarano, Mario 225
  Hildegart's mentor, as 51
  Liga foundation members 66
Menopause 140
Morata, Javier 225
  Hildegart's funeral 158
  publishing activities 66–67, 69
Motherhood SEE ALSO Maternology
  Aza, Vital, on 109
  definitions of perverse 156
  eugenic ideal of perfect form of 29
  hygienic 29
  Key, Ellen, on 13
  'Latin' eugenics, and 17
  legal aspects of conscious 120
  pathologies of 136–138
Mutterrecht
  theories of Bachofen 13, 135
Navarro Fernández, Antonio 1, 43–44, 49, 104, 225
  infanticide, on 52

Nelken, Margarita 225
  education of Spanish mothers 45
Neo-Malthusianism
  Eugenics Education Society, and 11
  Haire and 69
  Leunbach and 69
  Malthusismo y neomalthusismo 56, 69
  Salud y Fuerza 46
Noguera, Enrique 45, 86, 106, 117, 120, 225
  1928 Eugenics Conference, and 54
  Gaceta Médica Española 58
Nordau, Max 224
  ideas of degeneration 8
Nóvoa Santos, Roberto 86, 226
  1931 Cortes members 64
  WLSR planks of belief, and 92
Onanism 32–33
Oriol Anguera, Antonio 67, 91, 226
Ortiz de Pinedo, José 38, 226
  novels, writing 76
Otaola y Richter, José María de 56, 86, 107, 108, 226
  Liga sections 95
  Sexus I editorial board 106
  Sexus II editorial board 111
Pascua, Marcelino 226
Perversion
  active player 141
  filicide as 156
  men, in 156
  state regulation of 93
  structure of 141–142
  women, in 156
Pestaña, Ángel 9, 226
Pi y Suñer, Augusto 91, 226
Pittaluga Fattorini, Gustavo 30, 57, 226

Archivos De Higiene y Sanidad,
  and 44
  articles by 38
  gendered behaviour, on 57
  Institute of Social Medicine,
    and 37–38, 58
  Liga membership 91
  Sexualidad, and 44
Prados Sach, Miguel 27, 227
  psychiatric report on Aurora
    125, 143, 156, 159
  defence witness, as 152
Proletariat
  La limitación de la prole: un deber del proletariado consciente 68
  La novela proletaria 9, 72, 75
  Roces, Wenceslao
    Proletariado y procreación 119
Prostitution 32–35
  abolition of 66
    Hildegart on 99
  authorities' lists of prostitutes 33
  conscious parenthood, and 73
  criminalization of pimping 34
  eugenic ideal of motherhood, and 29
  Hildegart, and 70
  Huerta's article on 113
  hygiene of 34
  La prostitución en la villa de Madrid 43
  legislation for 32, 53
    Hildegart on 143
  Liga sections 87, 95
  masturbation, and 32–33
  penalties for rape, and 53
  regulation of 34
    abolition of 34–35, 66
  Russia, in 114
  'special hygiene', and 33
  VD clinics, and 34
WLSR planks of belief, and 17, 93
Psychiatry
  Archivos de neurobiología, psicología, fisiología, histología, neurología y psiquiatría 59
  Los senderos de la locura (Divulgaciones psiquiátricas) 57
Psychoanalysis
  importation of 6
  Los horizontes de la psicoanalisis 57
Psychology
  Archivos de neurobiología, psicología, fisiología, histología, neurología y psiquiatría 59
  Estudios de Psicología Sexual 46
  Estudio psicológico del cubismo y expresionismo 59
  Hildegart's references to 126
  sex, of
    'recreational' attitude to 87
  Siete ensayos sobre sociología sexual 46
  Studies in the Psychology of Sex 13, 15, 29, 125
Puericulture
  'Latin' eugenics, and 10, 28
  meaning 19
  positive aims of eugenics, as 14
Ramón y Cajal, Santiago 227
Recaséns, Sebastián 55, 57, 227
  1928 Eugenic Conference
    lecture 30, 119–120
  Institute of Social Medicine 38, 58
  Sexualidad, and 44
Remartínez, Roberto 91, 227
Residencia de Estudiantes 6, 8, 9, 51
Revista de Occidente 6

foundation of 8
Lafora's writings in 66
Ortega y Gasset, José 45
Pittaluga's articles in 57
prominent names associated
    with 119
Rivas Cherif, Cipriano 78, 227
Rocamora 45, 57, 227
Rodríguez, Aurora
  article on Cain and Abel
    137
  Ciempozuelos 26, 31–32, 74, 80,
    137, 149, 152
  defence at trial 27–28, 152–153
  experimental community, and
    28, 34
  family background 31–32
  father for Hildegart, and 33–34
    'ideal' father, whether 27
    mason, as 26
  father's library 1, 23–24, 26, 70
  freemasonry, and 26, 32
    desire for daughter to follow
      ideals of 26
    father as mason 26
    persecution of grandfather
      because of 26
  Gillett-Gatty, Katherine, and
    128
  homosexuality, and
    descriptions of her sister
      32
    reasons for murdering
      Hildegart 155
    views of 80
  lesbianism, sense of suppressed
    80
  menopause, and 141
  murder of Hildegart, and 2, 26,
    72, 98–99, 127–129,
    148–151
  paranoia, and 99
  Pepito Arriola, and 26, 31, 136,
    157
  sex education, and
    decision to have eugenic
      child 28
  sexual pleasure, and 36
  sister Josefina, and 26
    complaints about 31–32
    son of 26
Rodriguez, Hildegart SEE
    Hildegart
Rodríguez Lafora, Gonzalo 38, 91,
    228
  Archivos de neurobiología,
    psicología, fisiología,
    histología, neurología y
    psiquiatría 59
  articles by 38–39
  criticisms of Hildegart's ideas
    158
  Luz articles 155
  place of gender in society, on
    66
  psychiatric assessment of
    Aurora 152
Ruiz Funes, Mariano 56, 67,
    228
  founding members of Liga
    86
  Liga sections 95
  Sexus I editorial board 106
  Sexus II editorial board 111
Russell, Bertrand 43
Russell, Dora 43
Sacristán, José María 57, 228
  Liga sections 95
  psychiatric report on Aurora
    27, 125, 143, 156, 158–159
  defence witness, as 152
Sainz de Aja, Enrique Álvarez 57,
    228
  committee on draft law on
    venereal disease 66
  Liga sections 95
  pamphlet by 36
  treatment of syphilis 38

Salazar Alonso, Rafael 229
Saldaña, Quintiliano 46–47, 56, 229
   Liga sections 95
   novels, writing 76
   Sexualidad, and 44, 46
   Sexus I, and 107, 110
   Sexus II, and 111
   source of Hildegart's interest in Ellis, as 129–130
   WLSR, definition and aims 86
   WLSR planks of belief, and 93
Salud y Fuerza 36, 46
Sánchez Covisa, José 57, 119, 229
   committee on draft law on venereal disease 66
   Liga sections 95
   Sexus I editorial board 106
   Sexus II editorial board 111
   work on syphilis 38
Sánchez de Rivera y Moset, Daniel 57, 229
   works by 57
Sánchez Taboada, Mario S. 44, 229
Sanchis Banús, José 54, 55, 57, 119, 229
   election to 1931 Cortes 64
   Sexus editorial boards, and 111
   'small fight' with Hildegart 96, 142
   WLSR planks of belief, and 92
Sanger, Margaret 229
   correspondence with Ellis 97–98
   Hildegart, and 130
   impressions of Ellis 130
Santullano, Luis 9, 230
Second Republic
   abolition of prostitution 66
   Azaña, president of 118
   co-operation between law and medicine 65
   divorce reform under 6–7
   divorce law 20
   doctors and lawyers
      participation in structures of power 64
   Hildegart, and
      opportunities offered by coming of 67
   leaders of as homosexuals
      Hildegart's accusations of 63–64, 79, 87
   Liga, organization of, and 1–2
      problems with Republic, and 104
   protection of women 66
   publishing activity, and 1–2, 59, 64
      contribution of publishers 66–67
      Hildegart's writings, and 69
      reformers participating in public power, and 64
   sex education, and 65
      legislation for 65–66
   Spanish sexual reform, and 89
   spirit of legal reform under 116
Sex education 35–39
   attitudes to among sex reformers 35
   Aurora, and
      decision to have eugenic child 28
   Catholic press attitudes to 65
   divorce reform under Second Republic, and 7
   Hildegart, and 35–36
      WLSR, and 86
   Instituto de Medicina Social 37–38
   'Latin' eugenics, and 35
   Liga sections 87, 95
   legislation, and 65–66
   new discourse of 36
   periodical publications 36–37
   Saldaña's view of 47

scope 37
  education in good eugenic
    practice, as 37
  statistics, use of 36
  translated works 37
  WLSR views on 73
Sex reform
  agenda 73
    WLSR planks of belief, and
      16–17, 73
  Code reform, and 54
  contribution of publishers to
    66–67
  Ellis, Havelock, and 109
    attitude to 15
    networking of different
      groups involved in 13
  Hildegart, and
    Hildegart's education 43
    tensions in Liga, and 86
  homosexuality, and 72–73
  importing from Europe 15–16
  integration of homosexual
    movement and 19
  international language,
    adoption of 44
  liberation of body 64
  Liga SEE Liga
  marriage, approach to 73
  professional rivalries causing
    problems in field of 65
  public examination of issues of
    64
  publications of movement 105
  rationale for 15
    Freud and 15
  reconciliation with religious
    beliefs 46
  regulation, arguments against
    34
  Russia, in 113
  science, and 107
    Sexus, and 107 SEE ALSO *Sexus*
  Second Republic, coming of 89

sex education, and 35–37
sexual crimes, and 116
sexual variation, and 73
specialist reviews 104
time line for development of 7
WLSR planks of belief, and
  16–17
World League for Sexual
  Reform (WLSR) SEE World
  League for Sexual Reform
Sexology
  Ellis, Havelock, and 125
  four areas of 18
  Hildegart's study of 130
  La sexología (Ensayos) 46
  Saldaña, and 47, 93, 129
Sexualidad
  audience envisaged in
    publication 104
  Haro, and 47–48
  Hildegart, and 45–46
    articles in 48
    brief encapsulating sentence,
      feature of articles by 51
    first hearing of WLSR 45
    number of appearances in 48
  participation of Liga members
    44–45
  people associated with,
    significance 48
  publication of activities of
    Hygiene Campaign 44
  Ripoll, Torrubiano 46
  Saldaña, Quintiliano 46, 130
  self-creation through
    publication 104
Sexuality
  attitudes to
    Aurora's comments on 77
    Aza, Vital and 'proper'
      sexuality 73–74
    Ellis, Havelock, and 13
    Hildegart's 35, 75–76
    Saldaña's 46–47

Sexus I, in 109
  WLSR planks of belief, and 17
  crimes linked to 116
  Eugenics Conference, and 117
  hygienists, work of early, and 28
  'Latin' eugenics, and 28
  Ripoll, Torrubiano, study of 46
  Saldaña, Quintiliano, study of 46
  scientific approach to 108
  Sexus, and 108
  sex education, and 65
Sexus
  balance of power, and 105–106
  designation of contributors to 107
    Hildegart's place in 107
  Eugenics Conference 1934 programme 117
  Hildegart, and
    'Criminología sexual' article in 155
    'Endocrinología, delincuencia y eugenesia' article in 80
    'Ensayos en torno a la criminología sexual' article in 80
    history of Liga in 55
    prominent role in second number of 98
    view of Haro in charge of 97
  publication dates 106
  publication of Liga's aims in 88, 94, 95
  reports of Beacon Hill school in 43
  Sexus I 108–111
    editorial board 106
    Hildegart's 'child', as 110
    self-promotion of Liga 108
  Sexus II 111–116
    composition and contents 112–116
    editorial board 111
    Haro's interventions and 112
    structure and content 107
    WLSR aims, and 20
Socialism
  Congreso de las Juventudes 43
  HG Wells 'Socialism and the Family' 15
  Hildegart, and
    'falling out' with socialism 71
    involvement in socialist activity 71
    late nineteenth-century socialist utopians 126
    membership of Socialist party 72
    mother's father's library, and 1
    resignation from activities associated with 72
  Spanish involvement in 5, 6
  WLSR's ten planks, and 92
    Sanchis Banús objections to plank two 92
Sterilization
  Anglo-American eugenics 14
  Aurora's insistence on strategy of 98
  Ellis, Havelock, on 12, 24
  Eugenics Education Society committee for legalizing compulsory sterilization 11, 12
  mentally feeble, of 35
  Ripoll, Torrubiano, views of 46
Stopes, Marie 230
Syphilis 28
  Degeneración por sífilis adquirida 57
  Eugenics Conference 1933 118
  Lafora's publications 59

Lo que todo el mundo debe saber sobre la sífilis 36
Sainz de Aja's work on 38
Sánchez Covisa's work on 38
Sífilis, blenorragia y matrimonio 36
Theosophy 11
Tomás y Samper, Rodolfo 230
  Sexus II editorial board 111
Torrubiano y Ripoll, Jaime 46, 56, 67, 86, 91, 230
  Liga sections 95
  Sexualidad, and 44, 46, 130
  Sexus II, and 111
  Teología sexual 46
Transvestites
  Die Transvestiten 18
Unión General de Trabajadores (UGT)
  Hildegart joining 43, 53, 68, 71
  resignation from 72
Van de Velde, Theodore H. 230
Varela Radio, Manuel 230
Venereal disease
  ¿Cómo se curan y cómo se evitan las enfermedades venéreas? 69
  compulsory treatment of 66
  conscious parenthood, and 73
  'crime of venereal infection' 66
  criminal act of contagion of 53
  draft law concerning 66
  Eugenics Education Society, and
    line on treatment of 11
  Haire on 115
  Liga sections 95
  prostitutes, and 32, 34
    abolition of prostitution, and 66
    legislation, and 32
    requirement to treat 34
  WLSR planks of belief, and 17, 93
Weisskopf, Joseph 230

Wells, H. G. 15, 96, 126, 230
  contact with Hildegart 125, 126
Wilde, Oscar 75, 147, 154
Winnicott, Donald W. 156
World League for Sexual Reform (WLSR) 16–20
  coming of Second Republic, and 89
  congresses 16
  dissolution 19
  Ellis, Havelock, and
    explanation of association with 15
    Grosskurth's biography, and 158
    honorary president, as 13
  emancipation of homosexuals, and 19
  Haire, and
    decision to dissolve WLSR 19
    interpretation of WLSR aims 19
    welcome address at London Congress 18–19
  Hildegart, and
    aims, and 86
    definition of 86
    espousal of more revolutionary aspects 86
    first hearing of 45
  Hirschfeld, Magnus, founder of 16
    Hildegart's interview with 110
  international context 69
  Le Problème Sexuel 105
  Liga as child of 108 SEE ALSO Liga
  membership 16
  mission 18
  organization of Spanish chapter 1
    Ellis' advice to Hildegart on 2, 87

planks of belief 16–17
  agendas contained in 18
  discussion of 88–89, 91–95, 111
  Ellis' view of homosexuality, and 109
  Hildegart, and 17, 97
  interests in common with eugenics 73
  Liga's 'Decalogue' 91
  Liga's 'Octologue' 93
  overlap between eugenics and sexual reform movement 17
  sexual variation, and 73
  tolerance for homosexuality 74
  portfolio of concerns 16
  programme of action 107
  sex education, and 37
  Sexus SEE *Sexus*
Zoroastrianism 50
Zozaya, Antonio 71–72, 230–231
  novels, writing 76
Zulueta, Luis de 78, 231